THE PLAYBOOK

52 Rules to Aim, Shoot, and Score in This Game Called Life

BY KWAME ALEXANDER

PHOTOGRAPHS BY THAI NEAVE

Houghton Mifflin Harcourt
Boston   New York

• • • • • • *With special thanks to* • • • • • •

JoEllen McCarthy, Aditya Kalia, Mary Rand Hess,
Trenton Hess, Castleton Elementary, Singapore American School,
Sid Reischer, and Angela Turnbull.

www.hmhco.com

The text was set in Adobe Garamond Pro.

Design by Lisa Vega

Library of Congress Cataloging-in-Publication data is on file.

ISBN: 978-0-544-57097-9

Manufactured in the United States of America

DOC 10 9 8 7 6 5 4 3 2 1

4500636040

IMAGE CREDITS:

Page(s) i: © Shutterstock; **1–2:** © Thai Neave; **5:** © Shutterstock; **7:** © Getty Images; **11:** © Shutterstock; **12–13:** © Thai Neave; **14:** © Shutterstock; **18–21:** © Thai Neave; **22:** © Shutterstock; **25–27:** © Thai Neave; **28–29:** © Shutterstock (ball), Getty Images (hand); **30–31:** © Getty Images (texture), Shutterstock (figure); **32–35:** © Thai Neave; **36–37:** © Shutterstock; **38–41:** © Thai Neave; **42–43:** © Shutterstock; **45–47:** © Thai Neave; **48–49:** © Shutterstock; **50:** © Getty Images; **53:** © Getty Images; **57:** © Shutterstock; **58–61:** © Thai Neave; **62, 65:** Shutterstock (ball); **66–67:** © Thai Neave; **69:** © Getty Images; **70–71:** © Shutterstock (line art); **71–73:** © Thai Neave; **74–75, 77:** © Shutterstock; **78–79:** © Thai Neave; **80–81:** © Shutterstock; **82–85:** © Thai Neave; **86:** Shutterstock (ball); **88–89:** © Shutterstock; **92–93:** © Thai Neave; **97:** © Shutterstock; **100–101:** © Thai Neave; **102:** Shutterstock (ball); **103–5:** © Thai Neave; **106:** © Shutterstock (line art); **108–11:** © Thai Neave; **112–13:** © Getty Images (texture), Thai Neave (photo); **116–17:** © Thai Neave; **119–21:** © Shutterstock; **122–23:** © Thai Neave; **124–25:** © Getty Images; **126–27:** © Thai Neave; **129–30:** © Shutterstock (ball); **134–35:** © Dreamstime; **136–37:** © Thai Neave; **139–41:** © Shutterstock; **142–43:** © Thai Neave; **144–45:** © Shutterstock; **146–46:** Getty Images (texture); **148–50:** © Shutterstock (line art); **150–51:** © Thai Neave; **152–53:** © Shutterstock; **154–55:** © Thai Neave; **156–57:** © Shutterstock; **158–61:** © Thai Neave; **162–63, 169:** © Shutterstock.

For Cedric Howard, the best teammate ever
• • • • • • • • *and* • • • • • • • •
Margaret Raymo, the best coach in the game

Warm-up: The Rules

Sports teaches you character, it teaches you to play by the rules, it teaches you to know what it feels like to win and lose—it teaches you about life.

—BILLIE JEAN KING, Hall of Fame thirty-nine-time Grand Slam tennis champion, founder of the Women's Tennis Association

In 1891, when James Naismith invented the game of basketball with a soccer ball and two peach baskets to use as goals, he also had to create some rules—13 of them in fact. Rules like:

THE BALL MAY BE THROWN IN ANY DIRECTION WITH ONE OR BOTH HANDS AND THE TIME SHALL BE TWO 15-MINUTE HALVES WITH FIVE MINUTES' REST BETWEEN.

Over the next 100-plus years, these rules would govern the hoops game and make basketball one of the most popular sports in the world.

I believe that sports are a great metaphor for life. In our games, we decide who the best players are to assist us, we flex our skills, and we test our will to win on and off the court. Our character is built during the times we are victorious and also during the times we are met with major challenges. This is when we find out what we're really made of. There are countless stories of athletes who faced defeat to accomplish historic feats. They, like you and me, had dreams. Big dreams. How do we make our dreams come true? I believe that we have to be passionate, determined, focused, and work hard, in order to succeed. But, we also have to master the rules of the game.

WANT TO BE A BALLER,
KNOW THE RULES.

WANT TO DO BETTER IN SCHOOL,
KNOW THE RULES.

WANT TO HAVE BETTER FRIENDSHIPS,
KNOW THE RULES.

WANT TO SUCCEED IN THE GAME OF LIFE,
KNOW THE RULES.

In eighth grade, I was eager to succeed. In sports and in popularity. I wanted people to know who I was, especially the girls. I wanted to walk down the halls and get *high-fives*, *daps*, and *hollas*. I wanted to be cool. I wanted to be *Da Man!* Thing was, I had no idea how to do it. Until a friend named Vince suggested basketball. I was tall and agile and my dad had been a star baller, so I figured what I lacked in actual talent, my genes would make up for. I tried out and made the team.

First game of the season, I bring the ball up the court, dribble the ball between my legs, behind my back, no defender in sight. I get to the half-court line and decide, in front of hundreds of classmates, teachers, parents . . . and girls, that I'm going to shoot, and hopefully score the first points of the game. I throw the ball up right there at the half-court line. It's the first play of the season, and if I make this, there will be newspaper clippings of me for my kids to read one day. If I make it, everyone will know *Kwame Alexander*.

I don't make it.

The ball goes over the backboard and hits the scoreboard. Me and my coolness get benched. So much for basketball. I finish out the season sitting mostly on the sidelines. One of the rules I'd learned growing up was to **never give up,** especially when you really want something. So, the following year—my freshman year—I try out for the junior varsity team.

I don't make it.

Cedric, my best friend, who was not as tall as I was, but ripped—he had muscles, y'all—suggested that we try out for the football team, because *everybody liked football players.* I said **yes!** We both made the team. Wide receivers.

First game of the season, he gallops down one sideline, I speed down the other. I eagerly await my chance to get the ball, **score,** hear the cheers. I see my mom in the stands, so I wave at her. The quarterback looks my way. Oh yes, it's about to go down. I'm about to score a **touchdown**—then everyone will know me. Thing is, I never get the ball. I get knocked flat on my butt by some monster whose actual nickname is, get this, "Monster." Lights out. *Crickets.* Cedric goes on to score many touchdowns as the star receiver of our football team. He even plays in college. My mom benches me after the hit. And it's no more football for me. Truth was, football wasn't really an interest of mine. I thought it might make me cool, but all it made me was sore. I guess the rule I learned that day was know your strengths, know your passion, know that if your heart isn't in it, the Monster will hurt you!

Then my mom suggests another sport. *Kwame, cool is what you make it,* I remember her saying. *If you're bent on playing a sport, why don't you try tennis?*

Tennis? The *uncoolest* sport on earth. My dad had played high school tennis too. He was a high school competitor of Arthur Ashe—the one exception to the *tennis isn't cool* rule. I thought my mom was bonkers. No way I was going to sport a pair of white shorts and an aluminum racket. Thing was, I trusted my mom. She was pretty smart and always had my back. She took me out to the courts, taught me some of the basics, practiced with me. I decided to give it a shot.

SOMETIMES, YOU MAY NOT AGREE WITH OR UNDERSTAND THE ADVICE YOU GET, BUT IF YOU HEED IT, IT JUST MIGHT STICK WITH YOU UNTIL YOU COME TO UNDERSTAND IT.

Until you live it and breathe it! But first you need to *say yes* to the possibility. You need to be open to new things. You have to *say yes* to yourself. The most important rule I think I've ever learned is that when you're presented with an opportunity that may seem different or challenging or unknown, sometimes you've got to summon the courage to trust yourself and SAY YES!

So, I said YES!

I tried out for the tennis team and made it. I was number twelve. On a roster of twelve. My father had purchased me a gold-plated tennis racket from K-mart to go along with my corduroy shorts and red Chuck Taylors. I looked nothing like a tennis player, and played even worse. Actually, I didn't play in one match that first year. I just watched. The next season, I moved up to number nine, and I got to play in my first match, which I won. Suddenly, my confidence was building, but my ego wasn't. I wanted to be a starter on the team, to play in every match, and that motivated me to keep playing, to keep trying, even when faced with the ridicule of some of my teammates. The older guys on the team didn't think I was that good, didn't think I was worthy to be a starter, and didn't take me seriously. So, I devised a plan. It involved practice. And more practice. And still, even more practice. Six hours every day during summer vacation, we practiced: Me and Shawn and Rob and Paul. And Claudia—the real reason I wanted to be cool.

We all have what it takes to do exactly what we want to do in life, no matter what anyone else says. If someone tells you, "You can't do this because you are [fill in the blank]," I say embrace the challenge. Wear it like a new pair of Converse or Jordans. Meet it head-on. Find your grit and put in the work to elevate your game.

CHAMPIONS TRAIN, CHUMPS COMPLAIN.

Be true to your unique, amazing, and awesome self. Motivate yourself, and powerfully step into your dreams to create the life you want, and do not let anyone or anything stop you!

PRACTICE. WORK HARD. FOCUS. PREPARE YOURSELF FOR THE THING THAT YOU WANT TO ACCOMPLISH—ACE A TEST, MAKE A TEAM, JOIN A CLUB, GO TO COLLEGE—WHATEVER IT IS, YOU SIMPLY MUST PUT. IN. THE. WORK. . . . . .

The next year, I was number four on the team. My dedication had paid off. I played in every match. I won every one. In the district tournament, the number one, two, and three seeds on our team all got beat. Guess who made it to the finals? Yep, ME! All because I said yes. All of a sudden, I felt cool. I had overcome a few challenges and succeeded beyond my wildest dreams. Of course, you want to know if I won . . . stay tuned.

The Playbook is a collection of short poems, divided into 4 quarters of 13 rules each, accompanied by uplifting quotes from famous people who have overcome challenges to achieve amazing things. They have each found their path to greatness.

Whether you're playing soccer or tennis, baseball or lacrosse, softball or basketball, you've got to find the right motivation and creativity to propel you to success. Think of *The Playbook* as a source of inspiration: *52 rules to aim, shoot, and score in this game called life.* Like James Naismith's, these are my rules, for basketball, for sports, and for life!

1st Quarter

Grit

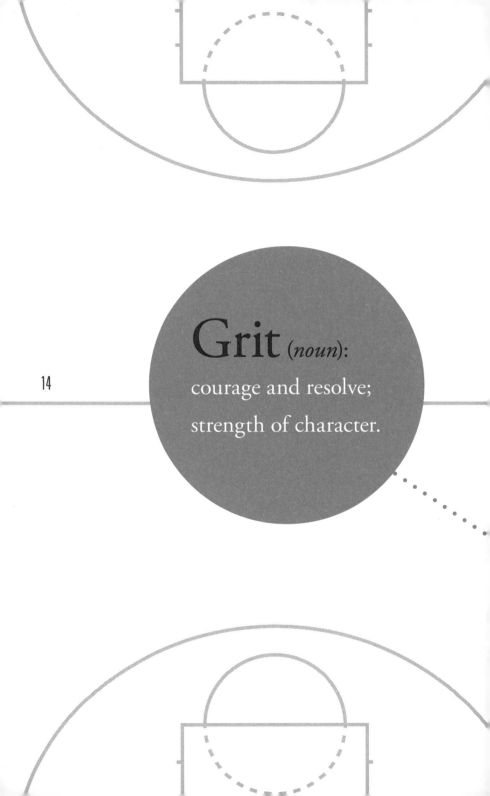

14

Grit *(noun)*:
courage and resolve;
strength of character.

In eighth grade, I had to do a book report, and I waited, as usual, until the very last minute. My house was pretty much a library, so I grabbed the first slim volume I saw off the shelf in our family room. It was a book about Wilma Rudolph, an Olympic track champion. It took me about an hour to read the book. Her story was remarkable. What I found out about her life changed mine.

When she was born, Wilma Rudolph weighed only four and a half pounds, and she spent the first eleven years of her childhood fighting illnesses such as scarlet fever, whooping cough, double pneumonia, and, get this, polio. Polio causes paralysis and has no cure. So, left with only one working leg, Wilma was fitted with a metal leg brace at around age five.

Every week, she and her mom took a Greyhound bus from their small town to Nashville, Tennessee, for her physical therapy, so that she could learn to walk with her brace. During these trips, Wilma witnessed and experienced the segregation of the Deep South—they always had to ride in the back of the bus, and they couldn't eat in most restaurants. Witnessing racial divides and experiencing her own disability gave Wilma grit and determination that would help her overcome some pretty huge challenges.

Often, Wilma would try to remove her leg brace so she could play like her friends and siblings. By age eleven, she finally kicked off that leg brace permanently and began practicing to walk, run, and play ball. It was painful and hard, but she was determined. Her brothers set up a basketball hoop in their yard, where she played every chance she got. After years and years of hard work and sheer willpower, she could not only walk well, but she could run faster than most kids. She became a star basketball player at her school, where Coach C. C. Gray gave her the nickname "Skeeter" because she was so fast. Imagine that: a girl who walked in special shoes with a leg brace for years was now given a nickname because of her speed.

Wilma became an all-state basketball player, setting the state record of forty-nine points in a single game. She was gifted, so gifted that word soon reached Ed Temple, track coach at Tennessee State University, who recruited her to start training with his team. Surprisingly, she qualified for the 1956 Olympic Games in Melbourne, Australia, where she became the youngest member of the U.S. track team at just sixteen years old. She flew home with a bronze medal.

After high school, Wilma went to Tennessee State, where she studied education and trained for the next Olympic Games. Within four years, she was back at the Olympics, this time in Rome, Italy, where she set world records in the 100-meter dash, 200-meter dash, and the 100-meter relay. The Olympics were a huge success and a game changer for Wilma, as she became the first American woman to win three gold medals in a single Olympics. She was soon known as the world's fastest woman.

She was later inducted into the U.S. Olympic Hall of Fame and founded the Wilma Rudolph Foundation to help inspire and encourage amateur athletics. Not bad for a girl whose doctors said she would always have trouble walking.

When I presented my book report to the class, I ended by saying that we all face challenges and defeats in our life, but if you are self-determined and committed to putting in the work, you can bounce back like Wilma Rudolph did. I got an $A+$ on the report, but more important, I realized that if she could overcome a paralyzed leg and become a track star, then I could work hard and excel in whatever sport I chose—and, perhaps, in life.

Rule #1

IT TAKES SKILL
TO MAKE
THE LAST SHOT,
BUT IT TAKES CONFIDENCE
TO TAKE IT.

I have missed more than 9,000 shots in my career. I have lost almost 300 games. On 26 occasions I have been entrusted to take the game-winning shot and missed. And I have failed over and over and over again in my life. And that is why I succeed.

—Michael Jordan, six-time NBA champion with the Chicago Bulls, five-time MVP

WHEN THE GAME IS ON
THE LINE,
DON'T FEAR.

GRAB THE BALL.

TAKE IT
TO THE HOOP.

22

I don't focus on what I'm up
against. I focus on my goals
and I try to ignore the rest.

—Venus Williams, seven-time
Grand Slam tennis champion,
Olympic gold medalist

23

THE SIZE OF YOUR HEART MATTERS MORE THAN THE SIZE OF YOUR OPPONENT.

It's not how big you are, it's how big you play.

—John Wooden, ten-time NCAA championship—winning coach with UCLA and six-time national coach of the year

The fight is won . . . behind the lines, in the gym, and out there on the road, long before I dance under those lights.

—Muhammad Ali, "The Greatest" world heavyweight boxing champion, philanthropist, social activist

PRACTICE
PREPARES YOU
FOR THAT GLORIOUS MOMENT
WHEN YOU HOLD
THE BALL
AND DESTINY
IN YOUR HANDS.

27

LEARN THE FUNDAMENTALS,
SO YOU CAN ALWAYS
BE IN A POSITION

TO DRIBBLE
PASS
OR SHOOT.

WHEN THE BALL
IS IN YOUR HANDS,
BE A TRIPLE TRIPLE TRIPLE
THREAT.

The glory of sport comes from dedication, determination, and desire. Achieving success and personal glory in athletics has less to do with wins and losses than it does with learning how to prepare yourself so that at the end of the day, whether on the track or in the office, you know that there was nothing more you could have done to reach your ultimate goal.

—Jackie Joyner-Kersee, three-time Olympic gold medalist, track and field, voted Greatest Female Athlete of the Twentieth Century by *Sports Illustrated*

PRACTICE
IS SO ROUTINE
AND SOMETIMES
ROUTINES ARE BORING.
BUT IF YOU DON'T PRACTICE
YOU WILL GET BEAT
ROUTINELY.

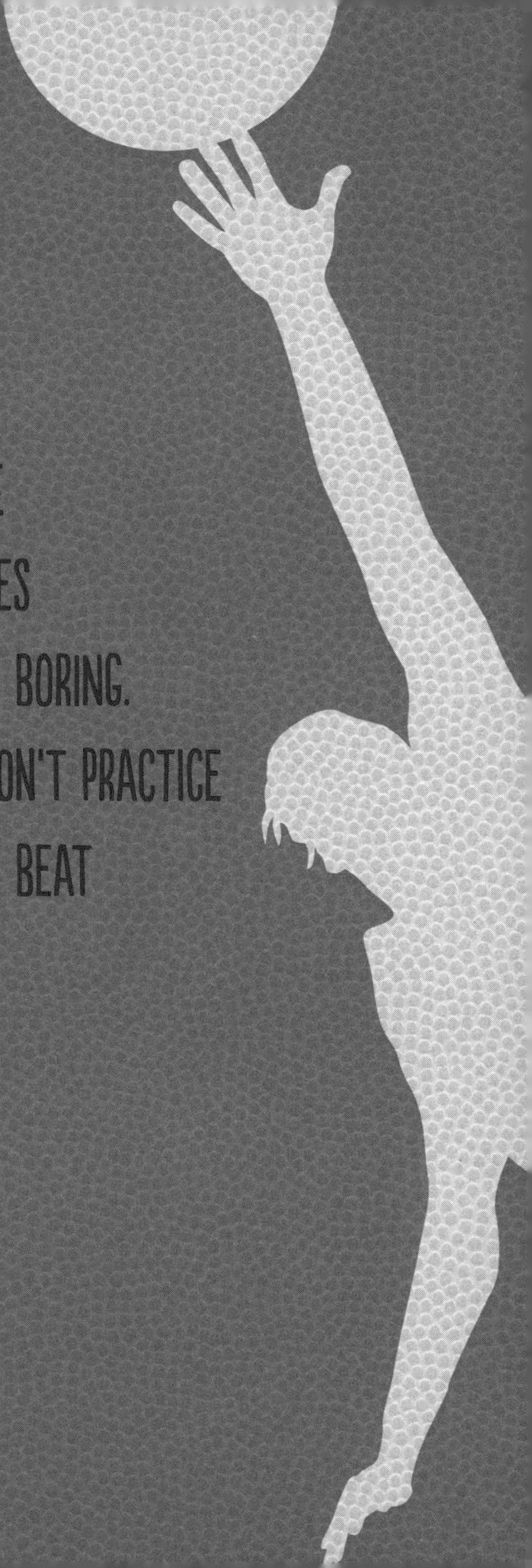

Hard work beats talent when
talent fails to work hard.

—Kevin Durant, seven-time
NBA all-star with the Oklahoma
City Thunder and the Golden
State Warriors

If you've given the greatest effort that you can expect from yourself, then you'll always get what you deserve.

—C. Vivian Stringer, Hall of Fame basketball coach, and assistant coach of the 2004 women's basketball Olympic team

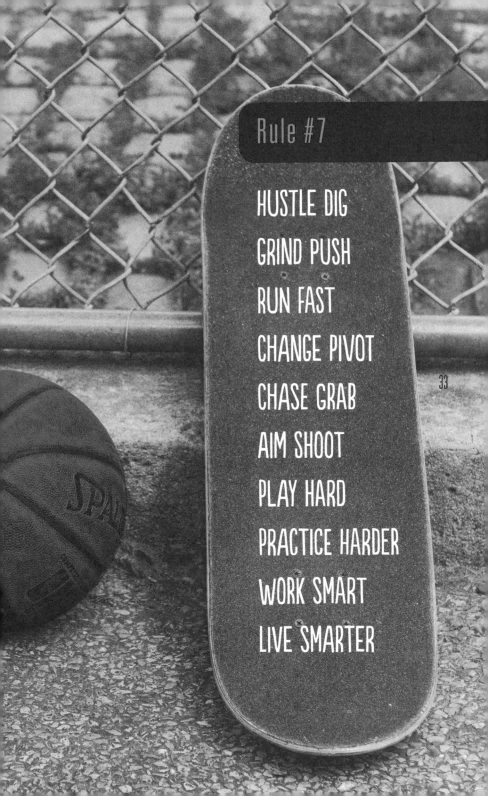

Rule #7

HUSTLE DIG

GRIND PUSH

RUN FAST

CHANGE PIVOT

CHASE GRAB

AIM SHOOT

PLAY HARD

PRACTICE HARDER

WORK SMART

LIVE SMARTER

33

I just keep fighting and try to be the last one standing.

—Li Na, French Open and Australian Open tennis
champion

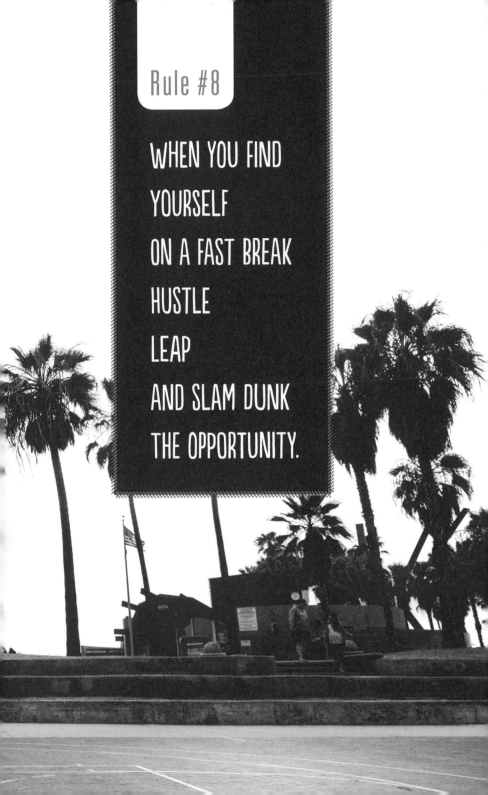

Rule #8

WHEN YOU FIND
YOURSELF
ON A FAST BREAK
HUSTLE
LEAP
AND SLAM DUNK
THE OPPORTUNITY.

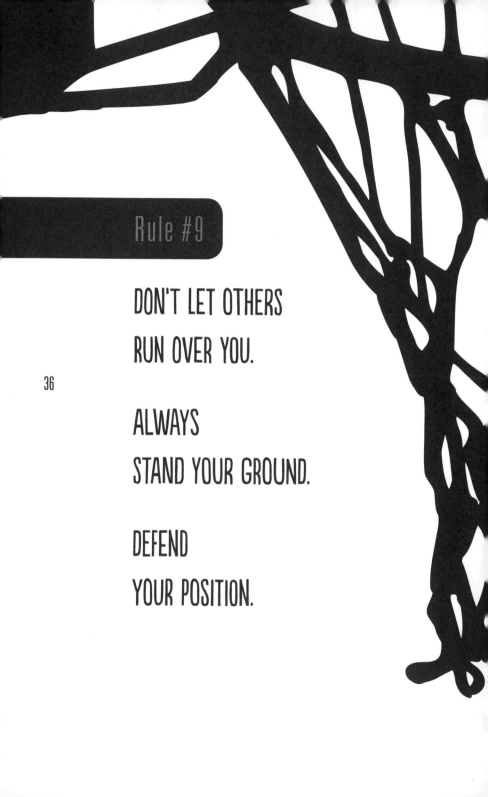

DON'T LET OTHERS
RUN OVER YOU.

36

ALWAYS
STAND YOUR GROUND.

DEFEND
YOUR POSITION.

I've worked too hard
and too long to let
anything stand in the way
of my goals. I will not let
my teammates down and I
will not let myself down.

—Mia Hamm, two-time
Olympic gold medalist
and FIFA Women's
World Cup champion

Success is no accident. It is hard work, perseverance, learning, studying, sacrifice, and, most of all, love of what you are doing or learning to do.

WHEN
YOU STOP
PLAYING
YOUR GAME
YOU'VE ALREADY
LOST.

—Pelé, three-time FIFA World Cup champion with
Brazil, most successful league goal scorer (541) in
the world

There's winning and there's losing, and in life you have to know they both will happen. But what's never acceptable to me is quitting.

—Magic Johnson, five-time NBA champion with the Los Angeles Lakers, successful American businessman

Rule #11

DON'T LET PAST MISTAKES
STOP YOU FROM PLAYING
THE CURRENT GAME.

PUT YOUR FULL HEART
PURE PASSION
UNSTOPPABLE FAITH

ON THE LINE
AS IF YOU'VE NEVER HIT
THE COURT BEFORE.

Rule #12

YOU CAN ALWAYS

DO BETTER THAN YOU DID
WORK HARDER THAN YOU WORKED
LEAP BROADER THAN YOU LEAPT

SO

DIG DEEPER
CLAW HARDER
REBOUND BETTER

There may be people who have
more talent than you, but there's
no excuse for anyone to work harder than you do.

—Derek Jeter, five-time MLB World Series
champion with the New York Yankees

Rule #13

FIND GRIT
WHEN YOU WANT TO
QUIT

44

COOLNESS
WHEN YOU GET
HEATED

AND DETERMINATION
WHEN YOU FEEL
DEFEATED.

Winning is great, sure, but if you are really going to do something in life, the secret is learning how to lose. Nobody goes undefeated all the time. If you can pick up after a crushing defeat and go on to win again, you are going to be a champion someday.

—Wilma Rudolph, three-time Olympic gold medalist, track and field

45

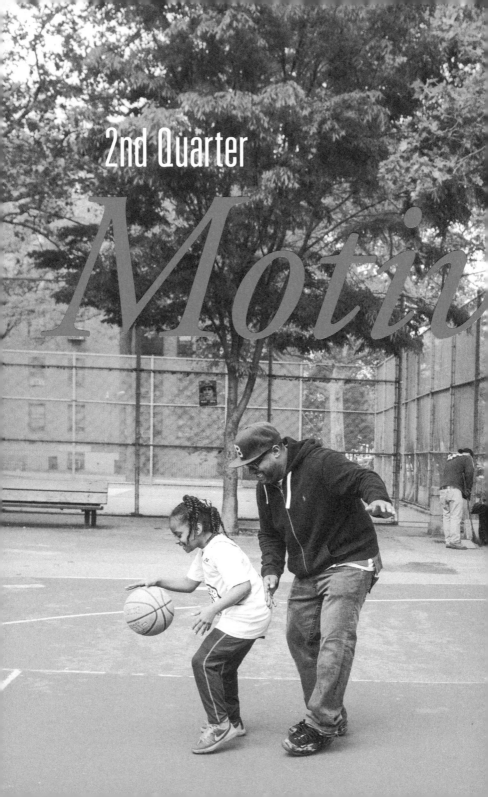

2nd Quarter

Motiv

Motivation *(noun)*: the desire or willingness of someone to do something.

50

Before I was born, my father was a star basketball and tennis player. They called him "Big Al." I remember looking through his photo albums and seeing newspaper clippings of his prowess on the court. His jump shot was sick. His serve-and-volley was lethal. His rebounding skills were *nasty*. And the pictures of him holding the championship trophies—in tennis and basketball—were inspiring to a young, budding athlete. I wanted trophies of my own. I wanted some of that cool.

All great players have to begin somewhere and must find the motivation deep inside of them to work harder, play harder, and win with heart. For me, it was wanting to be like my dad. For my favorite baller, LeBron James, who didn't have a father around to inspire him, it was something else.

LeBron James was born in 1984 in Akron, Ohio, to a teen mother, who raised him alone. He's talked about how his father not being in his life affected him, motivated him:

"Dad, you know what? I don't know you. I have no idea who you are. . . . The fuel that I use today—you not being there— it's part of the reason I grew up to become who I am. It's part of the reason why I want to be hands-on with my endeavors."

His mother struggled to find steady jobs, and the family moved from housing project to housing project. Growing up, James faced all the adversity that comes with living in impoverished conditions. When LeBron was nine years old, his mother made a life-changing decision to give her son a better chance at success. She let LeBron move in with his local football coach. It was in his new home that LeBron quickly found an outlet for his dreams and hopes—basketball. He excelled in AAU (Amateur Athletic Union) basketball as a middle school student, and a few years later led his high school team—composed of many of his Akron friends with whom he played AAU—to three straight championships. By his senior year, LeBron was named Gatorade National Player of the Year. In 2003, the same year he graduated high school, James made a decision to enter the NBA draft, where he became the number one pick for, get this, his hometown Cleveland Cavaliers.

The first seven years of his NBA career were met with praise—he lived up to the ball-handling, passing, and dunking skills that were characteristic of his stellar high school career. There was also heavy skepticism—could The King ever live up to the comparisons to His Airness, Michael Jordan? Did he possess the skill and will to win a championship or two? Would Ohio's Mr. Basketball reverse Cleveland's fifty-two-year sports curse? Cleveland, Ohio, has three major sports teams: the Cleveland Browns of the NFL, the Cleveland Indians of the MLB, and the Cleveland Cavaliers of the NBA. None of these teams had won a championship in 147 seasons, since 1964 when the Browns won the NFL championship.

In 2010, when he left Cleveland and joined the Miami Heat, the naysayers and haters multiplied, with many people—in Cleveland and beyond— insisting that he would never win a championship because 1) he wasn't a clutch player like Michael Jordan, and, more significantly, 2) he'd betrayed his hometown. It didn't matter that he remained committed to Ohio in general and Cleveland and Akron in particular, as evidenced by the $41 million he pledged to provide scholarships to students in Akron who grew up in challenging environments like he had. The city where he grew up and honed his skills, on and off the court, didn't care that he still considered himself one of them. They now saw him as the enemy.

Motivation can come from inspiration and encouragement, but it can also come from opposition and discouragement. LeBron took the good with the bad, used it as the driving force for the next four years of his career. He won back-to-back

NBA championships as a member of the Miami Heat. While his game elevated and his championship rings increased, the Cleveland Cavaliers got worse, with one losing season after another. And then, in 2014, LeBron surprised everyone. He left Miami and went back to, get this, Cleveland. The impetus for this decision: He wanted to bring a championship to his hometown.

Of course, those who were angry with him for leaving Cleveland in the first place were now his biggest fans and supporters. The King had come home. In his first year back, he led his team to the NBA Finals, but was beaten pretty handily by the incredibly shooting Golden State Warriors in six games. After the win, fans and media anointed the Warriors star Stephen Curry as one of the best players in the league. And when the next season came around and Golden State won seventy-three games—a new NBA record— Steph Curry was now considered *the best player* in the league. All of a sudden, the boy from Cleveland, who had been a star since middle school, who had carried teams on his back all the way to the Finals six straight years, was being surpassed by "the new face of the NBA."

In that next season, the Cavaliers again made it to the Finals, where they faced the Golden State Warriors. With a 3-1 deficit, staring defeat in the face, LeBron dug deep. Critics said the series was over, that no other team in the history of the NBA had ever come back and won a championship after being down like this, that LeBron's leadership had failed the team again and that the Warriors would repeat. In games five and six, LeBron scored 41 points each to force a 3-3 tie. In a nail-biting game seven, he hustled, scored, defended, and played the best game of his life to overcome adversity and lead the Cavaliers to what has been called the greatest comeback victory in the sports history.

He was determined to silence all the critics and prove the doubters wrong. He was driven, beyond what many thought was humanly possible, by the desire to, after a fifty-two-year sports curse, bring a championship to the city of Cleveland. Skill is something you can learn. Will is something you earn over time, by overcoming challenges. LeBron James has faced challenges on and off the court, and used those experiences to motivate himself beyond compare, to become perhaps the greatest player in NBA history.

Rule #14

NEVER LET ANYONE
LOWER YOUR GOALS.
OTHERS' EXPECTATIONS
OF YOU ARE DETERMINED
BY THEIR LIMITATIONS
OF LIFE.
THE SKY IS YOUR LIMIT.
ALWAYS SHOOT
FOR THE SUN
AND YOU *WILL* SHINE.

I'll always be number 1 to myself.

—Moses Malone, three-time NBA MVP
and NBA champion with the
Philadelphia 76ers

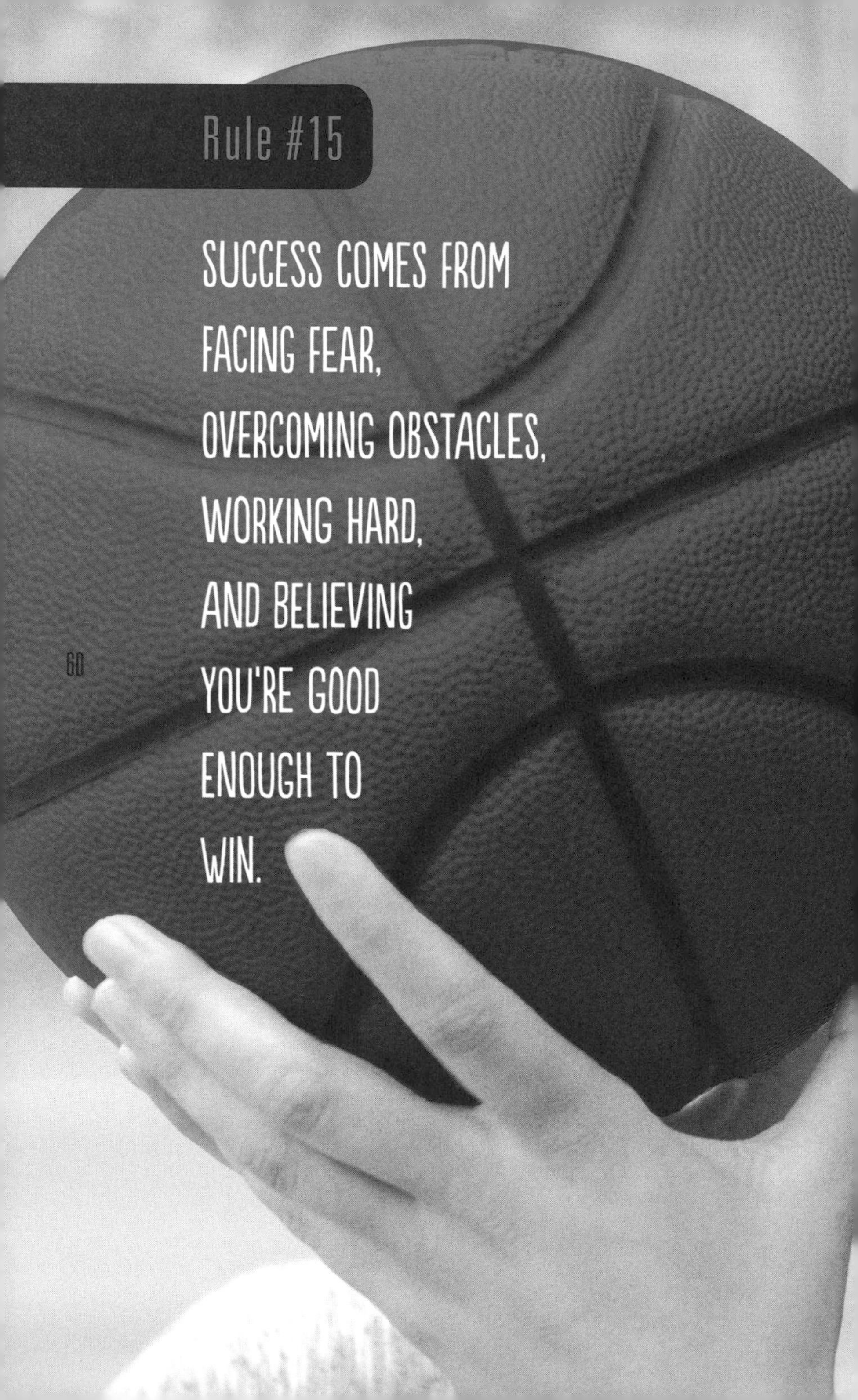

SUCCESS COMES FROM
FACING FEAR,
OVERCOMING OBSTACLES,
WORKING HARD,
AND BELIEVING
YOU'RE GOOD
ENOUGH TO
WIN.

Luck has nothing to do with it, because I have spent many, many hours, countless hours, on the court working for my one moment in time, not knowing when it would come.

—Serena Williams, number one world tennis player (ATP rankings), twenty-one-time Grand Slam tennis champion

Rule #16

YOU MAY NOT BE

A STARTER

BUT ALWAYS

BE A STAR

IN YOUR MIND

READY TO SHINE

AT ANY TIME.

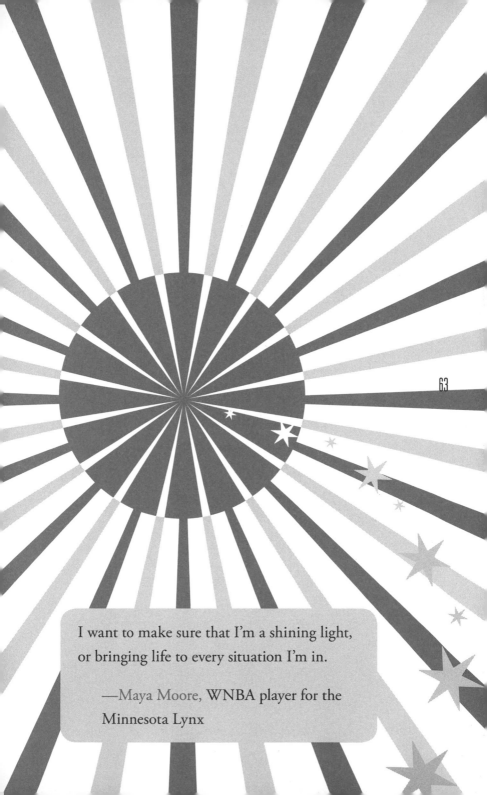

I want to make sure that I'm a shining light, or bringing life to every situation I'm in.

—Maya Moore, WNBA player for the Minnesota Lynx

SOMETIMES, WE NEED
OTHERS
TO MOTIVATE US
TO HELP US DREAM
TO BOUNCE IDEAS OFF
REBOUND WITH
GROW WITH.

A TEAM.
A DREAM TEAM.

No matter what accomplishments you make,
somebody helped you.

—Althea Gibson, eleven-time Grand Slam
tennis champion

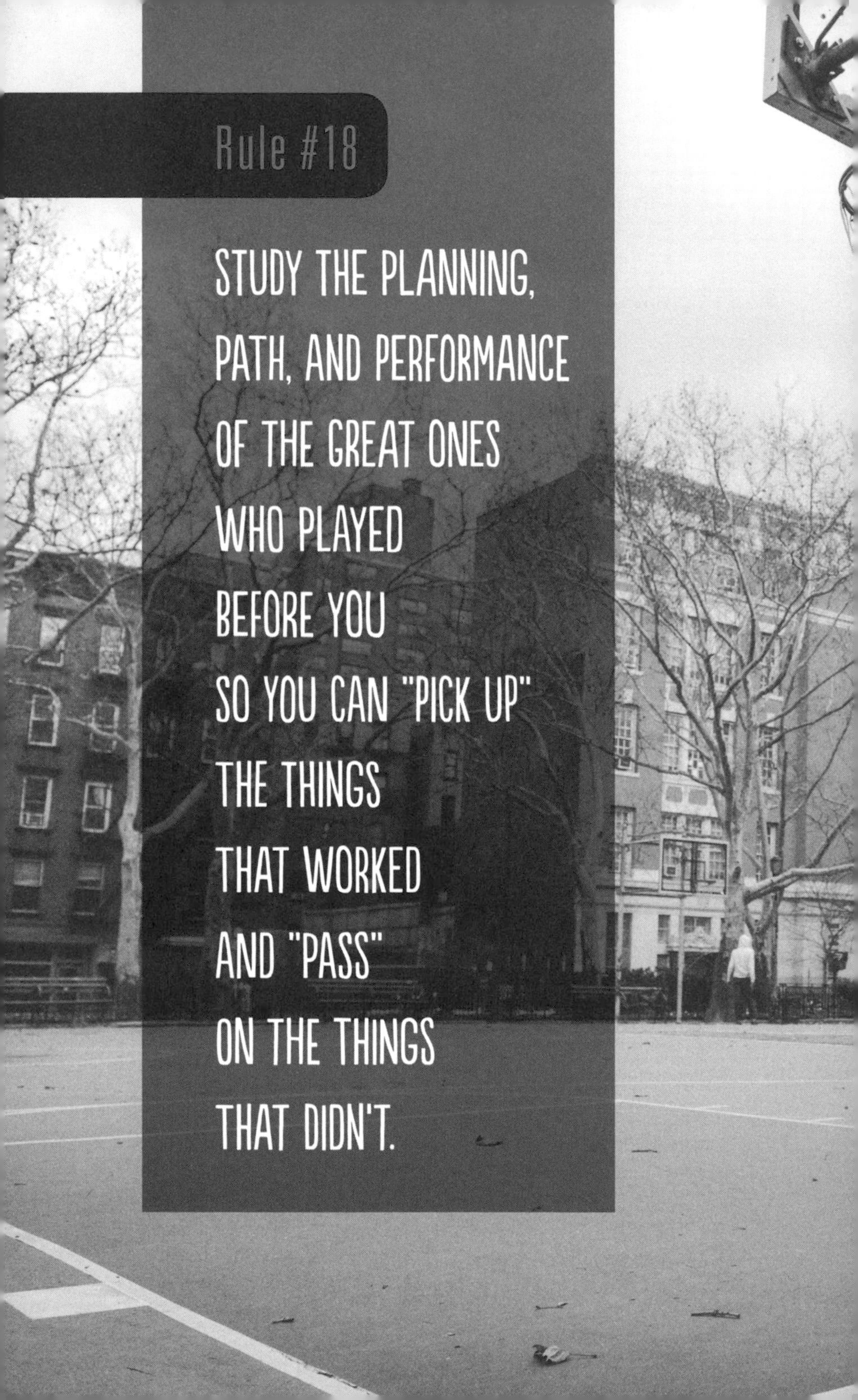

STUDY THE PLANNING,
PATH, AND PERFORMANCE
OF THE GREAT ONES
WHO PLAYED
BEFORE YOU
SO YOU CAN "PICK UP"
THE THINGS
THAT WORKED
AND "PASS"
ON THE THINGS
THAT DIDN'T.

Champions
behave like
champions
before they
are champions.

—Bill Walsh,
three-time NFL
Super Bowl
champion coach
of the San
Francisco 49ers

WHEN YOU'RE HOT, SHOOT.
WHEN YOU'RE NOT, PASS.
CHAMPIONS HIDE
THEIR WEAKNESSES
WITH THEIR STRENGTHS.

Start where you are. Use what you have. Do what you can.

—Arthur Ashe, number one world tennis player (ATP rankings), winner of three Grand Slam titles

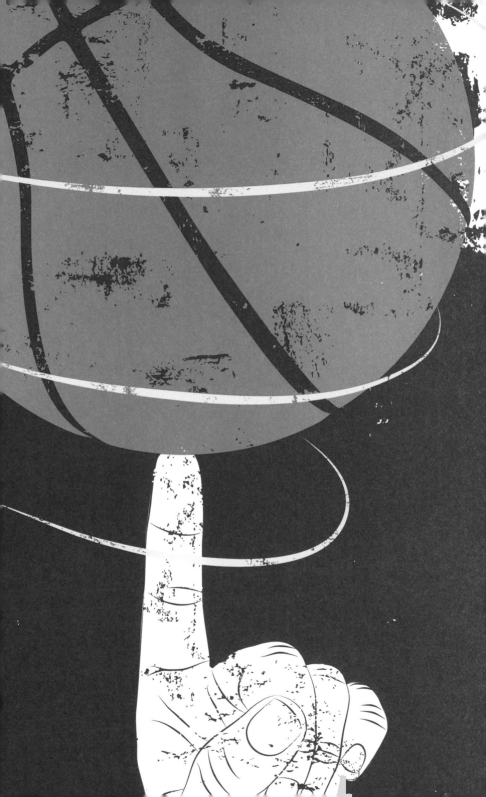

A GOOD COACH LEADS THE TEAM.

A GREAT COACH CREATES LEADERS.

You can't force your will on people. If you want them to act differently, you need to inspire them to change themselves.

—Phil Jackson, eleven-time NBA championship–winning coach with the Chicago Bulls and the Los Angeles Lakers

KNOW THE COURT
KNOW WHERE TO GO
WHERE TO BE
FIND THE OPEN SPOT
BE IN THE RIGHT PLACE
AT THE RIGHT TIME
TO CREATE
YOUR BEST SHOT
FOR GREATNESS

Never underestimate the power of dreams
and the influence of the human spirit. We
are all the same in this notion: the potential
for greatness lives within each of us.

—Wilma Rudolph, three-time Olympic gold
medalist, track and field

EVEN IF
YOU'RE AFRAID,
WHEN YOU GET THE CHANCE
TO SHOOT,
LAUNCH
YOUR BEST
SHOT.

74

If you're afraid to fail, then you're probably
going to fail.

—Kobe Bryant, five-time NBA champion
with the Los Angeles Lakers

AT JUMP BALL
WHEN THE GAME BEGINS
BE ON YOUR TOES.
BE PREPARED
MENTALLY
AND PHYSICALLY
TO TAKE
THE LEAP.

Practice creates confidence.
Confidence empowers you.

—Simone Biles, four-time
Olympic gold medalist,
gymnastics

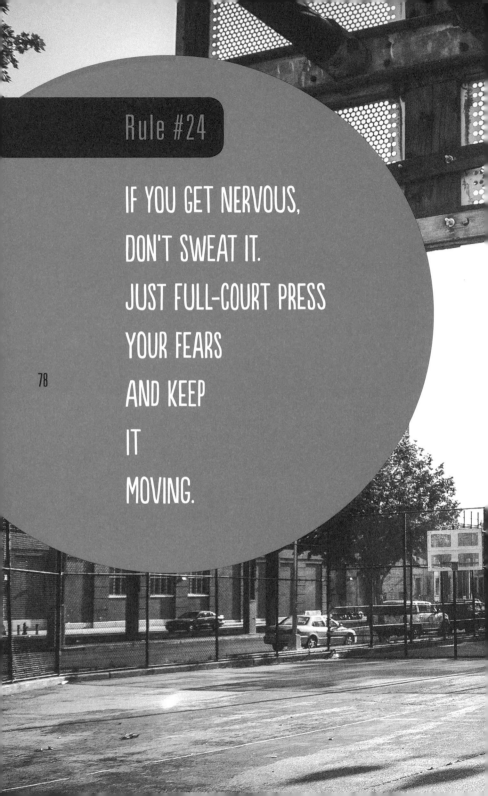

Rule #24

IF YOU GET NERVOUS,
DON'T SWEAT IT.
JUST FULL-COURT PRESS
YOUR FEARS
AND KEEP
IT
MOVING.

78

Never let the fear of striking out get in your way.

—Babe Ruth, seven-time World Series champion with the New York Yankees and the Boston Red Sox

IN THE FACE OF OPPOSITION, A WELL-TIMED CROSSOVER

Make it work no matter what you have to work with—that's something that stuck with me very early on as a point guard. Adjust. Get creative. Try a different angle, a different lane,

JUST MIGHT
GIVE YOU
ENOUGH SPACE
TO EXECUTE
THE PLAY
AND SCORE.

81

a different move or a different shot—just make it work.
—Stephen Curry, NBA champion, two-time MVP
with the Golden State Warriors

IN THIS GAME OF LIFE
YOUR FAMILY IS THE COURT
AND THE BALL IS YOUR HEART.
NO MATTER HOW GOOD YOU ARE,

NO MATTER HOW DOWN YOU GET,
ALWAYS LEAVE
YOUR HEART
ON THE COURT.

All I ever wanted really, and continue to want out of life, is to give 100 percent to whatever I'm doing and to be committed to whatever I'm doing and then let the results speak for themselves. Also, to never take myself or people for granted and always be thankful and grateful to the people who helped me.

—Jackie Joyner-Kersee, three-time Olympic gold medalist in track and field, voted Greatest Female Athlete of the Twentieth Century by *Sports Illustrated*

Halftime

Pas

Passion

(noun):

a strong feeling of enthusiasm or excitement for something or about doing something.

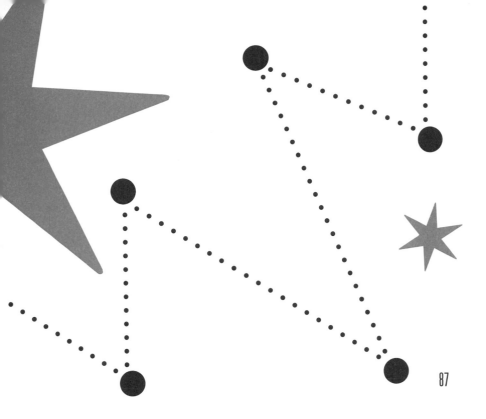

So having made it to the district tournament finals my junior year, I gave it my all. My parents came to the match. All my friends came.

And, I lost.

Losing is a test none of us has studied for. It's one of the hardest things to deal with in our young lives. Especially in the finals. But here's the thing: It's as much a part of life as winning, and true champions are resilient and learn how to rebound. To most of my friends, basketball and football were surefire ways to get noticed, to become cool, to be somebody. Basketball and football didn't work out, but I rebounded. I found my own path, and it worked for me. And while losing in the finals was almost unbearable, it was just a setback. Like the famous motivational speaker Willie Jolley says,

A SETBACK IS A SETUP FOR A COMEBACK.

I got right back out on the court to perfect my game. The summer before my senior year in high school, I played tennis nine, ten hours a day. I took more lessons. And I loved every minute of it. My parents were working, and my friends didn't feel like driving way out to my house to pick me up, so I'd take two buses to the courts, a few times even walking the five miles to serve and volley under the summer sun. I did this because I loved playing tennis. It's what I dreamed about at night. It's what I watched on television when it rained. It's what I thought about while I cut the grass. It's what I did every day. And night. It was, quite simply, my passion.

I played numerous tournaments during the summer and

fall, and came in first place more than ten times. There was a collection of trophies sitting in my room that I was quite proud of. When the spring came and the season started, I found myself the number one seed on my high school tennis team. The front page of our local newspaper had a picture of me in my new white shorts, white shirt, white sneakers, and graphite tennis racket with the following headline:

CAN THIS ALEXANDER BE GREAT?

I was the best player, not only at my school but in the district. I'd walk around school and people would high-five me. Even the girl that I liked smiled at me. All of sudden, everybody knew me, wanted to chat and hang out.

The season began and I won my first match. Then I won my second. And before long, I was undefeated. In the district tournament, I wanted nothing more than to redeem the previous year's loss in the finals, to get that first-place trophy. Well, I had the opportunity, and I gave it my all. And I lost again.

But it wasn't over. My teammate and I had made it to the doubles final. Excelling at singles requires individual skill and will. It's almost like singing your favorite song, in tune, on key, for an hour (or two). You keep the ball in the court, don't commit unforced errors, play your game well, don't choke, and you stand a good chance of being victorious.

Playing doubles is all that . . . plus playing in tandem with a partner. Now you have to sing a song with someone else . . . in harmony. It requires two people to think and act as one. Above all, it requires complete trust. My partner, Rob, and I had been winning doubles tournaments all summer, and our games were in sync. The trust and confidence we shared in each other was electric each time we stepped on the court. We ended up winning the district tennis tournament, and I got my first-place trophy.

All along, I'd thought basketball was going to be my sport. My father played it. I was tall. I thought I could ball. To this day, it's my favorite sport to watch. I even wrote a book called *The Crossover*, an homage to hoops, family, and friendship. Turns out, my passion was on a different court. Once I figured that out, I was relentless in my pursuit to excel. I was determined to succeed and be the best player. And, my serve was killer—fast, hard, and tricky. My teammates even gave me a nickname:

"The Big Ace."

Foc

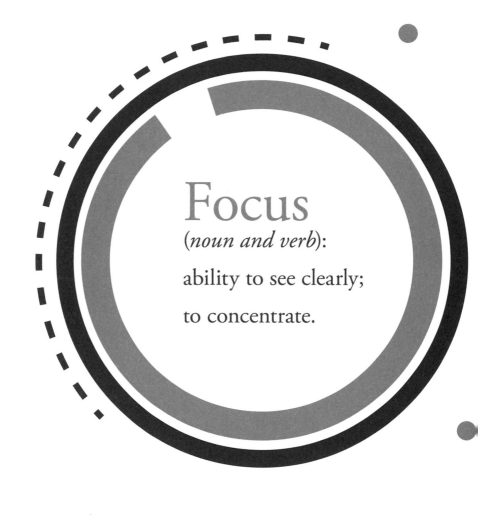

Focus
(*noun and verb*):
ability to see clearly;
to concentrate.

If there is a recipe for success, then one of the main ingredients is focus. And if there is a sport that requires consistent concentration, it's the ninety-minute game of *fútbol*.

On October 23, 1940, in Três Corações, Brazil, the soccer legend Edson Arantes do Nascimento, soon known as Pelé, was born into humble beginnings. It is said his parents, João (Dondinho) Ramos and Dona Celeste, named the future soccer star after history's most famous inventor, Thomas Edison. It seems they knew their son was destined to shine as bright as the sun.

LIGHTNING EYES FIXED ON THE ZOOOOOM CAN'T NOBODY STOP YOU YOU STOP FAST AND FREE FROM 12 YARDS OUT WINDING DOWN FIELD EYES FIXED ON THE CHECKERED BALL NOBODY YOU STRIKE ON THE GOAL

When Pelé was just a little boy, his parents moved to the city of Bauru, where his father was a struggling soccer player. The family was so poor, Dondinho created a soccer ball for Pelé made of a rolled-up sock stuffed with rags and newspaper and tied with a string. Pelé would run through the streets of Bauru barefoot, happily kicking the ball, practicing what would one day become his destiny. He would often skip school to practice in nearby fields. He sold peanuts and shined shoes to earn enough money to buy a real soccer ball. He and his friends formed their own team called the "Shoe-less Ones" because they played barefoot on streets and in vacant lots. These street games gave Pelé the rough edge he needed to eventually compete and be noticed as he perfected his own unique dribbling moves that would pay off later down the road. Pelé was expelled from school in fourth grade because he was caught skipping in favor of playing his beloved sport. He had to take a job as a cobbler's apprentice, making just a couple dollars a day, but it didn't stop him from playing soccer.

Pelé was discovered at age eleven by Waldemar de Brito, a former member of the Brazilian national soccer team, who secretly trained Pelé and encouraged him to join a junior football club. At the age

of fifteen, Pelé got permission from his family to leave home and try out for Santos, a top professional soccer team. At the beginning of his second season with Santos, he became a starter and top scorer in the league. In 1957, Pelé was selected for Brazil's national team, and he worked overtime playing for both Santos and Brazil. His dream had become a reality. But sometimes reality becomes even bigger than our dreams.

Before the 1958 World Cup match against Sweden, Pelé had been sidelined for a few games due to a knee injury. Feeling helpless and a bit hopeless, he sat on the bench, encouraging his teammates and summoning the focus to envision the contributions he would make once he was able to return to the pitch. He imagined helping his team to victory. After receiving treatment from doctors, and with the support of his teammates, he insisted that he play, and he was cleared. At just seventeen years old, Pelé, an unknown in the world of soccer, became the youngest athlete to play in the World Cup, leading his team to a 5–2 victory against Sweden.

Over time, he earned the nicknames "Gasoline" for his high, explosive energy, "The Executioner" for his ability to finish a play and score, and "The Black Pearl" because he was a rare and precious gift to his country and the world. The boy who ran through the rough streets of Bauru had his place in history as the greatest soccer player of all time, proving that with heart, focus, commitment, and talent, you can achieve greatness.

I think that in order to get better . . . you have to make goals. Whether you write them down or tell someone about them, it's important to set goals for yourself in order to achieve any kind of success.

—Abby Wambach, two-time Olympic gold medalist and FIFA Women's World Cup champion.

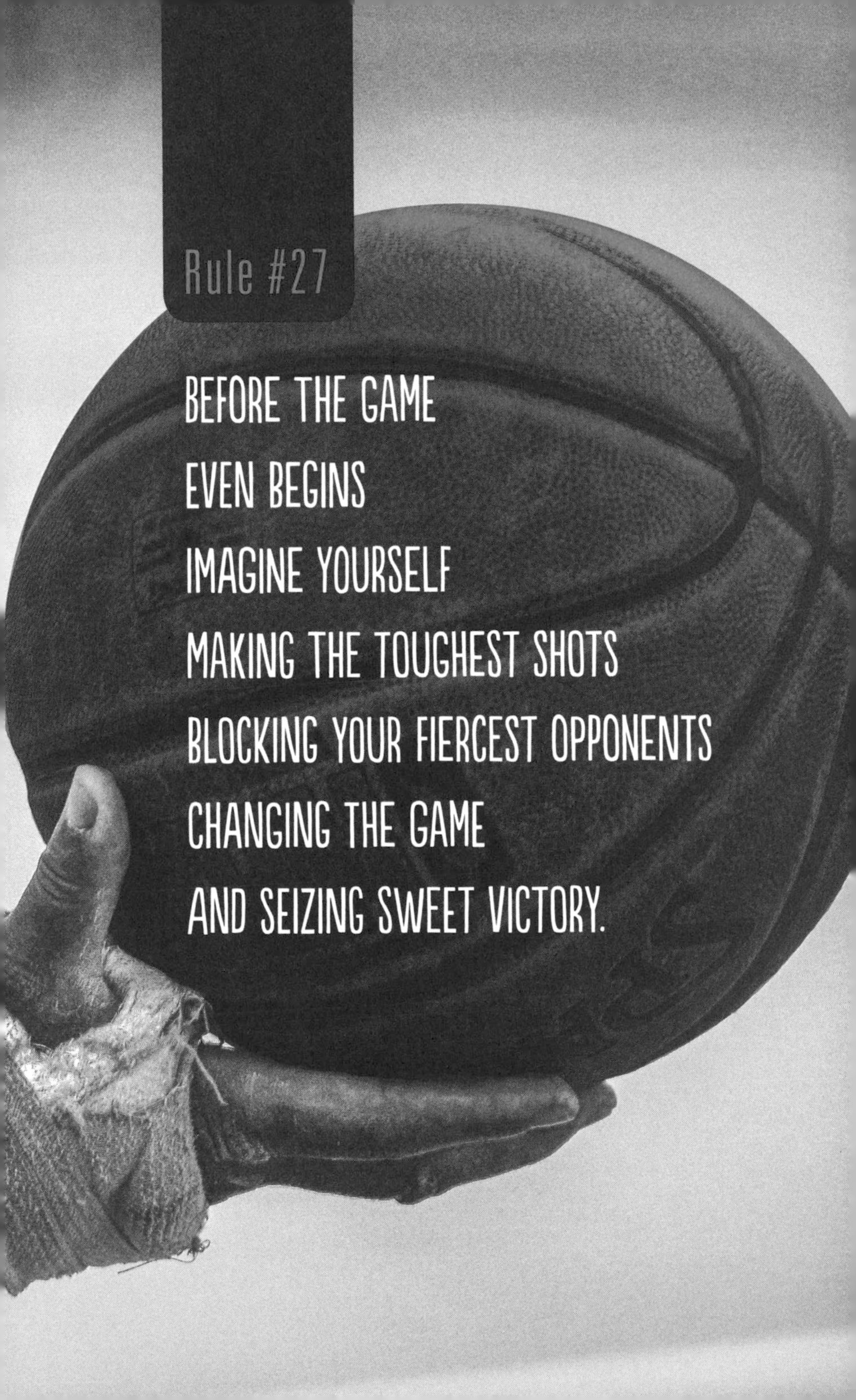

BEFORE THE GAME
EVEN BEGINS
IMAGINE YOURSELF
MAKING THE TOUGHEST SHOTS
BLOCKING YOUR FIERCEST OPPONENTS
CHANGING THE GAME
AND SEIZING SWEET VICTORY.

FOCUS.
KEEP YOUR EYES
ON THE BALL.
DON'T LOSE SIGHT.
DON'T OVERPLAY.

DON'T GET CROSSED-UP.
KEEP YOUR EYES
ON THE BALL.
FOCUS.

Concentration and mental toughness are the margins of victory.

—Bill Russell, Hall of Fame player/coach, five-time MVP and centerpiece of eleven NBA championships with the Boston Celtics

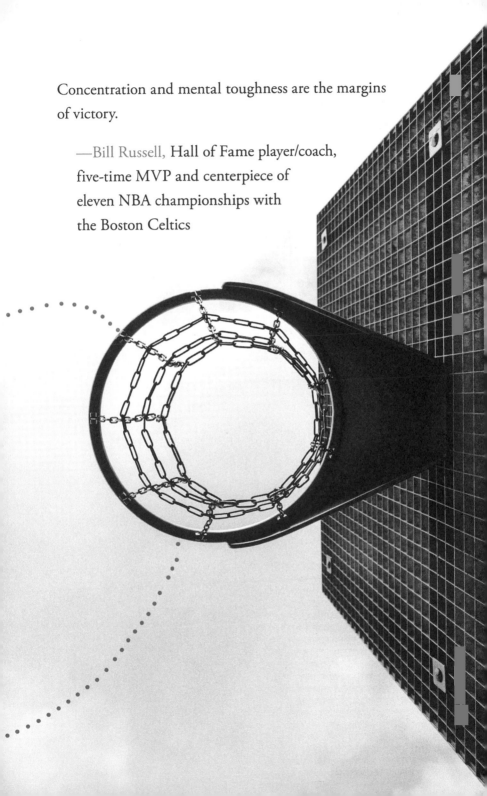

Rule #29

WHEN YOU FIND YOURSELF LOSING AND THE GAME IS OUT OF CONTROL TAKE A TIME-OUT.

When you come off something really disappointing, you want to come back and kind of regroup and get involved in something positive right away.

—Andy Roddick, number one tennis player (ATP rankings), U.S. Open champion

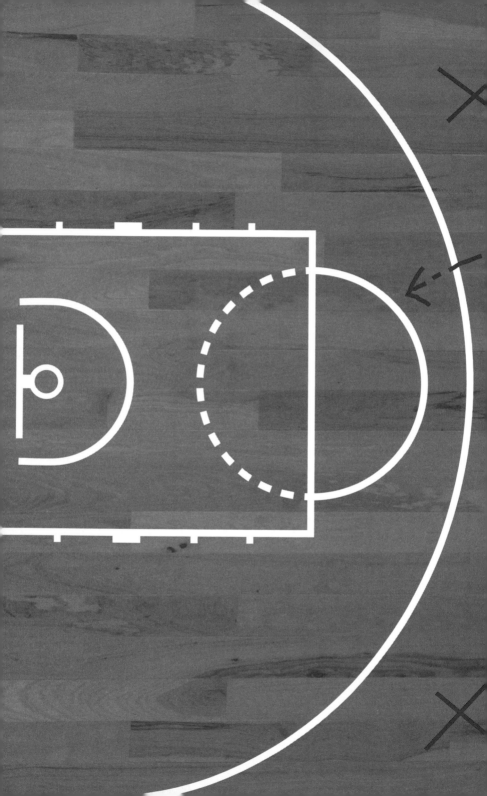

THERE IS NO SINGLE FORMULA FOR WINNING BUT YOU MUST HAVE A GAME PLAN.

I never worry about the problem. I worry about the solution.

—Shaquille O'Neal, four-time NBA champion with the Los Angeles Lakers and the Miami Heat, fifteen-time NBA all-star

108

WHEN YOU GET BENCHED,
STEP YOUR MENTAL GAME UP,
GET YOURSELF READY TO RETURN.

YOU MIGHT FOUL UP,
BUT DON'T FOUL OUT.

109

Excellence is the gradual result of always
striving to do better.

—Pat Riley, five-time NBA champion
head coach of the Los Angeles Lakers
and the Miami Heat

Every time you fall down,
it gives you an opportunity to question
yourself, question your integrity. . . . It's not about
the actual failure itself—it's how you respond to it.

—Abby Wambach, two-time Olympic gold medalist
and FIFA Women's World Cup champion

Rule #32

SOMETIMES
YOU HAVE TO
LEAN BACK
A LITTLE
AND
FADE AWAY
TO GET
THE BEST
SHOT.

111

IF YOU'RE OFF-BALANCE
OR DON'T FEEL COMFORTABLE
NEVER RUSH YOUR SHOT.

KICK THE BALL OUT.

RESTART.

TAKE THE TIME

YOU NEED
TO GET A
BETTER POSITION.

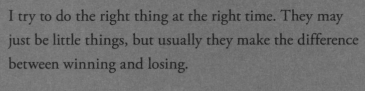

I try to do the right thing at the right time. They may just be little things, but usually they make the difference between winning and losing.

–Kareem Abdul-Jabbar, six-time NBA champion with the Los Angeles Lakers and the Milwaukee Bucks, six-time MVP

Rule #34

THE ROAD
TO
WINNING
THE BIG CHAMPIONSHIPS
IS FILLED WITH
BUMPS AND DIPS.

The harder you work and the more prepared you
are for something, you're going to be able to
persevere through anything.

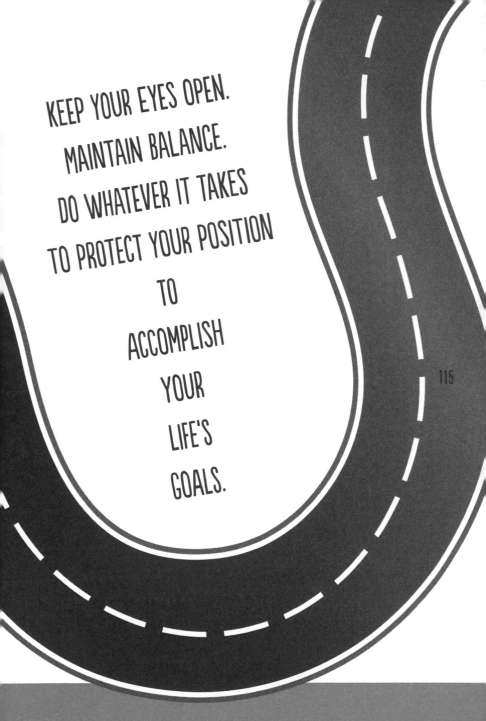

KEEP YOUR EYES OPEN.
MAINTAIN BALANCE.
DO WHATEVER IT TAKES
TO PROTECT YOUR POSITION
TO
ACCOMPLISH
YOUR
LIFE'S
GOALS.

—Carli Lloyd, two-time Olympic gold medalist, FIFA Women's
World Cup champion, and 2015 FIFA Women's Player of the Year

Rule #35

CONCENTRATE YOUR EFFORTS.

MOTIVATE YOUR TEAMMATES.

COMMUNICATE YOUR STRATEGY.

COORDINATE YOUR PLAYS.

DOMINATE YOUR OPPONENTS.

ORCHESTRATE YOUR WIN.

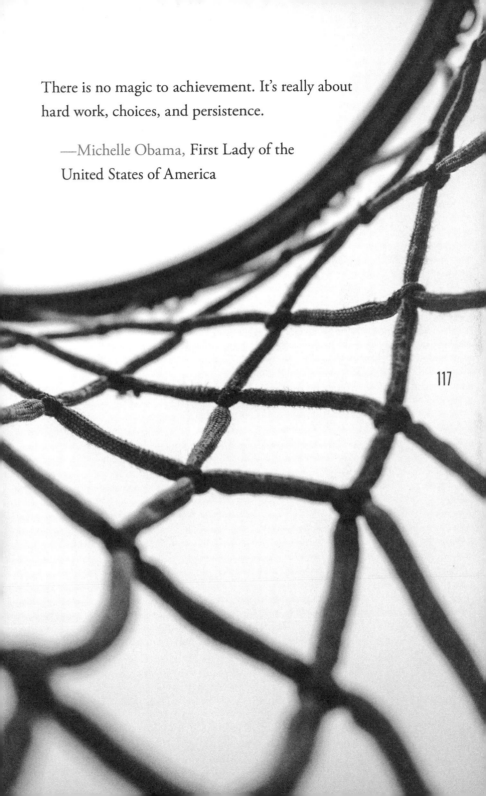

There is no magic to achievement. It's really about hard work, choices, and persistence.

—Michelle Obama, First Lady of the United States of America

117

IF YOU'RE THE POINT GUARD
YOU HAVE A SPLIT SECOND
TO READ THE COURT
ACT SWIFTLY
AND SET THE PLAY
THAT COULD CHANGE
THE GAME.

If you have a chance to accomplish something
that will make things better for people coming
behind you, and you don't do that, you are wasting
your time on this earth.

—Roberto Clemente, two-time World
Series champion and twelve-time MLB
all-star with the Pittsburgh Pirates

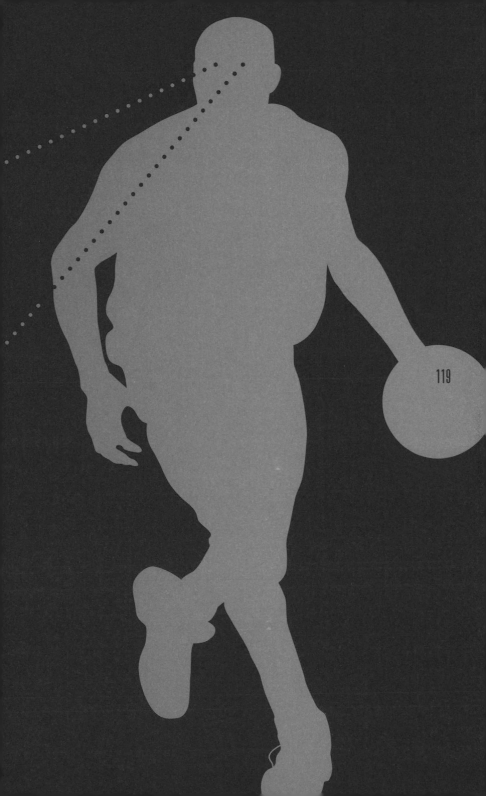

STARTING
WITH A SIMPLE MOVE
LIKE A LAY-UP
CAN BUILD CONFIDENCE
AS YOU MOVE
THROUGH THE HARD SCREENS
AND TOUGH CHALLENGES
ON YOUR WAY
TO THE GOAL.

A surplus of effort could overcome a deficit of confidence.

—Sonia Sotomayor, U.S. Supreme Court justice

THE FIRST STEP
IN ACHIEVING
POSITIVE RESULTS
IS PLANNING
TO ACHIEVE
POSITIVE
RESULTS.

THE SECOND STEP
IS ACTUALLY WORKING
THE PLAN.

You have to expect things of yourself
before you can do them.

—Michael Jordan, six-time NBA
champion with the Chicago Bulls,
five-time MVP

IT'S OKAY TO
TAKE TIME OUT
SLOW DOWN
HUDDLE
BREATHE
REGROUP
REFOCUS
RESTART.

All great achievements require time.

—Maya Angelou, acclaimed poet and author
of *I Know Why the Caged Bird Sings*

4th Quarter

Team

work

and Resilience

Teamwork *(noun)*:

the combined
action of
a group
of people,
especially
when
effective.

X

Resilience (*noun*):

the ability to
recover quickly
from difficulty;
toughness.

130

If you've never seen Venus and Serena Williams play against each other, go watch the 2000 Wimbledon Finals or the 2002 French Open Finals. *Stunning, powerful,* and *tense* are the best words to describe it. When they first played each other in 1999, Venus beat her younger sister. But, later that year, Serena bounced back and defeated Venus. I watched all these matches, and many more, and their resilience is awe-inspiring. They simply never give up.

Venus and Serena were the youngest two of five sisters born to Richard and Oracene (Brandi) Williams, and they spent much of their childhood in and around Compton, California. Richard was a superfan of tennis and was determined to help his daughters learn the finer points of the game. He put rackets in all his daughters' hands, teaching them how to power serve and rally and volley.

The girls were homeschooled by their mother, and practiced their tennis skills with their father for hours every day. They didn't wear hip and cool tennis outfits or fancy sneakers, because they couldn't afford them. So they practiced in their jeans on Compton courts, which had potholes and missing nets, under the

cloud of violence, home-lessness, and drug crimes that hovered over the city. Sometimes the girls had to take cover to avoid being hit in the crossfire of gang-related activity.

There weren't just the dangers of Compton, though—there were the emotional challenges the girls faced at games in other cities and places where they stood out as being different. They were often the only African Americans at a tournament. In order to prepare Venus and Serena for the harsh realities of playing tennis in front of racist crowds, Richard sometimes paid other children to yell out rude and demeaning comments to his daughters during their practices. Venus and Serena developed focus and a thick skin for the long, arduous journey to tennis stardom.

At seven years old, Venus started receiving attention from tennis elites such as Pete Sampras and John McEnroe, both of whom encouraged her to keep playing. By age ten, she was already ranked the number one player in the Under-12 division in Southern California. *Sports Illustrated* and *Tennis* magazine wrote stories about the young tennis star from the dangerous streets of Compton. Serena was not far behind, racking up accolades with the same distinction. Their hard work paid off. When they finally turned pro, Venus would go on to win nine Grand Slam championships, and Serena a whopping twenty-one. Together, they also accomplished something that very few players have done: The sisters teamed up to win thirteen Grand Slam doubles titles, including the prestigious Golden Slam—winning an Olympic gold medal and all four Grand Slam titles in their career.

From the tough courts of Compton to the world stage of tennis, the Williams sisters—models of raw, undeterred resilience—have broken barriers and changed the game of tennis forever. And they did it together. No matter whether they are playing against each other or cheering the other on during a match, the Williams sisters understand the value and importance of having someone in your corner, of supporting and encouraging each other. As Venus says, "My first job is big sister and I take that very seriously."

Who's got *your* back?

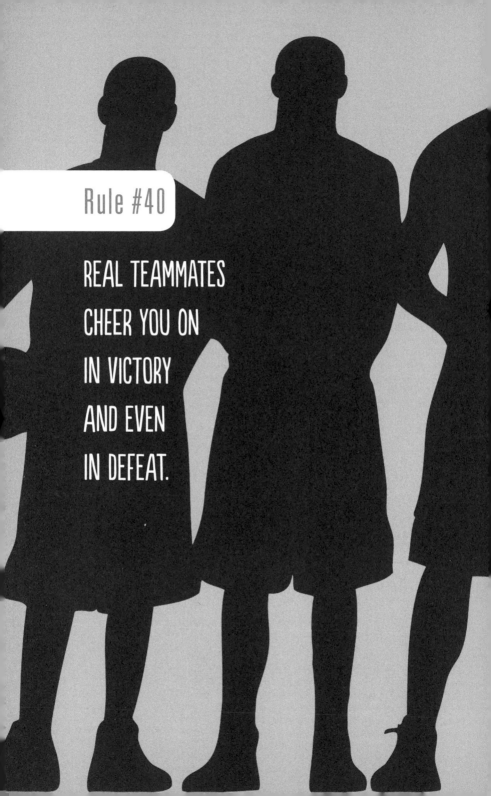

Rule #40

REAL TEAMMATES
CHEER YOU ON
IN VICTORY
AND EVEN
IN DEFEAT.

The strength of the team is each individual member. The strength of each member is the team.

—Phil Jackson, eleven-time NBA championship–winning coach with the Chicago Bulls and the Los Angeles Lakers

A GREAT TEAM
HAS A GOOD SCORER
WITH A TEAMMATE
WHO'S ON POINT
AND READY
TO ASSIST.

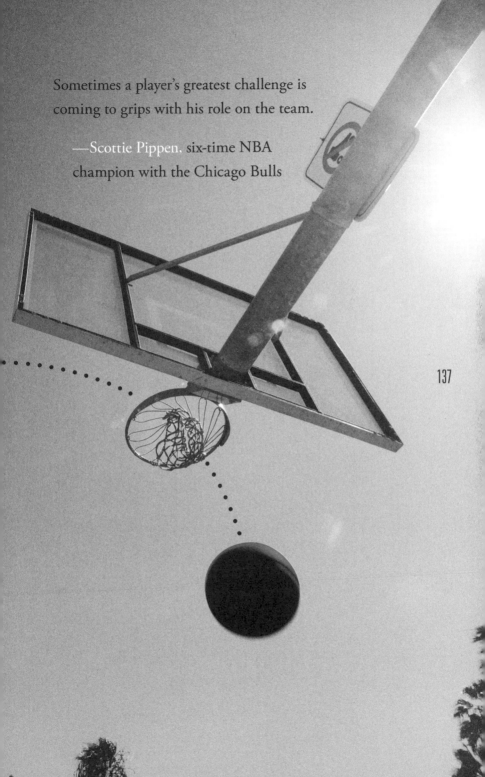

Sometimes a player's greatest challenge is coming to grips with his role on the team.

—Scottie Pippen, six-time NBA champion with the Chicago Bulls

137

BE UNSELFISH.
SHARE THE BALL.

WORK TOGETHER.
WIN TOGETHER.

138

The most important measure of how good a game I played was how much better I'd made my teammates play.

—Bill Russell, Hall of Fame player/coach, five-time MVP and centerpiece of eleven NBA championships with the Boston Celtics

139

Rule #43

WINNING HAPPENS WHEN FIVE PLAYERS ON THE COURT PLAY WITH ONE HEART.

Talent wins games, but teammates
and intelligence win championships.

—Michael Jordan, six-time
NBA champion with the
Chicago Bulls, five-time MVP

TEAMMATES ARE LIKE FAMILY, CELEBRATING WINS, CONSOLING LOSSES, ALWAYS A NET TIED TOGETHER.

142

Surround yourself with only people who are going to lift you higher.

—Oprah Winfrey, studio executive, producer, talk show host, actress, philanthropist

A LOSS IS INEVITABLE, LIKE RAIN IN SPRING. TRUE CHAMPIONS LEARN TO DANCE THROUGH THE STORM.

144

It's what you get from games you lose that is extremely important.

—Pat Riley, five-time NBA champion head coach of the Los Angeles Lakers and the Miami Heat

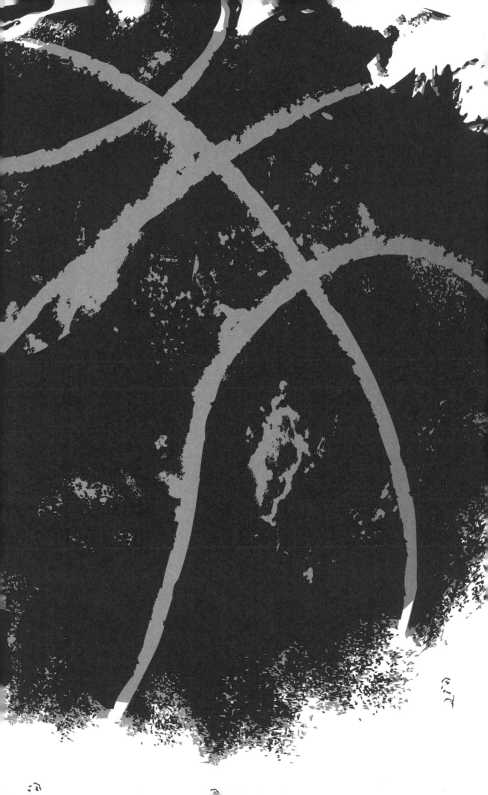

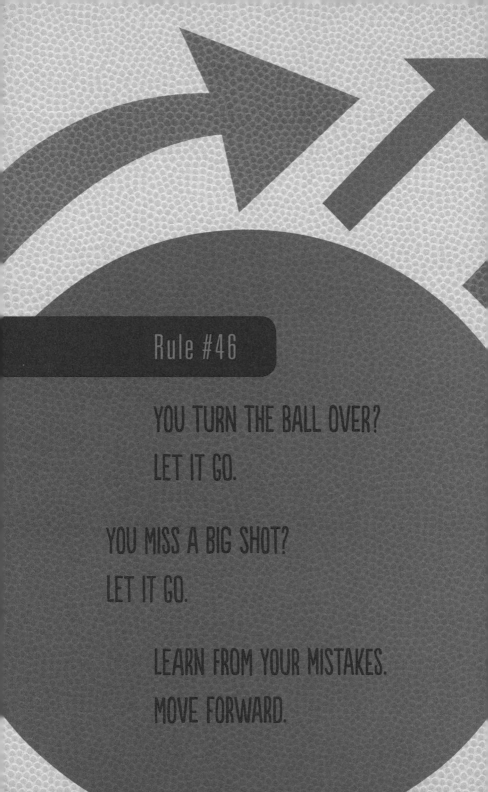

Rule #46

YOU TURN THE BALL OVER?
LET IT GO.

YOU MISS A BIG SHOT?
LET IT GO.

LEARN FROM YOUR MISTAKES.
MOVE FORWARD.

What to do
with a mistake: recognize it,
admit it, learn from it, forget it.

—Dean Smith, two-time NCAA
championship–winning head
coach at the University of
North Carolina

Rule #47

IF YOU MISS
ENOUGH OF LIFE'S
FREE THROWS
YOU WILL PAY
IN THE END.

Mistakes are a fact of life. It is the response to the error that counts.

—Nikki Giovanni, acclaimed poet, author of *Ego-Tripping and Other Poems for Young People*

WHEN YOUR SHOT
GETS BLOCKED
DON'T FEAR.
YOU'VE GOT TO GET
THE BALL BACK
REESTABLISH POSITION
AND PLAN
YOUR NEXT MOVE.

I learned that courage was not the absence of fear, but the triumph over it. The brave man is not he who does not feel afraid, but he who conquers that fear.

—Nelson Mandela, president of South Africa, Nobel Peace Prize winner

151

Persistence can change failure into extraordinary achievement.

—Matt Biondi, U.S. Olympic swimmer, eight-time gold medalist

Rule #49

DRIBBLE FAKE SHOOT MISS

DRIBBLE FAKE SHOOT MISS

DRIBBLE FAKE SHOOT MISS

DRIBBLE FAKE SHOOT SWISH!

153

Rule #50

LOSING
IS AN OPPORTUNITY
TO GET BETTER,
TO LEARN
WHAT TO DO
TO WIN.

We may encounter many defeats but we must not be defeated.

—Maya Angelou, acclaimed poet and author of *I Know Why the Caged Bird Sings*

REBOUNDING
IS THE ART
OF ANTICIPATING,
OF ALWAYS BEING PREPARED
TO GRAB IT.
BUT YOU CAN'T
DROP THE BALL.

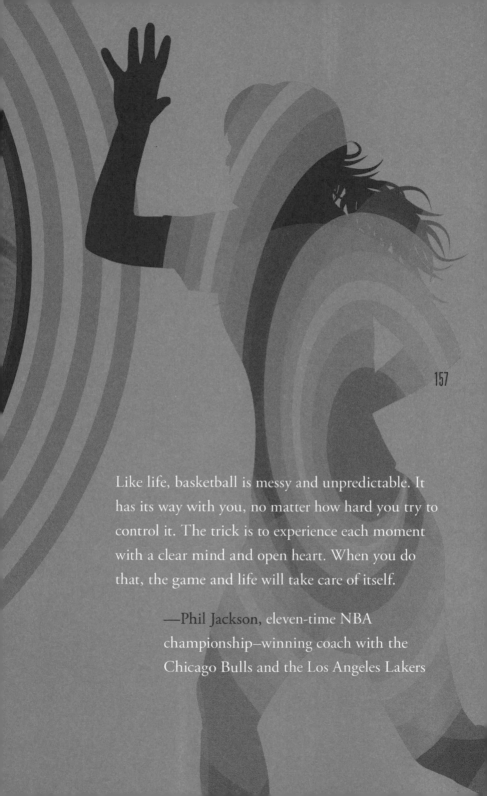

Like life, basketball is messy and unpredictable. It has its way with you, no matter how hard you try to control it. The trick is to experience each moment with a clear mind and open heart. When you do that, the game and life will take care of itself.

—Phil Jackson, eleven-time NBA championship–winning coach with the Chicago Bulls and the Los Angeles Lakers

Rule #52

IT MIGHT LOOK
LIKE A
LONG SHOT
BUT YOU'LL NEVER
MAKE IT
IF YOU DON'T
KEEP SHOOTING.

159

You miss 100 percent of the shots you don't take.

—Wayne Gretzky, four-time Stanley Cup
winner, recognized as the greatest hockey
player of all time by many sportswriters

162

Tenacity (*noun*):
determination, persistence.

When Lew Alcindor started playing basketball in college for UCLA, the NCAA officials felt that he was too dominant a player—because at seven feet, two inches he could dunk the ball too easily (not to mention way too FIERCELY). They felt he would be unstoppable. So in 1967 they changed the rules to forbid dunking in college games. This was called the "Alcindor Rule." Can you imagine the game of basketball without dunking? No way the NCAA's March Madness or the NBA would be so popular without Michael Jordan tongue wagging and soaring to the hoop for a *dunkalicious* slam!

As a result of the rule, Alcindor developed a great hook shot, which he used effectively during his playing days in college and the NBA to win three consecutive NCAA championships and six NBA championships. Lew Alcindor did not let the new no-dunking rule change thwart him. He *rebounded*, simply made up his own rule, and created the most lethal shot in hoops history—the hook. Shortly after he started playing professional basketball, he changed his name to Kareem Abdul-Jabbar. The

Alcindor rule was rescinded in 1975, and players were allowed to dunk again.

From Kareem Abdul-Jabaar to Steph Curry (who many college coaches said was too small to play for their team); from Venus and Serena to Tamika Catchings—the ten-year WNBA all-star, MVP, and WNBA champion who is also deaf—there are tales of athletes who have defied the odds and achieved greatness. And they've all had a few things in common: they know the rules and never give up! And *you* shouldn't either. I'm not saying it's easy, but I am saying that the hard work, grit, and *say yes* attitude is well worth it in the end. Just remember:

BE TENACIOUS.

BELIEVE IN YOURSELF
EVEN WHEN IT SEEMS THAT NO ONE ELSE DOES.

SOMETIMES YOU HAVE TO CHOOSE YOUR OWN MOVES.

SURROUND YOURSELF
WITH THE RIGHT TEAM, WITH PEOPLE WHO SUPPORT YOU, WHO ARE EQUALLY—IF NOT MORE—PASSIONATE AND AMBITIOUS.

OWN YOUR POSITION,
CONTROL IT, MOVE YOUR FEET, ROTATE, PUT YOUR NAME ON THE BALL.

CREATE YOUR OWN PLAY.

HONOR THE ONES WHO'VE COME BEFORE YOU.

HONOR THE GREATNESS
THAT IS YOU.

PRACTICE...

...FACE DEFEAT.

REBOUND.

EXPECT TO WIN.

WIN.

WALK THROUGH UNFAMILIAR DOORS.

KNOW THE RULES.

MASTER THE RULES.

SAY YES

TO THE POSSIBILITY

OF SOMETIMES

MAKING UP

YOUR OWN.

RULES!

ABOUT THE AUTHOR

KWAME ALEXANDER is a poet, educator, and *New York Times* best-selling author of twenty-one books, including *Booked* and *The Crossover,* which received the 2015 John Newbery Medal for the Most Distinguished Contribution to American Literature for Children, the Coretta Scott King Author Award Honor, the NCTE Charlotte Huck Honor, the Lee Bennett Hopkins Poetry Award, and the Paterson Poetry Prize.

A regular speaker at schools and conferences, he travels the world planting seeds of literary love. Each year, Alexander leads a delegation of writers, educators, and activists to Ghana as part of LEAP for Ghana, an international literacy program he co-founded that builds libraries and provides literacy professional development for teachers. He lives in Virginia. Visit him at kwamealexander.com.

Also by Kwame Alexander

THE CROSSOVER

In this Newbery Medal–winning middle grade novel in verse, twelve-year-old twin basketball stars Josh and Jordan wrestle with highs and lows on and off the court.

Newbery Medal Winner
Coretta Scott King Honor Award Winner
A *New York Times* Bestseller

"A beautifully measured novel of life and lines."
—*New York Times Book Review*

"Alexander's at the top of his poetic game in this taut, complex tale of the crossover from brash, vulnerable boy to young adult."—*Washington Post*

BOOKED

In this middle grade novel in verse, soccer, family, love, and friendship take center stage as twelve-year-old Nick learns the power of words, wrestles with problems at home, stands up to a bully, and tries to impress the girl of his dreams.

A *New York Times* Bestseller
National Book Award Longlist Nominee

"To pick up *Booked* is to find yourself turning page after page, swept along as Nick spills out his story."—*New York Times Book Review*

ABOUT THE PHOTOGRAPHER

THAI NEAVE is a former SportsCenter anchor for ESPN and now works as a freelance photographer and director. He currently resides between New York and Los Angeles. Follow his work at instagram.com/shootinghoops.

THE
YOUNG
ELITES

Also by Marie Lu

LEGEND

PRODIGY

CHAMPION

THE
YOUNG
ELITES

MARIE LU

G. P. Putnam's Sons

An Imprint of Penguin Group (USA)

G. P. PUTNAM'S SONS
Published by the Penguin Group
Penguin Group (USA) LLC
375 Hudson Street
New York, NY 10014

USA | Canada | UK | Ireland | Australia
New Zealand | India | South Africa | China
penguin.com
A Penguin Random House Company

Library of Congress Cataloging-in-Publication Data is available upon request.

Printed in the United States of America.
ISBN 978-0-399-16783-6
1 3 5 7 9 10 8 6 4 2

Design by Marikka Tamura.
Text set in Palatino Linotype.

To my aunt, Yang Lin, for all that you do

SKYLANDS

BELDAIN
Hadenbury

KENETTRA

The
Sun
Sea

Anfou
Campagnia
Serrata
Estenzia
Golden Valley
Triese di Mare
Udara
Dalia
Falls of
Laetes
Petra

The
Sacchi
Sea

SEALANDS

The Ember Isles

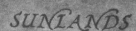

SUNLANDS

Four hundred have died here. I pray that yours are faring better. The city has canceled celebrations of the Spring Moons on quarantine orders, and the typical masquerades have become as scarce as the meat and eggs.

Most of the children in our ward are emerging from their illness with rather peculiar side effects. One young girl's hair turned from gold to black overnight. A six-year-old boy has scars running down his face without ever having been touched. The other doctors are quite terrified. Please let me know if you see a similar trend, sir. I sense something unusual shifting in the wind, and am most anxious to study this effect.

Letter from Dtt. Siriano Baglio to Dtt. Marino Di Segna

31 Abrie, 1348

Southeastern districts of Dalia, Kenettra

13 JUNO, 1361

City of Dalia
Southern Kenettra
The Sealands

Some hate us, think us outlaws to hang at the gallows.

Some fear us, think us demons to burn at the stake.

Some worship us, think us children of the gods.

But *all* know us.

—*Unknown source on the Young Elites*

Adelina Amouteru

I'm going to die tomorrow morning.

That's what the Inquisitors tell me, anyway, when they visit my cell. I've been in here for weeks—I know this only because I've been counting the number of times my meals come.

One day. Two days.

Four days. A week.

Two weeks.

Three.

I stopped counting after that. The hours run together, an endless train of nothingness, filled with different slants of light and the shiver of cold, wet stone, the pieces of my sanity, the disjointed whispers of my thoughts.

But tomorrow, my time ends. They're going to burn me at the stake in the central market square, for all to see. The Inquisitors tell me a crowd has already begun to gather outside.

1

I sit straight, the way I was always taught. My shoulders don't touch the wall. It takes me a while to realize that I'm rocking back and forth, perhaps to stay sane, perhaps just to keep warm. I hum an old lullaby too, one my mother used to sing to me when I was very little. I do my best to imitate her voice, a sweet and delicate sound, but my notes come out cracked and hoarse, nothing like what I remember. I stop trying.

It's so damp down here. Water trickles from above my door and has painted a groove into the stone wall, discolored green and black with grime. My hair is matted, and my nails are caked with blood and dirt. I want to scrub them clean. Is it strange that all I can think about on my last day is how filthy I am? If my little sister were here, she'd murmur something reassuring and soak my hands in warm water.

I can't stop wondering if she's okay. She hasn't come to see me.

I lower my head into my hands. How did I end up like this?

But I know how, of course. It's because I'm a murderer.

✦✦✦

It happened several weeks earlier, on a stormy night at my father's villa. I couldn't sleep. Rain fell and lightning reflected off the window of my bedchamber. But even the storm couldn't drown out the conversation from downstairs. My father and his guest were talking about me, of course. My father's late-night conversations were always about me.

I was the talk of my family's eastern Dalia district. *Adelina Amouteru?* they all said. *Oh, she's one of those who survived the fever a decade ago. Poor thing. Her father will have a hard time marrying her off.*

No one meant because I wasn't *beautiful*. I'm not being arrogant, only honest. My nursemaid once told me that any man who'd ever laid eyes on my late mother was now waiting curiously to see how her two daughters would blossom into women. My younger sister, Violetta, was only fourteen and already the budding image of perfection. Unlike me, Violetta had inherited our mother's rosy temperament and innocent charm. She'd kiss my cheeks and laugh and twirl and dream. When we were very small, we'd sit together in the garden and she would braid periwinkles into my hair. I would sing to her. She would make up games.

We loved each other, once.

My father would bring Violetta jewels and watch her clap her hands in delight as he strung them around her neck. He would buy her exquisite dresses that arrived in port from the farthest ends of the world. He would tell her stories and kiss her good night. He would remind her how beautiful she was, how far she would raise our family's standing with a good marriage, how she could attract princes and kings if she desired. Violetta already had a line of suitors eager to secure her hand, and my father would tell each of them to be patient, that they could not marry her until she turned seventeen. *What a caring father,* everyone thought.

Of course, Violetta didn't escape *all* of my father's cruelty.

He purposely bought her dresses that were tight and painful. He enjoyed seeing her feet bleed from the hard, jeweled shoes he encouraged her to wear.

Still. He loved her, in his own way. It's different, you see, because she was his investment.

I was another story. Unlike my sister, blessed with shining black hair to complement her dark eyes and rich olive skin, I am flawed. And by flawed, I mean this: When I was four years old, the blood fever reached its peak and everyone in Kenettra barred their homes in a state of panic. No use. My mother, sister, and I all came down with the fever. You could always tell who was infected—strange, mottled patterns showed up on our skin, our hair and lashes flitted from one color to another, and pink, blood-tinged tears ran from our eyes. I still remember the smell of sickness in our house, the burn of brandy on my lips. My left eye became so swollen that a doctor had to remove it. He did it with a red-hot knife and a pair of burning tongs.

So, yes. You could say I am flawed.

Marked. A *malfetto*.

While my sister emerged from the fever unscathed, I now have only a scar where my left eye used to be. While my sister's hair remained a glossy black, the strands of *my* hair and lashes turned a strange, ever-shifting silver, so that in the sunlight they look close to white, like a winter moon, and in the dark they change to a deep gray, shimmering silk spun from metal.

At least I fared better than Mother did. Mother, like every

infected adult, died. I remember crying in her empty bed-chamber each night, wishing the fever had taken Father instead.

My father and his mysterious guest were still talking downstairs. My curiosity got the best of me and I swung my legs over the side of my bed, crept toward my chamber door on light feet, and opened it a crack. Dim candlelight illumi-nated the hall outside. Below, my father sat across from a tall, broad-shouldered man with graying hair at his temples, his hair tied back at the nape of his neck in a short, custom-ary tail, the velvet of his coat shining black and orange in the light. My father's coat was velvet too, but the material was worn thin. Before the blood fever crippled our country, his clothes would have been as luxurious as his guest's. But now? It's hard to keep good trade relations when you have a *malfetto* daughter tainting your family's name.

Both men drank wine. Father must be in a negotiating mood tonight, I thought, to have tapped one of our last good casks.

I opened the door a little wider, crept out into the hall, and sat, knees to my chin, along the stairs. My favorite spot. Some-times I'd pretend I was a queen, and that I stood here on a palace balcony looking down at my groveling subjects. Now I took up my usual crouch and listened closely to the conversa-tion downstairs. As always, I made sure my hair covered my scar. My hand rested awkwardly on the staircase. My father had broken my fourth finger, and it never healed straight. Even now, I could not curl it properly around the railing.

"I don't mean to insult you, Master Amouteru," the man said to my father. "You were a merchant of good reputation. But that was a long time ago. I don't want to be seen doing business with a *malfetto* family—bad luck, you know. There's little you can offer me."

My father kept a smile on his face. The forced smile of a business transaction. "There are still lenders in town who work with me. I can pay you back as soon as the port traffic picks up. Tamouran silks and spices are in high demand this year—"

The man looked unimpressed. "The king's dumb as a dog," he replied. "And dogs are no good at running countries. The ports will be slow for years to come, I'm afraid, and with the new tax laws, your debts will only grow. How can you possibly repay me?"

My father leaned back in his chair, sipped his wine, and sighed. "There must be something I can offer you."

The man studied his glass of wine thoughtfully. The harsh lines of his face made me shiver. "Tell me about Adelina. How many offers have you received?"

My father blushed. As if the wine hadn't left him red enough already. "Offers for Adelina's hand have been slow to come."

The man smiled. "None for your little abomination, then."

My father's lips tightened. "Not as many as I'd like," he admitted.

"What do the others say about her?"

"The other suitors?" My father rubbed a hand across his

face. Admitting all my flaws embarrassed him. "They say the same thing. It always comes back to her . . . markings. What can I tell you, sir? No one wants a *malfetto* bearing his children."

The man listened, making sympathetic sounds.

"Haven't you heard the latest news from Estenzia? Two noblemen walking home from the opera were found burned to a crisp." My father had quickly changed tack, hoping now that the stranger would take pity on him. "Scorch marks on the wall, their bodies melted from the inside out. Everyone is frightened of *malfettos*, sir. Even *you* are reluctant to do business with me. Please. I'm helpless."

I knew what my father spoke of. He was referring to very specific *malfettos*—a rare handful of children who came out of the blood fever with scars far darker than mine, frightening abilities that don't belong in this world. Everyone talked about these *malfettos* in hushed whispers; most feared them and called them demons. But *I* secretly held them in awe. People said they could conjure fire out of thin air. Could call the wind. Could control beasts. Could disappear. Could kill in the blink of an eye.

If you searched the black market, you'd find flat wooden engravings for sale, elaborately carved with their names, forbidden collectibles that supposedly meant *they* would protect you—or, at the least, that they would not hurt you. No matter the opinion, everyone knew their names. *The Reaper. Magiano. The Windwalker. The Alchemist.*

The Young Elites.

The man shook his head. "I've heard that even the suitors who refuse Adelina still gape at her, sick with desire." He paused. "True, her markings are . . . unfortunate. But a beautiful girl is a beautiful girl." Something strange glinted in his eyes. My stomach twisted at the sight, and I tucked my chin tighter against my knees, as if for protection.

My father looked confused. He sat up taller in his chair and pointed his wineglass at the man. "Are you making me an offer for Adelina's hand?"

The man reached into his coat to produce a small brown pouch, then tossed it onto the table. It landed with a heavy clink. As a merchant's daughter, one becomes well acquainted with money—and I could tell from the sound and from the size of the coins that the purse was filled to the brim with gold talents. I stifled a gasp.

As my father gaped at the contents, the man leaned back and thoughtfully sipped his wine. "I know of the estate taxes you haven't yet paid to the crown. I know of your new debts. And I will cover all of them in exchange for your daughter Adelina."

My father frowned. "But you have a wife."

"I do, yes." The man paused, then added, "I never said I wanted to *marry* her. I am merely proposing to take her off your hands."

I felt the blood drain from my face. "You . . . want her as your mistress, then?" Father asked.

The man shrugged. "No nobleman in his right mind would make a wife of such a marked girl—she could not

possibly attend public affairs on my arm. I have a reputation to uphold, Master Amouteru. But I think we can work this out. She will have a home, and you will have your gold." He raised a hand. "One condition. I want her *now*, not in a year. I've no patience to wait until she turns seventeen."

A strange buzzing filled my ears. *No* boy or girl was allowed to give themselves to another until they turned seventeen. This man was asking my father to break the law. To defy the gods.

My father raised an eyebrow, but he didn't argue. "A mistress," he finally said. "Sir, you must know what this will do to my reputation. I might as well sell her to a brothel."

"And how is your reputation faring now? How much damage has she already done to your professional name?" He leaned forward. "Surely you're not insinuating my home is nothing more than a common brothel. At least your Adelina would belong to a noble household."

As I watched my father sip his wine, my hands began to tremble. "A mistress," he repeated.

"Think quickly, Master Amouteru. I won't offer this again."

"Give me a moment," my father anxiously reassured him.

I don't know how long the silence lasted, but when he finally spoke again, I jumped at the sound. "Adelina could be a good match for you. You're wise to see it. She is lovely, even with her markings, and . . . spirited."

The man swirled his wine. "And I will tame her. Do we have a deal?"

I closed my eye. My world swam in darkness—I imagined the man's face against my own, his hand on my waist, his sickening smile. Not even a wife. A *mistress.* The thought made me shrink from the stairs. Through a haze of numbness, I watched my father shake hands and clink wineglasses with the man. "A deal, then," he said to the man. He looked relieved of a great burden. "Tomorrow, she's yours. Just . . . keep this private. I don't want Inquisitors knocking on my door and fining me for giving her away too young."

"She's a *malfetto,*" the man replied. "No one will care." He tightened his gloves and rose from his chair in one elegant move. My father bowed his head. "I'll send a carriage for her in the morning."

As my father escorted him to our door, I stole away into my bedchamber and stood there in the darkness, shaking. Why did my father's words still stab me in the heart? I should be used to it by now. What had he once told me? *My poor Adelina,* he'd said, caressing my cheek with a thumb. *It's a shame. Look at you. Who will ever want a* malfetto *like you?*

It will be all right, I tried telling myself. *At least you can leave your father behind. It won't be so bad.* But even as I thought this, I felt a weight settle in my chest. I knew the truth. *Malfettos* were unwanted. Bad luck. And, now more than ever, feared. I would be tossed aside the instant the man tired of me.

My gaze wandered around my bedchamber, settling finally on my window. My heartbeat stilled for a moment. Rain drew angry lines down the glass, but through it I could

still see the deep blue cityscape of Dalia, the rows of domed brick towers and cobblestone alleys, the marble temples, the docks where the edge of the city sloped gently into the sea, where on clear nights gondolas with golden lanterns would glide across the water, where the waterfalls that bordered southern Kenettra thundered. Tonight, the ocean churned in fury, and white foam crashed against the city's horizon, flooding the canals.

I continued staring out the rain-slashed window for a long while.

Tonight. Tonight was the night.

I hurried to my bed, bent down, and dragged out a sack I'd made with a bedsheet. Inside it were fine silverware, forks and knives, candelabras, engraved plates, anything I could sell for food and shelter. That's another thing to love about me. I steal. I'd been stealing from around our house for months, stashing things under my bed in preparation for the day when I couldn't stand to live with my father any longer. It wasn't much, but I calculated that if I sold all of it to the right dealers, I might end up with a few gold talents. Enough to get by, at least, for several months.

Then I rushed to my chest of clothes, pulled out an armful of silks, and hurried about my chamber to collect any jewelry I could find. My silver bracelets. A pearl necklace inherited from my mother that my sister did not want. A pair of sapphire earrings. I grabbed two long strips of silk cloth that make up a Tamouran headwrap. I would need to cover up my silver hair

while on the run. I worked in feverish concentration. I added the jewelry and clothes carefully into the sack, hid it behind my bed, and pulled on my soft leather riding boots.

I settled down to wait.

An hour later, when my father retired to bed and the house stilled, I grabbed the sack. I hurried to my window and pressed my hand against it. Gingerly, I pushed the left pane aside and propped it open. The storm had calmed some, but rain still came down steadily enough to mute the sound of my footsteps. I looked over my shoulder one last time at my bedchamber door, as if I expected my father to walk in. *Where are you going, Adelina?* he'd say. *There's nothing out there for a girl like you.*

I shook his voice from my head. Let him find me gone in the morning, his best chance at settling his debts. I took a deep breath, then began to climb through the open window. Cold rain lashed at my arms, prickling my skin.

"Adelina?"

I whirled around at the voice. Behind me, the silhouette of a girl stood in my doorway—my sister, Violetta, still rubbing sleep from her eyes. She stared at the open window and the sack on my shoulders, and for a terrifying moment, I thought she might raise her voice and shout for Father.

But Violetta watched me quietly. I felt a pang of guilt, even as the sight of her sent a flash of resentment through my heart. Fool. Why should I have felt sorry for someone who had watched me suffer so many times before? *I love you, Adelina,* she used to say, when we were small. *Papa loves you*

too. He just doesn't know how to show it. Why did I pity the sister who was valued?

Still, I found myself rushing to her on silent feet, taking one of her hands in mine, and putting a slender finger up to her lips. She gave me a worried look. "You should go back to bed," she whispered. In the dim glow of night, I could see the gloss of her dark, marble eyes, the thinness of her delicate skin. Her beauty was so pure. "You'll get in trouble if Father finds you."

I squeezed her hand tighter, then let our foreheads touch. We stayed still for a long moment, and it seemed as if we were children again, each leaning against the other. Usually Violetta would pull away from me, knowing that Father did not like to see us close. This time, though, she clung to me. As if she knew that tonight was something different. "Violetta," I whispered, "do you remember the time you lied to Father about who broke one of his best vases?"

My sister nodded against my shoulder.

"I need you to do that for me again." I pulled far away enough to tuck her hair behind her ear. "Don't say a word."

She didn't reply; instead, she swallowed and looked down the hall toward our father's chambers. She did not hate him in the same way that I did, and the thought of going against his teaching—that she was too good for me, that to love me was a foolish thing—filled her eyes with guilt. Finally, she nodded. I felt as if a mantle had been lifted from my shoulders, like she was letting go of me. "Be careful out there. Stay safe. Good luck."

We exchanged a final look. *You could come with me*, I thought. *But I know you won't. You're too scared. Go back to smiling at the dresses that Father buys for you.* Still, my heart softened for a moment. Violetta was always the good girl. She didn't choose any of this. *I do wish you a happy life. I hope you fall in love and marry well. Good-bye, sister.* I didn't dare wait for her to say anything else. Instead I turned away, walked to the window, and stepped onto the second-floor ledge.

I nearly slipped. The rain had turned everything slick, and my riding boots fought for grip against the narrow ledge. Some silverware fell out of my sack, clattering on the ground below. *Don't look down.* I made my way along the ledge until I reached a balcony, and there I slid down until I dangled with nothing but my trembling hands holding me in place. I closed my eye and let go.

My legs crumpled beneath me when I landed. The impact knocked the breath from my chest, and for a moment I could only lie there in front of our house, drenched in rain, muscles aching, fighting for air. Strands of my hair clung to my face. I wiped them out of my way and crawled onto my hands and knees. The rain added a reflective sheen to everything around me, as if this were all some nightmare I couldn't wake from. My focus narrowed. I needed to get out of here before my father discovered me gone. Finally, I scrambled to my feet and ran, dazed, toward our stables. The horses paced uneasily when I walked in, but I untied my favorite stallion, whispered some soothing words to him, and saddled him.

We raced into the storm.

I pushed him hard until we had left my father's villa behind and entered the edge of Dalia's marketplace. The market was completely abandoned and flooded with puddles—I'd never been out in the town at an hour like this, and the emptiness of a place usually swarming with people unnerved me. My stallion snorted uneasily at the downpour and took several steps backward. His hooves sank into the mud. I swung down from the saddle, ran my hands along his neck in an attempt to calm him, and tried to pull him forward.

Then I heard it. The sound of galloping hooves behind me.

I froze in my tracks. At first it seemed distant—almost entirely muted by the storm—but then, an instant later, it turned deafening. I trembled where I stood. *Father.* I knew he was coming; it had to be him. My hands stopped caressing the stallion's neck and instead gripped his soaked mane for dear life. Had Violetta told my father after all? Perhaps he'd heard the sound of the silverware falling from the roof.

And before I could think anything else, I saw him, a sight that sent terror rushing through my blood—my father, his eyes flashing, materializing through the fog of a wet midnight. In all my years, I'd never before seen such anger on his face.

I rushed to jump back on my stallion, but I wasn't fast enough. One moment my father's horse was bearing down on us, and the next, he was *here,* his boots splashing into a puddle and his coat whipping out behind him. His hand closed around my arm like an iron shackle.

"What are you doing, Adelina?" he asked, his voice eerily calm.

I tried in vain to escape his grasp, but his hand only gripped tighter until I gasped from the pain. My father pulled hard—I stumbled, lost my balance, and fell against him. Mud splashed my face. All I could hear was the roar of rain, the darkness of his voice.

"Get up, you ungrateful little thief," he hissed in my ear, yanking me forcefully up. Then his voice turned soothing. "Come now, my love. You're making a mess of yourself. Let me take you home."

I glared at him and pulled my arm away with all my strength. His grip slipped against the slick of rain—my skin twisted painfully against his, and for an instant, I was free.

But then I felt his hand close around a fistful of my hair. I shrieked, my hands grasping at the empty air. "So ill-tempered. Why can't you be more like your sister?" he murmured, shaking his head and hauling me off toward his horse. My arm hit the sack I'd tied to my horse's saddle, and the silverware rained down around us with a thunderous clatter, glinting in the night. "Where were you planning on going? Who else would want *you*? You'll never get a better offer than this. Do you realize how much humiliation I've suffered, dealing with the marriage refusals that come your way? Do you know how hard it is for me, apologizing for you?"

I screamed. I screamed with everything I had, hoping that my cries would wake the people sleeping in the buildings all

around me, that they would witness this scene unfolding. Would they care? My father tightened his grip on my hair and pulled harder.

"Come home with me now," he said, pausing for a moment to stare at me. Rain ran down his cheeks. "Good girl. Your father knows best."

I gritted my teeth and stared back. "I hate you," I whispered.

My father struck me viciously across the face. Light flashed across my vision. I stumbled, then collapsed in the mud. My father still clung to my hair. He pulled so hard that I felt strands being torn from my scalp. *I've gone too far,* I suddenly thought through a haze of terror. *I've pushed him too much.* The world swam in an ocean of blood and rain. "You're a disgrace," he whispered in my ear, filling it with his smooth, icy rage. "You're going in the morning, and so help me, I'll *kill* you before you can ruin this deal."

Something snapped inside me. My lips curled into a snarl.

A rush of energy, a gathering of blinding light and darkest wind. Suddenly I could see everything—my father motionless before me, his snarling face a hairsbreadth away from my own, our surroundings illuminated by moonlight so brilliant that it washed the world of color, turning everything black and white. Water droplets hung in the air. A million glistening threads connected everything to everything else.

Something deep within me told me to pull on the threads. The world around us froze, and then, as if my mind had crept out of my body and into the ground, an illusion of

towering black shapes surged up from the earth, their bodies crooked and jolting, their eyes bloody and fixed straight on my father, their fanged mouths so wide that they stretched all across their silhouetted faces, splitting their heads in two. My father's eyes widened, then darted in bewilderment at the phantoms staggering toward him. He released me. I fell to the ground and crawled away from him as fast as I could. The black, ghostly shapes continued to lurch forward. I cowered in the midst of them, both helpless and powerful, looking on as they passed me by.

I am Adelina Amouteru, the phantoms whispered to my father, speaking my most frightening thoughts in a chorus of voices, dripping with hatred. *My* hatred. *I belong to no one. On this night, I swear to you that I will rise above everything you've ever taught me. I will become a force that this world has never known. I will come into such power that none will dare hurt me again.*

They gathered closer to him. *Wait,* I wanted to cry out, even as a strange exhilaration flowed through me. *Wait, stop.* But the phantoms ignored me. My father screamed, swatting desperately at their bony, outstretched fingers, and then he turned around and ran. Blindly. He smashed into his horse and fell backward into the mud. The horse shrieked, the whites of its eyes rolling. It reared on its mighty legs, pawing for an instant at the air—

And then down came its hooves. Onto my father's chest.

My father's screams cut off abruptly. His body convulsed. The phantoms vanished instantly, as if they were never

there in the first place. The rain suddenly grew heavy again, lightning streaked across the sky, and thunder shook my bones. The horse untangled itself from my father's broken body, trampling the corpse further. Then it tossed its head and galloped into the rain. Heat and ice coursed through my veins; my muscles throbbed. I lay there in the mud, trembling, disbelieving, my gaze fixed in horror on the sight of the body lying a few feet away. My breaths came in ragged sobs, and my scalp burned in agony. Blood trickled down my face. The smell of iron filled my nose—I couldn't tell whether it came from my own wounds or my father's. I waited, bracing myself for the shapes to reappear and turn their wrath on me, but it never happened.

"I didn't mean it," I whispered, unsure whom I was talking to. My gaze darted up to the windows, terrified that people would be watching from every building, but no one was there. The storm drowned me out. I dragged myself away from my father's body. *This is all wrong.*

But that was a lie. I knew it, even then. Do you see how I take after my father? I had enjoyed every moment. "I didn't mean it!" I shrieked again, trying to drown out my inner voice. But my words only came out in a thin, reedy jumble. "I just wanted to escape—I just wanted—to get away—I didn't—I don't—"

I have no idea how long I stayed there. All I know is that, eventually, I staggered to my feet. I picked up the scattered silverware with trembling fingers, retied the sack, and pulled myself onto my stallion's saddle. Then I rode away, leaving

behind the carnage I'd created. I ran from the father I'd murdered. I escaped so quickly that I never stopped to wonder again whether or not someone had been watching me from a window.

I rode for days. Along the road, I bartered my stolen silverware to a kind innkeeper, a sympathetic farmer, a softhearted baker, until I'd collected a small pouch of talents that would keep me in bread until I reached the next city. My goal: Estenzia, the northern port capital, the crowning jewel of Kenettra, the city of ten thousand ships. A city large enough to be teeming with *malfettos*. I'd be safer there. I'd be so far away from all of this that no one would ever find me.

But on the fifth day, my exhaustion finally caught up to me—I was no soldier, and I'd never ridden like this before. I crumpled in a broken, delirious heap before the gates of a farmhouse.

A woman found me. She was dressed in clean brown robes, and I remember being so taken by her motherly beauty that my heart immediately warmed to her in trust. I reached a shaking hand up to her, as if to touch her skin.

"Please," I whispered through cracked lips. "I need a place to rest."

The woman took pity on me. She cupped my face between her smooth, cool hands, studied my markings for a long moment, and nodded. "Come with me, child," she said. She led me to the loft of their barn, showing me where I could sleep, and after a meal of bread and hard cheese, I immediately fell unconscious, safe in the knowledge of my shelter.

In the morning, I woke to rough hands dragging me from the hay.

I startled, trembling, and looked up to see the faces of two Inquisition soldiers staring down at me, their white armor and robes lined with gold, their expressions hard as stone. *The king's peacekeepers.* In desperation, I tried to summon the same power I'd felt before my father died, but this time the energy did not course through me, and the world did not turn black and white, and no phantoms rose from the ground.

There was a girl standing beside the Inquisitors. I stared at her for a long moment before I finally believed the sight. Violetta. My younger sister. She looked as if she'd been crying, and dark circles under her eyes marred her perfection. There was a bruise on her cheek, turning blue and black.

"Is this your sister?" one of the Inquisitors asked her.

Violetta looked silently at them, refusing to acknowledge the question—but Violetta had never been able to lie well, and the recognition was obvious in her eyes.

The Inquisitors shoved her aside and focused on me. "Adelina Amouteru," the other Inquisitor said as they hauled me to my feet and bound my hands tightly behind my back. "By order of the king, you are under arrest—"

"It was an accident"—I gasped in protest—"the rain, the horse—"

The Inquisitor ignored me. "For the murder of your father, Sir Martino Amouteru."

"You said if I spoke for her, you would let her go," Violetta snapped at them. "I spoke for her! She's innocent!"

They paused for a moment as my sister clung to my arm. She looked at me, her eyes full of tears. "I'm so sorry, mi Adelinetta," she whispered in anguish. "I'm *so sorry*. They were on your trail—I never meant to help them—"

But you did. I turned away from her, but I still caught myself gripping her arm in return until the Inquisitors wrenched us apart. I wanted to say to her, *Save me. You have to find a way.* But I couldn't find my voice. Me, me, me. Perhaps I was as selfish as my father.

✾

That was weeks ago.

Now you know how I ended up here, shackled to the wall of a wet dungeon cell with no windows and no light, without a trial, without a soul in the world. This is how I first came to know of my abilities, how I turned to face the end of my life with the blood of my father staining my hands. His ghost keeps me company. Every time I wake up from a feverish dream, I see him standing in the corner of my cell, laughing at me. *You tried to escape from me,* he says, *but I found you. You have lost and I have won.* I tell him that I'm glad he's dead. I tell him to go away. But he stays.

It doesn't matter, anyway. I'm going to die tomorrow morning.

Enzo Valenciano

The dove arrives late in the night. It lands on his gloved hand. He turns away from the balcony and brings it inside. There, he removes the tiny parchment from the dove's leg, caresses the bird's neck with one blood-flecked glove, and unfurls the message. It is written in a beautiful, flowing script.

I've found her. Come to Dalia at once.

Your faithful Messenger

He remains expressionless, but he folds the parchment and tucks it smoothly inside his armguard. In the night, his eyes are nothing but darkness and shadow.

Time to move.

They think they can keep me out, but it does not matter how many locks they hang at the entrance. There is *always* another door.
—The Thief Who Stole the Stars, *by Tristan Chirsley*

Adelina Amouteru

Footsteps in the dark corridor. They stop right outside of my cell, and through the gap in the door's bottom, an Inquisitor slides in a pan of gruel. It careers into a black puddle in the cell's corner, and dirty water splashes into the food. If you can call it such a thing.

"Your final meal," he announces through the door. I can tell that he's already walking off as he says, "Better eat up, little *malfetto*. We'll come for you within the hour."

His footsteps fade, then disappear altogether.

From the cell next to mine, a thin voice calls out for me. "Girl," it whispers, making me shiver. "*Girl.*" When I don't respond, he asks, "Is it true? They say you're one of them. You're a Young Elite."

Silence.

"Well?" he asks. "Are you?"

I stay quiet.

He laughs, the sound of a prisoner locked away for so long that his mind has begun to rot. "The Inquisitors say you summoned the powers of a demon. *Did* you? Were you twisted by the blood fever?" His voice breaks off to hum a few lines of some folk song I don't recognize. "Maybe you can get me out of here. What do you think? Break me out?" His words dissolve again into a fit of laughter.

I ignore him as best as I can. A Young Elite. The idea is so ridiculous, I feel a sudden urge to laugh along with my crazy dungeon mate.

Still, I try once again to summon whatever strange illusion I'd seen that night. Again, I fail.

Hours pass. Actually, I have no idea how long it's been. All I know is that eventually I hear the footsteps of several soldiers coming down the winding stone steps. The sound grows nearer, until there is the scrape of a key in my cell's door and the creak of a rusty hinge. *They're here.*

Two Inquisitors enter my cell. Their faces are hidden in shadows beneath their hoods. I scramble away from them, but they grab me and pull me to my feet. They unlock my shackles, letting them fall to the floor.

I struggle with what little strength I have left. *This isn't real. This is a nightmare.* This isn't a nightmare. This is real.

They drag me up the stairs. One level, two levels, three. That's how far underground I was. Here, the Inquisition Tower comes into better view — the floors change from wet,

moldy stone into polished marble, the walls decorated with pillars and tapestries and the Inquisition's circular symbol, the eternal sun. Now I can finally hear the commotion coming from outside. Shouts, chanting. My heart leaps into my throat, and suddenly I push back with my feet as hard as I can, my ruined riding boots squeaking in vain against the floor.

The Inquisitors yank harder on my arms, forcing me to stumble forward. "Keep moving, girl," one of them snaps at me, faceless under his hood.

Then we're stepping out of the tower, and for an instant, the world vanishes into blinding white. I squint. We must be in the central market square. Through my tearing vision, I make out an ocean of people, all of whom have come out to see me executed. The sky is a beautiful, annoying blue, the clouds blinding in their brightness. Off in the distance, a stake of black iron looms in the center of a raised wooden platform, upon which a line of Inquisitors wait. Even from here, I can see their circular emblems shining on their breastplates, their gloved hands resting on their sword hilts. I try harder to drag my feet.

Boos and angry shouts come from the crowd as the Inquisitors lead me closer to the execution platform. Some throw rotten fruit at me, while others spit insults and curses at my face. They wear rags, torn shoes, and dirty frocks. So many poor and desperate, come to see me suffer in order to distract themselves from their own hungry lives. I keep my gaze down. The world is a blur, and I cannot think. Before me, the stake that looked so far away now draws steadily nearer.

"Demon!" someone yells at me.

I'm hit in the face with something small and sharp. A pebble, I think. "She's a creature of evil!"

"Bringer of bad fortune!"

"Monster!"

"Abomination!"

I keep my eye closed as tightly as I can, but in my mind, everyone in the square looks like my father and they all have his voice. *I hate you all.* I imagine my hands at their throats, choking, silencing them, one by one. I want peace and quiet. Something stirs inside me—I try to grab at it—but the energy disappears immediately. My breath starts to come in ragged gasps.

I don't know how long it takes for us to reach the platform, but it startles me when we do. I'm so weak at this point that I can't go up the stairs. One of the Inquisitors finally picks me up and swings me roughly over his shoulder. He sets me down at the top of the platform, and then forces me toward the iron stake.

The stake is made of black iron, a dozen times as thick as a man's arm, and a noose hangs from its top. Chains for hands and feet dangle from the stake's sides. Piles of wood hide the bottom from view. I see it all in a cloudy haze.

They shove me against the stake—they clap the chains onto my wrists and ankles, and loop the noose around my neck. Some in the crowd continue to chant curses at me. Others throw rocks. I glance uneasily at the roofs that surround the square. The chains feel cold against my skin. I reach out

in vain, again and again, in an attempt to call on something that can save me. My chains rattle from my trembling.

As I look at the other Inquisitors, my gaze settles on the youngest of them. He stands front and center on the platform, his shoulders squared and chin high, his hands folded behind his back. All I can see of his face is his profile.

"Master Teren Santoro," one of the other Inquisitors now introduces him with formal flair. "Lead Inquisitor of Kenettra."

Master Teren Santoro? I look at him again. The Lead Inquisitor of Kenettra has come to see me die?

Teren approaches me now with calm, confident steps. I shrink away from him until my back is pressed solidly against the iron stake. My chains clink against each other. He lowers his head to meet my gaze. His white robes are embellished with more gold than the others I've seen, definitely clothing befitting his status, and an elaborate chain of gold winds from shoulder to shoulder. He's surprisingly young. His hair is the color of wheat, pale for a Kenettran, and cut in a stylish fashion I haven't seen much in southern Kenettra— shorter on the sides, fuller on the top, with a slender tail wrapped in gold metal trailing down the nape of his neck. His face is lean and chiseled as if from marble, handsome in its coldness, and his eyes are pale blue. *Very* pale blue. So pale that they seem colorless in the light. Something about them sends a chill down my spine. There is madness in those eyes, something violent and savage.

He uses one delicately gloved hand to brush bloody

strands of my hair from my face, and then lifts my chin. He studies my scar. The edges of his mouth tilt up into a strange, nearly sympathetic grin.

"What a shame," he says. "You would have been a pretty little thing."

I jerk my chin out of his grasp.

"A temperamental one too." His words drip with pity. "You don't have to be afraid." Then quietly, his face close to mine, "You will find your redemption in the Underworld."

He steps away from me, turns to the crowd, and raises his arms to call for silence. "Settle now, my friends! I'm sure we're all excited." When the crowd's noise fades to a hush, he straightens, then clears his throat. His words ring out across the square. "Some of you may have noticed a recent rash of crimes on our streets. Crimes committed by people—twisted imitations of people—that feel more than . . . human. Some of you have taken to calling these new outlaws 'Young Elites,' as if they're exceptional, *worth* something. I've come here today to remind you all that they are *dangerous* and demonic. They are murderers, eager to kill their own loved ones. They have no regard for law and order."

Teren glances back at me. The square has fallen deathly silent now. "Let me reassure you: When we find these demons, we bring them to justice. Evil must be punished." He scans the crowd. "The Inquisition is here to protect you. Let this be a warning to you all."

I struggle feebly against my chains. My legs are shaking violently. I want to hide my body from all of these people,

hide my flaws from their curious eyes. Is Violetta somewhere in this crowd? I scan the faces for her, then look up toward the sky. It's such a beautiful day—how can the sky possibly be this blue? Something wet rolls down my cheek. My lip quivers.

Gods, give me strength. I am so afraid.

Teren now takes a lit torch from one of his men. He turns to me. The sight of the fire sends a greater terror through my veins. My struggles turn frantic. I'd fainted when the doctors removed my left eye with fire. *What kind of pain must it be to let fire consume your entire body?*

He touches his fingers to his forehead in a formal gesture of farewell. Then he tosses the torch onto the pile of wood at my feet. It sends up a shower of sparks, and immediately the dry kindling catches fire. The crowd erupts with cheers.

Rage surges through me, mixing with my fear. *I'm not dying here today.*

This time, I reach deep into my mind and finally grasp the strange power I've been searching for. My heart closes desperately around it.

The world stops.

The flames freeze, their trails of fire left painted, unmoving, stripped of color, hanging black and white in the air. The clouds in the sky stop floating by, and the breeze against my skin dies. Teren's smile wavers as he whirls around to look at me. The crowd stills, confused.

Then something rips open inside my chest. The world snaps back into place—the flames roar against the wood.

And overhead, the bright blue sky collapses into darkness.

The clouds turn black. Their outlines take on strange, frightening shapes, and through it all, the sun still shines, an eerie, bright beacon against a midnight canvas. The crowd screams as night falls on all of us, and the Inquisitors draw their swords, their heads tilted upward like the rest of ours.

I can't catch my breath. I don't know how to make it stop.

In the midst of the darkness and panic, something moves in the sky. And just like that, the black clouds twist—they scatter into a swarm of a million moving flecks that swirl across the sky and then dive down, down, down at the crowd. A nightmare of *locusts*. They descend on us with merciless efficiency, their buzzing drowning out the people's cries. The Inquisitors swing their swords uselessly at them.

The flames lick my feet, their heat searing me. *It's coming for me—it's going to devour me.*

As I struggle to keep away from the flames, I notice the strangest thing. The locusts come near, then pass straight through my body. As if they aren't really there at all. I watch the scene before me—the insects pass right through the Inquisitors too, as well as the crowd of people below.

This is all an illusion, I suddenly realize. *Just like the phantom silhouettes that attacked Father. None of it is real.*

One Inquisitor has staggered to his feet, his eyes burning from the smoke, and points his sword in my direction. He lurches toward me. I find my last reserves of strength and

pull as hard as I can against my chains. Hot blood trickles down my wrists. As I struggle, he draws closer, materializing from a sea of locusts and darkness.

Suddenly—

A rush of wind. Sapphire and silver. The fire at my feet flickers out into curls of smoke.

Something streaks across my vision. A figure appears between me and the oncoming Inquisitor, moving with deadly grace. It's a boy, I think. *Who is this?* This boy is *not* an illusion—I can sense his reality, the solidity of his figure that the black sky and the locusts don't have. He is clad in a whirlwind of hooded blue robes, and a metallic silver mask covers his entire face. He crouches in front of me, every line of his body tense, his focus entirely on the Inquisitor. A long dagger gleams in each of his gloved hands.

The Inquisitor skids to a halt before him. Uncertainty darts across his eyes. "Stand aside," he snaps at the newcomer.

The masked boy cocks his head to one side. "How impolite," he mocks, his voice velvet and deep. Even in the midst of chaos, I can hear him.

The Inquisitor lunges at him with his sword, but the boy dances out of its path and strikes with one of his daggers. It buries itself deep into the Inquisitor's body. The man's eyes bulge—he lets out a squeal like a dying pig. I'm too stunned to utter a sound. Something in me sparks with strange delight.

Inquisitors see the battle and rush to their fallen comrade. They draw their swords at the boy. He just nods at them,

taunting them to come closer. When they do, he slips through them like water between rocks, his body a streak of motion, blades flashing silver in the darkness. One of the Inquisitors nearly cuts him in half with a swing of his sword, but the boy slices the man's hand clean off. The sword clatters to the ground. The boy kicks the fallen sword up into the air with one flick of his boot, then catches it and points it at the other Inquisitors.

When I look harder, I notice that other masked figures flicker among the soldiers—others dressed in the same dark robes as the boy. He didn't come here alone.

"It's the Reaper!" Teren shouts, pointing at the boy with a drawn sword. He starts heading toward us. His pale eyes are mad with glee. "Seize him!"

That name. I'd seen it before on the Young Elite carvings. *The Reaper.* He's one of *them.*

More Inquisitors rush up the platform. The boy pauses for a moment to look at them, his blades dripping with blood. Then he straightens, lifts one arm high over his head, and sweeps it down again in a cutting arc.

A column of fire explodes from his hands, slicing a line across the platform and dividing the soldiers from us with a wall of flame stretching high into the blackened sky. Shouts of terror come from behind the fiery curtain.

The boy approaches me. I stare in fright at his hooded face and silver mask, the outline of his features lit by the inferno behind him. The only part of his face not hidden by his mask are his eyes—hard, midnight dark, but alight with fire.

He doesn't say a word. Instead, he kneels at my feet, then grabs the chains that shackle my ankles to the stake. The chains in his grasp turn red, then white hot. They quickly melt, leaving my legs freed. He straightens and does the same to the noose around my neck, then to the chains binding my wrists.

Black scorch marks on the walls. Bodies melted from the inside out.

My arm shackles break. Immediately I collapse, too weak to hold myself up, but the boy catches me and lifts me effortlessly into his arms. I tense, half expecting him to sear my skin. He smells like smoke, and heat emanates from every inch of his body. My head leans wearily against his chest. I'm too tired to fight, but I still try. My surroundings swim in an ocean of darkness.

The boy brings his face close to mine. "Stay still," he whispers into my ear. "And hold on."

"I can walk," I find myself muttering, but my words slur together and I'm too exhausted to think clearly. I think he's taking me away from this place, but I can't concentrate. As darkness descends, the last thing I remember is the silver insignia on his armguard.

The symbol of a dagger.

City of Estenzia
Northern Kenettra
The Sealands

To the north, the snowy Skylands. To the south, the sweltering Sunlands. Between them lie the island nations of the Sealands, jewels of wealth and trade in a world of extremes.

—Nations of Sky, Sun, and Sea, *by Étienne of Ariata*

Adelina Amouteru

I dream of Violetta. It's late spring. She is eight, I am ten, and we are still innocent.

We play together in the small garden behind our home, a blanket of green surrounded on all sides by an old, crumbling stone wall and a bright red gate with a rusty latch. How I love this garden. Over the wall climb blankets of ivy, and along the ivy bloom tiny white flowers that smell like fresh rain. Other flowers grow in bouquets along the wall's edges, brilliant orange roses and cornflower patches, red oleander and grape-colored periwinkle, stalks of white lilies.

Violetta and I always loved to play among the clusters of ferns that sprouted here and there, huddled together in the shade. Now I spread my skirts on the grass and sit patiently while Violetta braids a crown of periwinkle blossoms into

my hair with her delicate fingers. The flowers' scent fills my thoughts with heavy sweetness. I close my eye, imagining a real crown of gold, silver, and rubies. Violetta's braiding tickles me, and I nudge her in the ribs, suppressing a grin. She giggles. A second later, I feel her tiny lips plant a playful kiss on my cheek, and I lean against her, lazy with contentment. I hum my mother's favorite lullaby. Violetta listens eagerly, as if I were this woman that she barely knew. Memories. It's one of the few things I have that my sister doesn't.

"Mother used to say that faeries live in the centers of white lilies," I tell her as she works. It's an old Kenettran folktale. "When the flowers fill with raindrops, you can see them bathing in the water."

Violetta's face lights up, illuminating her fine features. "Can you really?" she asks.

I smile at how she hangs on my words. "Of course," I reply, wanting to believe. "I've seen them."

Something distracts my sister. Her eyes widen at the sight of a creature moving under the shade of a fern leaf. It's a butterfly. It drags itself between blades of grass under the fern's shelter, and when I pay it closer attention, I notice that one of its shining turquoise wings has been torn from its body.

Violetta whimpers in sympathy, hurries to the struggling creature, and scoops it into her hands. She coos at it. "Poor thing." The butterfly's remaining wing flutters weakly in her palm, and as it does, tiny clouds of glittering gold dust float

up in the air. The frayed edges of its torn wing look like teeth marks, as if something had tried to devour it. Violetta turns her wide dark eyes to me. "Do you think I can save it?"

I shrug. "It's going to die," I say gently.

Violetta holds the creature closer to her. "You don't know that," she declares.

"I'm just telling you the truth."

"Why don't you want to save it?"

"Because it's beyond saving."

She shakes her head at me sorrowfully, as if I've disappointed her.

My irritation rises. "Why did you ask me my opinion, then, if you've already made up your mind?" My voice turns cold. "Violetta, soon you're going to realize that things don't end well for everyone. Some of us are broken and there's nothing you can do to fix it." I glance down at the poor creature struggling in her hands. The sight of its ripped wing, its crippled, deformed body, sends a jolt of anger through me. I slap the butterfly out of her hands. It lands upside down in the grass, legs clawing at the air.

I'm instantly sorry. *Why did I do that?*

Violetta bursts into tears. Before I can apologize, she clutches her skirts and jumps to her feet, leaving periwinkle blossoms scattered in the grass. She spins around.

And there behind her stands my father, the smell of wine hovering about him in an invisible cloud. Violetta hurriedly brushes away her tears as he stoops to her eye level. He

frowns. "My sweet Violetta," he says, touching her cheek. "Why are you crying?"

"It's nothing," she whispers. "We were just trying to save a butterfly."

Father's eyes settle on the dying creature on the grass. "Both of you?" he says to Violetta, his eyebrows raised. "I doubt your sister would do that."

"She was showing me how to care for it," Violetta insists, but it's too late. His gaze wanders to me.

Fear hits me and I start to scramble away. I know what's coming. When the blood fever first passed through, killing a third of the population and leaving scarred, deformed children everywhere, we were pitied. *Poor things.* Then, a few parents of *malfetto* children died in freak accidents. The temples called the deaths acts of demons and condemned us. *Stay away from the abominations. They're bad fortune.* So the pity toward us quickly turned to fear. The fear, mixed with our frightening appearances, became hate. Then word spread that if a *malfetto* had powers, they would manifest when he or she was provoked.

This interested my father. If I had powers, at least I could be worth something. My father could sell me off to a circus of freaks, gather a ransom from the Inquisition for turning me in, use my power to his advantage, *anything.* So he has been trying for months now to awaken something in me.

He motions for me to come to him, and when I do as he says, he reaches toward me and holds my chin in his cold

palms. A long, silent moment passes between us. *I'm sorry for upsetting Violetta*, I want to say. But the words are choked by my fear, leaving me quiet, numb. I imagine myself disappearing behind a dark veil, vanishing to somewhere he can't see. My sister hides behind Father, her eyes wide. She looks back and forth between us with growing unease.

His eyes shift to where the dying butterfly is still struggling in the grass. "Go ahead," he says, nodding at it. "Finish the job."

I hesitate.

His voice coaxes me on. "Come now. It's what you wanted, isn't it?" His grip on my chin tightens until it hurts. "Pick up the butterfly."

Shaking, I do as he says. I grasp the butterfly's lone wing between two fingers and lift it into the air. The glittering dust smears on my skin. Its legs scramble, still fighting. My father smiles. Tears shine in Violetta's eyes. She had not intended this. She never intends anything.

"Good," he says. "Rip off the wing."

"Don't, Father," Violetta protests. She puts her arms around him, trying to win him over. But he ignores her.

I try not to cry. "I don't want to," I whisper, but my words fade away at the look in my father's eyes. I take the butterfly's wing between my fingers, then rip it from its body, my own heart tearing as I go. Its naked, pitiful form crawls in my palm. Something about it stirs a darkness within me.

"Kill it."

In a daze, I crush the creature under my thumb. Its broken carcass twitches slowly against my skin, before finally growing still.

Violetta cries.

"Very good, Adelina. I like it when you embrace your true self." He takes one of my hands in his. "Did you enjoy that?"

I start to shake my head, but his eyes make me freeze. He wants something out of me that I don't know how to give. My shake changes to a nod. *Yes, I enjoyed that. I loved it. I will say anything to make you happy, just please don't hurt me.*

Nothing happens, and my father's scowl deepens. "There must be something more inside you, Adelina." He picks out my ring finger, then runs one hand along it. My breaths quicken. "Tell me I've at least been given a *malfetto* daughter of some use."

I'm confused. I don't know how to answer. "I'm sorry," I finally manage to utter. "I didn't mean to upset her. I just—"

"No, no. You can't help yourself." He glances over his shoulder at my sister. "Violetta," he says gently, nodding for her to come close. She inches forward. "Come. Let's see if your sister has any value." *Let's see if she has any powers.*

"No, Father, don't—please—" Violetta begs, then tugs at his arm. "She didn't do anything. We were just playing." My heartbeat quickens to a frenzied pace. We exchange a frantic look. *Save me, Violetta.*

My father shakes her off, then turns his attention back to

me and tightens his grip around my ring finger. "Are you worthless like that butterfly, Adelina?"

I shake my head in panic. *No. Please. Give me a chance.*

"So *show me*. Show me what you can do."

Then he breaks my finger at the joint.

❧

I bolt awake, a silent scream on my tongue. My crooked finger throbs, as if it'd been broken only a moment ago instead of six years earlier, and I rub it instinctively, trying as always to straighten it out. Dark tides churn in my stomach, the familiar ugliness that my father liked to nurture.

Then I squint in the light. Where am I? Sunlight slants into my unfamiliar bedchamber from arched windows, filling the space with a cream-colored haze, and gossamer curtains ripple in the breeze. On a nearby table, an open book lies beside a quill and inkwell. Plates of jasmine blossoms sit on dressers and balcony ledges. Their sweet scent was probably the reason why I dreamed of my sister and me in our garden. I shift gingerly, then realize I'm lying in a bed piled high with blankets and embroidered pillows. I blink, disoriented for a moment.

Perhaps I died. This room doesn't really look like the waters of the Underworld, though. What had happened at the burning? I remember the Inquisitors lined up on the platform, and my hands struggling against iron shackles. I look down at my hands—white bandages cover both of my wrists,

and when I move them, I can feel the burn of chafed skin underneath. My torn, dirty clothes are gone now, replaced by a clean silk robe of blue and white. Who cleaned and changed me? I touch my head, then wince. Someone also wrapped a cloth tightly around my head, right where my father had pulled at my hair, and when I gingerly comb a hand through my hair, I realize that it's been scrubbed clean of its filth. I frown, trying to remember more.

Teren, the Lead Inquisitor. A beautiful, blue day. There were the iron stake, the soldiers, and the lit torch. They had thrown the torch onto the pile of wood at my feet.

And then I turned the sky black. My eye widens as the memory comes rushing back.

A knock at my chamber door startles me. "Come in," I call out, surprised at the sound of my voice. It feels strange to give orders in a bedchamber that isn't my own. I brush locks of my hair over the left side of my face, hiding my scar.

The door opens. A young maid peers inside. When she sees me, she brightens and comes bustling in, holding a tray laden with food and a glass of sparkling cordial. Flaky rose bread, still giving off warm clouds of steam; a thick stew swimming with golden chunks of meat and potatoes; iced fruit; fat tarts of raspberry and egg. The rich smell of butter and spices sends my head spinning—I haven't eaten real food in weeks. I must look amazed at the slices of fresh peaches, because she smiles at me.

"One of our traders connects us with the finest fruit trees in the Golden Valley," she explains. She sets the tray on the

dresser next to my bed and checks my bandages. I find my-self admiring her robe, like the merchant's daughter that I am. It's made out of a shimmering satin trimmed with gold thread, *very* fine for a servant. This is not coarse cloth you buy for a handful of copper lunes. This is material worth real gold talents, imported straight from the Sunlands.

"I'll send word that you're awake," she says as she care-fully unwinds the bandage on my head. "You look much better after a few days' rest."

Everything she says confuses me. "Send word to whom? How long have I been asleep?"

The servant blushes. When she touches her face with her hands, I notice how impeccably polished her nails are, her skin pampered and shiny from scented oils. What place is this? I can't be in an ordinary household if the servants look as impressive as she does. "I'm sorry, Mistress Amouteru," she replies. So. She also knows my name. "I'm not sure how much I'm allowed to tell you. You're safe, rest assured, and he should be here shortly to explain everything to you." She pauses to reach toward the tray. "Have a bite, young mis-tress. You must be starving."

Hungry as I am, I hesitate to eat her offering. The fact that she seems to be treating my injuries doesn't explain what she's healing me *for.* I think back to the woman who took me in after that night, how I thought she would help me. How she threw me instead to the Inquisition. Who knows what poisons might be in this food? "I'm not hungry," I lie with a polite smile. "I'm sure I'll feel up to it soon."

She returns my smile, and I think I see a hint of sympathy behind it. "You don't need to pretend," she replies, patting my hand. "I'll leave the tray here for when you're ready."

She pauses at the sound of footsteps down the hall. "That must be him. He must already know," she says. She releases my hand and offers me a quick bow. Then she hurries toward the door. But before she can leave, a boy steps inside.

Something about him looks familiar. An instant later, I realize I recognize his eyes—dark as midnight, with thick lashes. This is my mysterious savior. Now, instead of wearing that silver mask and his hooded robes, he's clad in finely spun linen and a black velvet doublet trimmed with gold, clothing exquisite enough to belong to the wealthiest aristocrats. He's tall. He has the warm brown skin of northern Kenettrans, and his cheekbones are high, his face narrow and beautiful. But his hair holds my attention the most. It looks dark red in the light, so dark it's almost black, a rich shade of blood that I've never seen before, tied back into a short, loose tail at the nape of his neck. It is a color not of this world.

He's marked, just like me.

The maid curtsies low for him and mumbles something I can't quite catch. Her face flushes scarlet. The tone she uses now is distinctly different from the tone she'd just used with me—where before she seemed relaxed, she now sounds meek and nervous.

The boy nods once in return. The maid needs no second dismissal; she curtsies again and immediately scurries into the hall. My unease grows. After all, I saw him toy with an

entire squadron of Inquisitors, grown men trained in the art of war, with no effort at all.

He walks around the chamber with that same deadly grace I remember. When he sees me struggling to a better sitting position, he waves one hand in nonchalance. A gold ring flashes on his finger. "Please," he says, glancing at me from the corner of his eyes. "Be at ease." I now recognize his voice too, soft and deep, sophisticated, a layer of velvet hiding secrets. He seats himself in a cushioned chair near the edge of my bed. Here he leans back and stretches out his body, rests his chin against one hand, and lets his other hand remain on a dagger hilt at his waist. Even indoors, he wears a pair of thin gloves, and when I look closer, I notice tiny flecks of blood on their surface. A chill runs down my spine. He doesn't smile.

"You're part Tamouran," he says after a moment of silence.

I blink. "Pardon?"

"Amouteru is a Tamouran family name, not a Kenettran one."

Why does this boy know so much about the Sunlands? Amouteru is not a common Tamouran surname. "There are many Tamouran immigrants in southern Kenettra," I finally answer.

"You must have a Tamouran baby name, then." He says this casually, idle chitchat that sounds strange to me after all that's happened.

"My mother used to call me *kami gourgaem*," I reply. "Her 'little wolf.'"

He tilts his head slightly. "Interesting choice."

His question brings back an old memory of my mother, months before the blood fever hit. *You have your father's fire in you,* kami gourgaem, she said, cupping my chin in her warm hands. She smiled at me in a way that hardened her usually soft demeanor. Then she leaned down and kissed my forehead. *I'm glad. You will need it in this world.* "My mother just thought wolves were pretty," I reply.

He studies me with quiet curiosity. A thin trickle of sweat rolls down my back. I get the vague sense again that I've seen him somewhere before, somewhere other than the burning. "You must be wondering where you are, little wolf."

"Yes, please," I reply, sweetening my words to let him know that I'm harmless. "I'd be grateful to know." The last thing I need is for a killer with blood-flecked gloves to dislike me.

His expression remains distant and guarded. "You're in the middle of Estenzia."

I catch my breath. "Estenzia?" The port capital of Kenettra that sits on the northern coast of the country—it's perhaps the farthest city from Dalia—and the place I'd originally wanted to escape to. I have an urge to rush out of bed and look out the open window at this fabled city, but I force myself to keep my focus on the young aristocrat seated across from me, to hide my sudden excitement.

"And who are you?" I say to him. "Sir?" I remember to add.

He bows his head once. "Enzo," he replies.

"They called you . . . that is, at the burning . . . they said you're the Reaper."

"I'm also known as that, yes."

The hairs rise on the back of my neck. "Why did you save me?"

His face relaxes for the first time as a small, amused smile emerges on his lips. "Some would thank me first."

"*Thank you.* Why did you save me?"

The intensity of Enzo's stare turns my cheeks pink. "Let me ease you into that answer." He uncrosses his legs, his boot hitting the floor, and leans forward. Now I can see that the gold ring on his finger bears the simple engraving of a diamond shape. "The morning of your burning. Was that the first time you've ever created something unnatural?"

I pause before I answer. Should I lie? But then he would know—he'd been there at my burning; he knew what I'd been arrested for. So I decide to tell the truth. "No."

He considers my answer for a moment. Then he holds one of his gloved hands out to me.

He snaps his fingers.

A small flame bursts to life on his fingertips, licking hungrily at the air above it. Unlike whatever it was that I created during my burning, this fire feels real, its heat distorting the space above it and warming my cheeks. Violent memories of my execution day flash through my mind. I shrink away from the fire in terror. *The wall of flames he pulled from midair during my burning.* That was real too.

Enzo twists his wrist, and the flame dies out, leaving only a tiny wisp of smoke. My heart beats weakly. "When I was twelve years old," he says, "the blood fever finally

hit Estenzia. It swept in and out within a year. I was the only one in my family affected. A year after the doctors pronounced me recovered, I still could not control my body's warmth. I'd turn desperately feverish one moment, freezing cold the next. And then, one day, this." He looks down at his hand, then back to me. "What's your story?"

I open my mouth, then close it. It makes sense. The fever had struck the country in waves for a full decade, starting with my home city of Dalia and ending here, in Estenzia. Out of all the Kenettran cities, Estenzia had been hit the hardest—forty thousand dead, and another forty thousand marked for life. Nearly a third of their population, when put together. The city's *still* struggling to get back on its feet. "That's a very personal story to tell someone you just met," I manage to reply.

He meets my stare with unwavering calm. "I'm not telling you my story so that you can get to know me," he says. I blush against my will. "I'm telling you to offer you a deal."

"You're one of . . ."

"And so are you," Enzo says. "You can create illusions. Needless to say, you caught my attention." When he sees my skeptical look, he continues, "Word has it that the temples in Dalia have been overflowing with terrified worshippers ever since the stunt with your father."

I can create illusions. I can summon images that aren't really there and I can make people believe they are real. A sickening feeling crawls from my stomach to the surface of my skin. *You are a monster, Adelina.* I instinctively brush my

hand down my arm, as if attempting to rid myself of a disease. My father tried so hard to provoke something like this in me. Now it's here. And he is dead.

Enzo waits patiently for me to speak again. I don't know how much time passes before I finally murmur, "I was four years old when I caught the blood fever. The doctors had to remove one of my eyes." I hesitate. "I've only done . . . *this* . . . twice before. Nothing seemed out of the ordinary during my childhood."

He nods. "Some manifest powers later than others, but our stories are the same. I know what it's like to grow up marked, Adelina. All of us understand what it is like to be abominations."

"*All* of us?" I ask. My mind wanders again to the black market's wooden carvings, to the growing rumors of the Young Elites. "There are others?"

"Yes. From around the world."

The Windwalker. Magiano. The Alchemist. "Who are they? How many?"

"Few, but growing. In the ten or so years since the blood fever died down in Kenettra, some of us have started making our presence known. A strange sighting here, an odd witness there. Seven years ago, villagers in Triese di Mare stoned a little girl to death because she had covered the local pond with ice in the middle of summer. Five years ago, people in Udara set fire to a boy because he had made a bouquet of flowers bloom right before his sweetheart's eyes." He tightens his gloves, and my eye again darts to the bloody flecks

that coat the leather. "As you can see, I kept my abilities a secret for obvious reasons. It wasn't until I met another who also possessed strange powers given to him by the fever that I changed my mind."

"So. You're a Young Elite." There. I've said it aloud.

"A name the people invented to refer to our youth and our unnatural abilities. The Inquisition hates it." Enzo smiles, a lazy expression of mischief. "I am the leader of the Dagger Society, a group of Young Elites who seek out others like ourselves before the Inquisition can. But we are not the only Elites—there are many others, I'm sure, scattered all across the world. My goal is to unite us. Burnings like yours happen every time the Inquisition thinks they've found a Young Elite. Some people abandon their own marked family members because they're afraid of 'bad luck.' The king uses *malfettos* as an excuse for his poor rule. As if we are to blame for the state of his impoverished nation. If we don't fight back, the king and his Inquisition Axis will kill us all, every child marked by the fever." His eyes harden. "But we *do* fight back. Don't we, Adelina?"

His words remind me of the strange whispers that have accompanied my illusions—something dark and vengeful, tempting and powerful. A weight presses on my chest. I am afraid. Intrigued.

"What will you do?" I whisper.

Enzo leans back and looks out the window. "We will seize the throne, of course." He sounds almost indifferent, like he's talking about his breakfast.

He wants to kill the king? What about the Inquisition? "That's impossible," I breathe.

He gives me a sideways look, something simultaneously curious and threatening. "Is it?"

My skin tingles. I peer closer at him. Then, suddenly, I cover my mouth with one hand. *I know where I've seen him before.*

"You—" I stammer. "You're the prince."

No wonder he looks familiar. I'd seen many portraits of Kenettra's firstborn prince as a child. He was the crown prince back then, our future king. The word was that he had nearly died from the blood fever. He came out of it marked instead. Unfit to be heir to the throne. That was the last we all heard about him, really. After his father the king died, Enzo's older sister stripped Enzo of his crown and banished him permanently from the palace, never again to set foot near the royal family. Her husband, a powerful duke, became king.

I lower my gaze. "Your Royal Highness," I say, bowing my head.

Enzo replies with a single, subtle nod. "Now you know the real reason why the king and queen denounce *malfettos*. It makes *malfettos* look like abominations, and it keeps me unfit for the throne."

My hands start to tremble. Now I understand. He is assembling a team, a team to help him reclaim his birthright.

Enzo leans close enough for me to see slashes of a brilliant red in his eyes. "I make you this offer, Adelina Amouteru. You can spend the rest of your life on the run, friendless

and alone, always fearful of the Inquisition Axis finding you and bringing you to justice for a crime you did not commit. Or we can see if you belong with *us*. The gifts the fever left with you are not as unreliable as they might seem. There is a rhythm and science to controlling your power. There's reason behind the chaos. If you wish, you can learn control. And you will be well paid for it."

When I stay silent, Enzo lifts one gloved hand and touches my chin. "How many times have you been called an abomination?" he whispers. "A monster? Worthless?"

Too many times.

"Then let me tell you a secret." He shifts so that his lips are close to my ear. A shiver dances down my spine. "You are not an abomination. You are not merely a *malfetto*. That is why they fear you. The gods gave us powers, Adelina, because *we are born to rule.*"

A million thoughts run through my mind—memories of my childhood, visions of my father and my sister, of the Inquisition's dungeons, the iron stake, Teren's pale eyes, the crowd chanting against me. I remember how I always crouched at the top of my stairs, pretending to rule from on high. *I can rise above all of this, if I become one of them. They can keep me safe.*

Suddenly, in the presence of this Young Elite, the power of the Inquisition Axis seems very far away.

I can tell that Enzo is watching how my hair and lashes shift colors ever so slightly with the light. His gaze lingers where my hair hides the scarred side of my face. I blush. He

reaches out a hand. It falters there, as if waiting for me to shy away, but I stay very still until he finally touches my hair and tucks it carefully away from my face, exposing my imperfections. Heat rushes instantly from his fingertips through my body, a thrilling sensation that sends my heart pounding.

He says nothing for a while. Then, he pulls the glove off one of his hands. I gasp. Underneath the leather, his hand is a mass of burned flesh, most of it healed over in thick layers of hideous scar tissue that must have accumulated over the years, while a few spots still remain red and angry. He replaces the glove, transforming the awful sight into one of black leather and flecks of blood. Of *power*.

"Embellish your flaws," he says softly. "They will turn into your assets. And if you become one of us, I will teach you to wield them like an assassin wields a knife." His eyes narrow. His subtle smile turns dangerous. "So. Tell me, little wolf. Do you want to punish those who have wronged you?"

Teren Santoro

Late afternoon in Estenzia.

Teren waits behind a pillar lining the palace's main courtyard, his heart in his throat, the white of his Lead Inquisitor cloak blending in with the marble. Shadows and sunlight play on his face. Farther up the courtyard's path and partially hidden from view by rose vines, the queen of Kenettra walks alone, her dark hair piled high on her head in a tumble of curls, her skin a warm hue under the sun. *Her Majesty, Queen Giulietta I of Kenettra.*

Teren waits until she's close enough. When she walks past, he grabs her wrist and pulls her gently into the shadows behind the pillar.

The queen lets out a soft gasp, then smiles at the sight of him. "You're back from Dalia," she whispers. "And up to your boyish antics, I see."

Teren presses her tightly against the pillar. His lips brush against the skin of her neck. Her dress seems cut particularly low today, emphasizing the swell of her breasts, and he wonders with a surge of jealousy whether she wears it as temptation for the king—or for him. The king is a grown man, well into his forties. Teren is nineteen. *Does she like me for my youth? Perhaps she sees me as a boy, four years too young for her.* He marvels again at how lucky he is, to have drawn the attention of royalty.

"I returned last night," he whispers back. He kisses her deeply. "You asked to see me, Your Majesty?"

The queen lets out a sigh as he kisses the line of her jaw. Her fingers run along the grooves of his silver belt, and he arcs toward her in longing. "Yes." She stops him for a moment to give him a level look. Her eyes are very dark, so dark that sometimes they seem wholly empty. Like he could fall to his death in them. "So. Did they take her?"

"They did."

"And will you be able to find her again?"

Teren nods once. "I don't know what curse the gods have brought down on us, to give us demons like this, but I promise you—she will be our advantage. She'll lead me to them. I've already gathered five patrols of my best men."

"And the girl's sister? You mentioned her in your report."

Teren bows his head. "Yes, Your Majesty. Violetta Amouteru is in my custody." He smiles briefly. "She's unharmed."

The queen nods in approval. She reaches out and undoes

a clasp on his uniform's collar, exposing the hollow of his throat, then traces it with one slender finger. A breath escapes him. *Gods, I want you. I love you. I'm not worthy of you.* She tightens her lips, lost in her own thoughts, and then meets his eyes again. "Let me know when you find the girl. I dislike the embarrassment these Elites are making of the crown."

I would do anything for you. "As you command, Your Majesty."

Giulietta touches his cheek affectionately. Her hand is cold. "The king will be pleased to hear it, as soon as he climbs out of his mistress's bed." She emphasizes her last words.

Teren's mood darkens at that. The king is supposed to be meeting with his council right now—not frolicking in bed with a lover. *He's no king. He's a duke the queen was forced to marry. A loud, arrogant, disrespectful duke.* He lowers his lips to hers, then steals another long kiss. His voice turns tender and aching. "When can you come to me again? Please."

"I'll come to you tonight." She gives him a careful smile, one full of calculated secrets. It is the smile of someone who knows exactly what to say to a boy soldier madly in love. She pulls him close enough to whisper in his ear. "I've missed you too."

There are four places where the spirits still wander . . .
the snow-covered Dark of Night, the forgotten paradise of
Sobri Elan, the Glass Pillars of Dumon, and the human mind,
that eternally mysterious realm where ghosts shall forever walk.
–An Exploration of Ancient and Modern Myths, *by Mordove Senia*

Adelina Amouteru

For a week, I never leave my bedchamber. I float in and out of consciousness, waking up only to eat the pastries and roasted quail brought daily into my room, and to let the maid change my robe and bandages.

Sometimes Enzo checks in on me, his face expressionless and his hands gloved, but no one aside from him and the maid visit. No more information about the Dagger Society. What they'll do with me now, I have no idea.

More days pass. Prosperiday. Aevaday. Moraday. Amareday. Sapienday. I imagine what Violetta is doing right now, and whether she's wondering the same about me. Whether she's safe or not. Whether she's searching for me, or moving on with her life.

By the time Prosperiday comes around again, I've recovered enough to go without bandages. The chafing on my wrists and ankles has faded into faint bruises, and the swelling in my cheek has disappeared, returning my face to normal. I'm thinner, though, and my hair has turned into a mess of knots, the spot where my father pulled at my scalp still tender. I study myself in front of the mirror every night, watching how the candlelight splashes orange on my face, how it illuminates the scarred skin over my missing eye. Dark thoughts swim in the far corners of my mind. Something is alive in those whispers, clawing for my attention, beckoning me deeper into the shadows, and I am afraid to listen to it.

I look the same. I also look like a complete stranger.

Voices outside my bedchamber pull me out of my sleep and into the gold of morning light. I lie very still, listening to the conversation that drifts in through the door.

I recognize the speakers immediately. Enzo and my maid.

"—business to attend to. Mistress Amouteru. How is she?"

"Much better." A pause. "What should I do with her today, Your Highness? She is well now, and growing restless. Shall I take her around the court?"

A brief pause. I imagine Enzo tightening his gloves, his face turned away from the maid, looking as disinterested as he sounds. Finally:

"Bring her to Raffaele."

"Yes, Your Highness."

The conversation ends there. I hear footsteps echoing down the hall outside, then fading away and disappearing altogether. A strange disappointment hits me at the thought that Enzo won't be around. I'd hoped to ask him more questions. *The court,* that's what the maid had called this building where we're all staying. What kind of court? A royal estate? Who is Raffaele?

I stay in bed and wait until the maid bustles in. "Good morning, mistress," she says from behind an armful of silks and a bowl of steaming water. "Look at that! So much pink in your cheeks. Lovely."

How odd, someone complimenting me all the time and catering to my every whim. But I smile my thanks. As she scrubs me all over and then dresses me in the white and blue shift, I comb strands of hair across my missing eye. I wince when she runs a brush along the injured part of my scalp.

Finally, we're ready. She guides me toward the door, and I take a deep breath as I step out of my bedchamber for the first time.

We head down a narrow hallway that branches into two. I study the walls. Paintings of the gods adorn them, tales of beautiful Pulchritas emerging from the sea and young Laetes falling from the heavens, the colors as vivid as if they had been commissioned only a week ago. Veined marble outlines the ceiling's arch. I stare at the hall for so long that I start to fall behind, and only when the maid calls for me to hurry do

I turn my gaze away and quicken my steps. As we walk, I try to think of something to say to her—but every time I open my mouth, the maid smiles politely at me and then looks away in disinterest. I decide to stay quiet. We take another turn, and then abruptly stop before what seems like a solid wall and a line of pillars.

She runs a hand along one side of a pillar, then pushes against the wall. I watch, stunned, as the wall swings aside to reveal a new hall behind it. "Come, young mistress," the maid says over her shoulder. Dumbstruck, I follow her. The wall closes behind us, as if nothing had ever existed beyond it.

The longer we walk, the more curious I grow. The layout makes sense, of course. If this is a place where the Young Elites stay—assassins wanted by the Inquisition—then they wouldn't have a door you could simply enter and exit straight from the street. The Elites are a secret hidden behind the walls of another building. But what is this court?

The maid finally stops at a tall set of doors at the end of a hall. The double doors are elaborately engraved with an image of Amare and Fortuna, god of Love and goddess of Prosperity, locked in an intimate embrace. I suck in my breath. Now I know where I am.

This place is a brothel.

The maid pulls the double doors open. We step into a gloriously decorated sitting room with a door along its walls that likely leads into a bedchamber. The thought reddens my cheeks. Part of the room is open to a lush courtyard.

Translucent lengths of silk drape low from the ceiling, stirring slightly, and trails of silver chimes sing in the breeze. The scent of jasmine hangs on the air.

The maid knocks on the bedchamber door.

"Yes?" someone answers. Even muffled through the doorway, I can tell how unusually lovely the voice is. Like a minstrel's.

The maid bows her head, even though there's no one but me to witness it. "Mistress Amouteru is here to see you."

Silence. Then I hear the soft shuffle of feet, and a moment later, the door opens. I find myself staring up at a boy who leaves me speechless.

A famous poet from the Sunlands once described a beautiful face as "one kissed by moon and water," an ode to our three moons and the loveliness of their light on the ocean. He gave exactly two people this compliment: his mother, and the last princess of the Feishen empire. If he were alive to see who I'm now looking at, he would add him as a third. Moon and water must love this boy desperately.

His hair, black and shining, drapes across one of his shoulders in a loose, silken braid. His olive skin is smooth, flawless, glowing. The faint musk of night lilies envelops him in a veil, intoxicating, promising something forbidden. I'm so distracted by his appearance that it takes me a moment to notice his marking—under canopies of long, dark lashes, one of his eyes is the color of honey under sunlight, while the other is the brilliant summer green of an emerald.

The maid nods a hurried farewell to us both, then disappears down the hall, leaving us alone. The boy smiles at me, exposing dimples. "It's good to meet you, mi Adelinetta." He takes my hands and leans down to kiss me on each cheek. I shiver at the softness of his lips. His hands are cool and smooth, his fingers slender and encircled with thin gold rings, his nails gleaming. His voice is as lyrical as it sounded through the door. "I'm Raffaele."

A movement behind him distracts me. Despite the dimly lit bedchamber, I make out the smooth outlines of another person turning over in his bed, his short brown locks catching the light. I glance back at Raffaele. It's a brothel, naturally. Raffaele must be a client.

Raffaele notices my hesitation, then blushes and lowers his lashes in a single sweep. Never in my life have I seen such a graceful gesture. "Apologies. My work frequently continues until morning."

"Oh," I manage to reply. I'm a fool. He isn't the client at all. The man inside is the client, and Raffaele is the *consort*. With a face like his, I should have known immediately—but to me, a consort means a street prostitute. Poor, desperate workers selling themselves on the sides of roads and in brothels. Not a work of art.

Raffaele looks back at his bedchamber again, and when it seems like his client has fallen back into a deep slumber, he steps outside and closes the door without a sound. "Merchant princes tend to sleep late," he says with a delicate smile. Then

he nods at me to follow him. I marvel at the simple elegance of his movements, fine-tuned to perfection in the way I suppose a high-class consort would be. Does this entire sitting room and courtyard belong to him?

"Sensing your energy this close is a bit overwhelming," he says.

"You can sense me?"

"I was the one who first discovered you."

I frown at that. "What do you mean?"

Raffaele guides us out of the sitting room and into the hall, until we reach a large courtyard of fountains. The breeze combs through his hair, revealing several brilliant sapphire strands glistening under the black, jeweled lines moving against a night canvas. A second marking. "The night you ran away from home," he says as we walk, "you paused in Dalia's central market."

I recoil at the memory. My father's rain-washed face, split into a menacing grin, flashes before me. "Yes," I whisper.

"Enzo sent me to southern Kenettra for several months, to find those like you. I could sense you the instant I arrived in Dalia. Your pull was faint, though, something that came and went, and it took me several weeks to narrow my search to your district." Raffaele pauses before the largest fountain in the courtyard. "But the first time I *saw* you was in that market. I watched you ride off into the rain. Naturally, I sent word back to His Highness right away."

Someone had indeed been watching me that night. *A boy*

who can sense those like me—like us. That must be his ability, just like Enzo to fire, myself to illusion. "You recruit Young Elites for the Dagger Society, then?"

"Yes. They call me the Messenger, and the hunt is always an adventure. Of every thousand *malfettos,* there's that *one.* After a potential recruit falls into the Inquisition's hands, though, it's difficult to save them in time. You're the first we've pulled straight from their grasp." Raffaele winks a jewel-toned eye at me. "Congratulations."

The Reaper. The Messenger. A society full of double names and hidden meanings. I take a deep breath, wondering about the other names I've heard rumors of.

"No one told me this place was a . . . a brothel," I say.

"A pleasure court," Raffaele specifies. "Brothels are for the poor and tasteless."

"A pleasure court," I echo.

"Our clients come to us for music and conversation, beauty and laughter and wit. They dine and drink with us. They forget their worries." He smiles demurely. "Sometimes outside the bedchamber. Sometimes within."

I give him a wary, sidelong look. "And I'm hoping I don't have to become a consort to join the Dagger Society? Not to offend you, of course," I add in a hurry.

Raffaele's gentle laugh answers me. Like everything else about him, his laughter is perfectly refined, as lovely as summer bells, a sound that fills my heart with light. "Where you sleep is not who you are. You aren't of age, mi Adelinetta. No

one at the Fortunata Court will force you to service clients—
unless, of course, such work interests you."

My face burns at the suggestion.

Raffaele leads us around the side of the courtyard. Out
here, the wind brings with it the sweet scent of spring. I can
tell that the brothel—*pleasure court*—is situated on the side of
a rolling hill, and when we reach a good outlook, I glimpse
the city below. I catch my breath.

Estenzia.

Redbrick domes and wide, clean roads. Curving spires,
sweeping archways. Narrow side streets overgrown with
colorful flowers and vines. Towering monuments that gleam
in the sun. People bustling from building to building, horses
pulling carts loaded with casks and crates. Marble statues
of the twelve gods and angels, their feet draped with flowers, line the main squares. Hundreds of ships pull into and
out of the harbor, fat galleons and thin, quicksilver *caravelas*,
their shining sails brown and white against the deep blue
of the sea, their flags a rainbow of kingdoms from all over
the world. Floating gondolas glide between them, fireflies
among giants. A bell chimes somewhere in the distance. Off
at the horizon, the misty outlines of a chain of islets appear
before the flatness of the Sun Sea. And up in the sky—

I gasp in delight as an enormous creature resembling an
ocean ray glides lazily across the city's harbor, its fleshy
wings smooth and translucent in the light, its tail stretched
out behind it in a long line. Someone—a tiny speck nearly

lost from sight—rides on its back. The creature lets out a haunting note that echoes across the city.

"A balira!" I exclaim.

Raffaele glances over his shoulder at me, his gesture so smooth and regal that one could mistake him for royalty. He smiles at my joy. "I would think you'd often see them shipping cargo in Dalia, given your location near the waterfall arc."

"Never this close."

"I see. Well, we have warm, shallow waters, so they gather here in the summer to give birth. You'll see your fill, trust me."

I shake my head and continue to take in the scene. "The city's beautiful."

"Only to a newcomer." His smile fades. "We are not like the Skyland nations, where the blood fever was mild and where their few marked people are celebrated. Estenzia was devastated by the fever. She has suffered ever since. Trade is down. Pirates plague our routes. The city grows poorer, and the people are hungry. *Malfettos* are the scapegoats. A *malfetto* girl was killed just yesterday, stabbed to death in the streets. The Inquisition turns a blind eye."

My excitement wanes. When I look again at the city below us, I notice the many boarded-up shops, the beggars, the white cloaks of Inquisitors. I turn away uncomfortably. "The story's not much different in Dalia," I mutter. A brief silence. "Where are the other Elites?"

We come upon a blank wall of stone behind a narrow corner of the courtyard, situated in such a way that you'd never think to stop here unless you knew better. Raffaele runs his fingers along the wall before pushing against it — and to my surprise, it slides silently open. A cold rush of air greets us. I peer inside. Stairs of weathered stone wind their way down into the darkness. "Don't think of them," he replies. "Today, it is just you and me." A strange, pleasant tingle runs down my neck. He says no more, and I decide not to press him for more information.

We head into the gloom. Raffaele pulls a small lantern from the wall and lights it, and the dim glow cuts black and orange shapes into the darkness. All I can see are the steps right before me and the folds of Raffaele's robes. A pleasure court with so many secret spaces.

After a while, the stairs come to an end in front of another blank wall. Raffaele unlocks this one too. It opens with a heavy groan. We step into a room lit by patches of light from a grating in its ceiling, the glow illuminating motes of dust floating in the air. Moss covers the grating's bars. In one corner, a table is overflowing with parchments and maps, strange orreries depicting the paths of the moons, and illuminated books. The space smells cool, damp.

Raffaele walks over to the table and pushes some of his papers aside. "Don't be alarmed," he says.

I suddenly tense. "Why? What are we doing here?"

Raffaele doesn't look at me. Instead, he opens a drawer

in the table and takes out several different kinds of stones. *Stones* actually isn't the best word. These are *gems*, raw and unpolished, freshly broken from the earth. Something seems familiar about this setup. Yes, I remember now — operators on the streets will, for two copper lunes, place painted stones before a child and then tell him about his personality.

"Are we playing some kind of game?" I ask.

"Not quite." He rolls up his sleeves. "Before you can become one of us, you must pass a series of tests. Today is the first of those tests."

I try to look calm. "And what's the test?"

"Every Elite responds to energy in a unique way, and every Elite has a different strength and weakness. Some people respond to strength and bravery. Others are wise and logical. Still others are ruled by passion." He glances down at the gems. "Today, we're going to figure out who *you* are. How *your* specific energy connects to the world."

"And what are the gemstones for?"

"We are the children of gods and angels." A kind smile touches Raffaele's face. "It's said that gems are lingering reminders of where the gods' hands touched the earth during creation. Certain gems will call to the specific type of energy that flows in you. They work best in their natural form." Raffaele holds up one of the gems. In the light, it looks jagged and clear. "Diamond, for instance." He puts it down and picks up another, this one with a blue tint. "Veritium too. There's prase quartz, moonstone, opal, aquamarine." He lays out one after another. Finally, twelve different gems sit

on the table, each glinting a different color under the light. "And nightstone," he finishes. "One for each of the gods and angels. Some will call to you more than others."

I look on, now more confused than wary. "Why do you tell me not to be alarmed?"

"Because in a moment, you're going to feel something very strange." Raffaele holds out a hand to me, gesturing for me to stand in the center of the room. Then he starts placing the gemstones in a careful circle around me. "Don't fight it. Just calm yourself and let the energy flow."

I hesitate, then nod.

He finishes placing the gems. I turn in place, looking at each of them with rising curiosity. Raffaele steps back, observes me for a moment, and then crosses his arms with a sweep of silk sleeves. "Now, I want you to relax. Clear your mind."

I take a deep breath, then try to do as he says.

Silence. Nothing happens. I still my thoughts, thinking of calm water, of night. Nearby, Raffaele lowers his head in a nearly imperceptible nod.

I feel an odd tingling in my arms and at the back of my head. When I look down at the stones, I now see that five of them have started to glow, as if lit from within, in shades of crimson, white, blue, orange, and black.

Raffaele glides around me in a slow circle, his eyes alight with curiosity. The way he's circling me feels almost predatory, especially when he passes to the weak side of my vision and I have to turn my face in order to keep him in view. He

lifts one foot slightly, his bejeweled slipper pushing away each stone that did not glow. He picks up the five remaining stones, returns to the desk, and lays them carefully out.

Diamond, roseite, veritium, amber, nightstone. I bite my lip, impatient to find out what the five mean.

"Good. Now, I want you to look at the diamond." For a moment, Raffaele doesn't move. All he does is stare straight at me, his gaze calm and level, his hands slack at his sides. The distance between us seems to hum with life. I try to concentrate on the stone and keep myself from trembling.

Raffaele tilts his head.

I gasp. A rush of energy courses through me, something strong and light that threatens to carry me off my feet. I steady myself against the wall. A memory rushes through my mind, so vivid and bright that I could swear I was reliving it:

I am eight years old, and Violetta is six. We run out to greet our father, who has just returned from a monthlong trip to Estenzia. He picks up Violetta, laughs, and spins her in a circle. She squeals in delight as I stand by. Later that afternoon, I challenge Violetta to a race through the trees behind our home. I pick a route that is full of rocks and crevices, knowing full well that she has just recovered from a fever and is still weak. When Violetta trips over a root, skinning her knees, I smile and don't stop to help her. I keep running, running, running until the wind and I become one. I don't need my father to spin me in a circle. I can already fly. Later that night, I study the scarred, eyeless side of my face, the

strings of my silver hair. Then I pick up my hairbrush and smash the mirror into a thousand pieces.

The memory fades away. The bright glow pulses inside the diamond for a moment before fading away. I take a shuddering breath, lost in a haze of wonder and guilt at the memory.

What was *that*?

Raffaele's eyes widen, then narrow. He looks down at the diamond. I glance at it too, half expecting it to glow with some color—but instead I see nothing. Maybe I'm too far away to tell. He looks at me. "Fortuna, goddess of Prosperity. Diamond shows your alignment to power and ambition, the fire inside you. Adelina, can you hold your arms out to either side?"

I hesitate, but when Raffaele gives me an encouraging smile, I do as he says—I hold out my arms so that they are parallel to the floor. Raffaele moves the diamond aside and replaces it with the veritium, now bathed in light. He studies me for a bit, then reaches out and pretends to pull at something invisible in the air. I feel an odd, pushing sensation, like someone is trying to shove me aside, searching for my secrets. I instinctively push back. The veritium flashes and lets off a brilliant blue glow.

The memory that comes to me this time:

I am twelve. Violetta and I sit together in our library, where I read to her from a book cataloging flowers. I can still remember those illuminated pages, the parchment crinkling like skeleton leaves. *Roses are so beautiful,* Violetta sighs in her

innocent way, admiring the book's images. *Like you.* I stay silent. A while later, when she goes off to play at the harpsichord with Father, I venture out to the garden to look at our rosebushes. I study one of the roses carefully, and then look at my crooked ring finger that my father broke years earlier. On a strange impulse, I reach out and close my hand tightly around the rose's stem. A dozen thorns slash into the flesh of my palm. Still, I clench my jaw and tighten my grip as hard as I can. *You're right, Violetta.* Finally I release the stem, staring in wonder at the blood that blooms on my hand. Scarlet stains the thorns. *Pain enhances beauty,* I remember thinking.

The scene fades. Nothing else happens. Raffaele tells me to turn back around, and when I do, I notice the veritium is glowing a faint blue. At the same time, it gives off a tremulous note of music that reminds me of a broken flute.

"Sapientus, god of Wisdom," Raffaele says. "You align with veritium for the truth in oneself, knowledge and curiosity."

He moves on to the roseite without another word. For this one, he beckons me over to him and tells me to hum in front of it. When I do, a faint tingling runs down my throat, numbing it. The stone glows red for a long moment, then fades in a shower of glitter. The memory that accompanies it:

I am fifteen. Father has arranged for several suitors to come to our home and take a look at both Violetta and me. Violetta stays demure and sweet the whole time, her tiny mouth puckered into a rosy smile. *I hate it when they look at me too,* she always tells me. *But you have to try, Adelina.* I catch her in front of her mirror, pulling her neckline down so that

it shows more of her curves, smiling at the way her hair falls over her shoulders. I don't know what to make of it. The men admire her at the dinner. They chuckle and clink glasses. I follow Violetta's example; I flirt and smile as hard as I can. I notice the hunger in their eyes whenever they glance at me, the way their stares linger on the line of my collarbone, my breasts. I know they want me too. They just don't want me as a wife. One of them jokes about cornering me the next time I walk alone in our garden. I laugh with him. I imagine mixing poison into his tea, then watching his face turn purple and anguished; I picture myself leaning over him, looking on patiently, with my chin resting in my hands, admiring his dying, writhing body as I count out the minutes. Violetta doesn't think such things. She sees happiness and hope, love and inspiration. She is our mother. I am our father.

Again the memory disappears into thin air, and again I find myself staring at Raffaele. There is a wariness in his gaze now, distance mixed with interest. "Amare, god of Love," he says. "Roseite, for the passion and compassion in oneself, blinding and red."

Finally, he holds up the amber and nightstone. The amber gives off a beautiful golden-orange color, but the nightstone is an ugly rock, dark and lumpy and dull. "What do I do this time?" I ask.

"Hold them." He takes one of my hands in his. I blush at how smooth the palm of his hand is, how gentle his fingers feel. When he brushes past my broken finger, I wince and flinch away. He meets my gaze. Although he doesn't ask

why I reacted to the touch, he seems to understand. "It will be okay," he murmurs. "Hold your hand open." I do, and he carefully places the stones in my hand. My fingers close around them.

A violent shock ripples through me. A wave of bitter fury. Raffaele jumps backward—I gasp, then collapse to the ground. The whispers in the dark corners of my mind now spring free of their cages and fill my thoughts with their noise. They bring a flurry of memories, of everything I've already seen and everything I've fought to suppress. My father breaking my finger, shouting at me, striking me, ignoring me. The night in the rain. His shattered ribs. The long nights in the Inquisition's dungeons. Teren's colorless eyes. The crowd jeering at me, throwing stones at my face. The iron stake.

I squeeze my eye shut and press my hands tightly to my ears in a desperate attempt to block it all out, but the maelstrom grows thicker, a curtain of darkness that threatens to pull me under. Papers fly up from the desk. The glass of Raffaele's lantern shatters.

Stop. Stop. STOP. I will destroy everything in order to make it stop. *I will destroy all of you.* I grit my teeth as my fury swirls around me, seething and relentless, yearning to burst free. Through the whirlwind, I hear my father's harsh whisper.

I know who you really are. Who will ever want you, Adelina?

My fury heightens. *Everyone. They will cower at my feet, and I will make them bleed.*

Then the shrieking fades. My father's voice vanishes, leaving memories of it trembling in the air. I stay on the ground, my entire body shaking with the absence of my unexpected anger, my face wet with tears. Raffaele keeps his distance. We stare at each other for a long time, until he finally walks over to help me to my feet. He gestures at the chair next to his table. I sit gratefully, soaking in the sudden peace. My muscles feel weak, and I can barely keep my head up. I have a sudden urge to sleep, to dream away my exhaustion.

After a while, Raffaele clears his throat. "Formidite and Caldora, the twin angels of Fear and Fury," he whispers. "Amber, for the hatred buried in one's chest. Nightstone, for the darkness in oneself, the strength of fear." He hesitates, then looks me in the eye. "Something blackens your heart, something deep and bitter. It has festered inside you for years, nurtured and encouraged. I've never felt anything like it."

My father was the one who nurtured it. I shiver, remembering the horrible illusions that have answered my call. In the corner of the room, my father's ghost lurks, partially hidden behind the ivy wall. *He's not really there, he's an illusion, he's dead.* But there's no mistaking it—I can see his silhouette waiting for me, his presence cold and haunting.

I look away from him, lest Raffaele think that I'm losing my mind. "What . . . ," I begin, then clear my throat. "What does it mean?"

Raffaele just gives me a sympathetic nod. He seems reluctant to discuss it any further, and I find myself eager to move on as well.

"We'll see how Enzo feels about this, and what this means for your training," he goes on in a more hesitant tone. He frowns. "It may take some time before you'll be considered a member of the Dagger Society."

"Wait," I say. "I don't understand. Am I not already one of you?"

Raffaele crosses his arms and looks at me. "No, not yet. The Dagger Society is made up of Young Elites who have proven themselves capable of calling upon their powers whenever needed. They can *control* their talents with a level of precision that you cannot yet grasp. Do you remember how Enzo saved you, the way he controlled fire? You need to be your ability's master. You will arrive there, I'm sure, but you're not there yet."

The way Raffaele says all this stirs a warning in me. "If I'm not a Dagger yet, then what am I? What happens next?"

"You're an apprentice. We need to see if we can train you to qualify."

"And what happens if I don't qualify?"

Raffaele's eyes, so warm and sweet earlier, now seem dark and frightening. "A couple of years ago," he says gently, "I recruited a boy into our society who could call the rain. He seemed promising at the time—we had high hopes for him. A year passed. He could not learn to master his abilities. Did you hear about the drought that hit northern Kenettra back then?"

I nod. My father had cursed the rise in wine prices, and

rumor had it that Estenzia was forced to cull a hundred prized horses because they couldn't afford to feed them. People starved. The king sent out the Inquisition and killed hundreds during the riots.

Raffaele sighs. "The boy caused that drought by accident, and he could not stop it. He fell into panic and frustration. People blamed *malfettos,* of course. The temples burned *malfettos* at the stake in hopes that sacrificing us would lift the drought. The boy started acting strange and erratic, causing a public scene by trying to conjure rain right in the middle of a market square, sneaking off to the harbor at night to try to pull at the waves, and so forth. Enzo was *not* pleased. Do you see? Someone who cannot learn to control his energy is a danger to us all. We do not operate for free. Keeping you safe here, feeding and clothing and sheltering you, training you . . . this all costs coin and time, but most of all, it costs our name and reputation to those loyal to us. You are an investment and a risk. In other words, you need to *prove* that you're worth it." Raffaele pauses to take my hand. "I don't like to frighten you. But I will not hide from you how seriously we take our mission. This is no game. We cannot afford a weak link in a country that wants us dead." His grip tightens. "And I will do everything in my power to make sure you are a strong link."

He is trying to comfort me, even in his honesty. But there's something he's not saying. In the brief, silent spaces between his words, I hear everything else I need to know. They'll be

watching me. I need to prove that I can conjure my powers again, and that I can wield them with precision. If for some reason I can't control my abilities, they won't just cast me out of the Dagger Society. I've seen their faces, where they stay, and what they do. I know that Kenettra's crown prince leads them. I know too much. *A weak link in a world that wants us dead.* That weak link could be me.

If I cannot pass their tests, then they will do to me what they must have done with the boy who could not control the rain. They will kill me.

Raffaele Laurent Bessette

Midnight. The entire Fortunata Court is asleep, and Raffaele sits alone in his bedchamber, turning the delicate pages of a book on the moons and tides. Waiting. Finally, a soft knock sounds at his door. He rises in one smooth motion, his beaded silks glittering in the candlelight, and walks on silent feet to let in the visitor. Enzo enters with a sweep of dark robes, bringing with him the scent of wind, night, and death. Raffaele bows respectfully.

Enzo closes the door behind him. "The Tournament of Storms," he whispers. "It's confirmed. The king and queen will make a rare appearance together there. It will be our best chance to strike both of them down."

Raffaele nods. "Perfect."

Enzo frowns at him. "You look tired," he says. "Are you all right?"

Raffaele's client for the evening had left over an hour ago. "I'm fine," he decides to reply.

"Did you see Adelina today?"

"Yes."

"And?"

He tells Enzo about Adelina's test. How she reacted to each gem. He touches on her alignment with the amber and nightstone, her overwhelming attraction to the twin rocks. As he feared, Enzo narrows his eyes in interest. Raffaele shivers at his expression. He has recruited many Elites for the young prince in the past few years, but none has ever shown Enzo's same alignment to diamond, such fiery ambition. Being near his energy is intoxicating.

"Fear and Fury," the prince says thoughtfully. In the candlelight, his eyes gleam. "Well. That's a first."

Raffaele takes a deep breath. "Are you sure you want to do this?" he asks.

Enzo keeps his gloved hands folded behind his back. "What do you advise?"

"Get rid of her. Now."

"After all that trouble, you are asking me to kill her?"

Raffaele's voice is pained, but firm. "Enzo. Every single one of her memories was laced with darkness. It is an infection of the mind. Something is *very wrong* with her. She should have manifested early, as a child, but only now has she started to find her power. It has built up inside her, and the energy feels twisted in a way that disturbs me. She doesn't

know it yet, but she is ravenous to use it. I don't know how she'll respond to our training."

"You're afraid of her," Enzo murmurs, intrigued. "Or perhaps you're afraid of your fascination with her."

Raffaele stays silent. *No. I'm afraid of* your *fascination with her.*

Enzo's eyes soften. "You know I trust you. I always have. But getting rid of her would be a waste. Adelina has the potential to be very useful."

"She *will* be very useful," Raffaele agrees. The sapphire strands in his hair catch the light. He casts Enzo a sideways look. "*If* she'll obey you."

"I will take back my throne soon," Enzo whispers. "And *malfettos* will no longer live in fear." Raffaele could feel the threat of fire emanating from Enzo's body. "Adelina has the potential to get us there, even if that potential lies within darkness. We've all seen what she can do. She has no reason to turn on us."

Raffaele hesitates. "Tread carefully, Reaper. We don't know the extent of her energy yet."

"Then train her. Let's see how she does. If your opinion of her remains, I'll get rid of her. But until then," he says, his eyes hardening, "she stays."

We are making a terrible mistake, Raffaele thinks, but bows anyway. "As you command, Your Highness." As he does, his hair tumbles forward and exposes his neck. Enzo leans closer. Then he reaches out and gently pushes Raffaele's collar aside.

Ugly red bruises circle the consort's lower neck, as if someone has tried to choke him. Only now, as Enzo touches Raffaele's chin and tilts his face in the direction of the light, does the faint purple bruising at the edges of his lips become noticeable.

Enzo looks Raffaele in the eyes. "Did one of your clients do this to you?"

Raffaele's eyes stay downcast. He adjusts his collar back into place, then brushes his hair across one shoulder in a glossy rope. He says nothing, knowing that his silence answers Enzo's question.

"Tell me the name," Enzo murmurs.

Raffaele doesn't speak for a moment. Most of his clients are gentle with him, even in their passion. But not all. Memories from earlier in the evening return, memories of rough hands on his neck, shoving him against the wall, striking his face, insults whispered harshly into his ear. It happened on very rare occasions, and he did not like troubling Enzo with the details. Raffaele's work is important to the Daggers, after all—he might not have the same powers that the others do, but while his power cannot kill, it *does* hypnotize. Many of his clients fall so feverishly in love with him that they become loyal patrons to the Daggers. Political alliances are made in his bed.

Still. The work comes with its dangers. *I should tell my madam first; she will privately fine my client for his abuse and ban him from seeing me.* Instead, he meets Enzo's gaze. His gentle

heart hardens. *But not this time. Some deserve punishment greater than a fine.* "Count Maurizio Saldana," he replies.

Enzo nods once. His expression doesn't change, but the scarlet streaks in his eyes burn bright. He presses a gloved finger against Raffaele's chest. His voice is a quiet command. "Next time, do not keep secrets from me."

❦

The next morning, Inquisitors find Count Maurizio Saldana's dismembered body nailed to his front door, his mouth suspended in a scream, his corpse burned black beyond recognition.

Magic is a shortened term derived from "Magiano's tricks," coined from the exploits of the famous young charlatan, Magiano, who was never captured by the Inquisition.

—Essays, *by Raffaele Laurent Bessette*

Adelina Amouteru

Violetta was afraid of thunder.

When we were very little, she would sneak into my bedchamber whenever a storm rolled through. She'd climb into my bed, wake me, and curl her little body against mine, and I'd wrap an arm around her and hum our mother's lullaby as the storm raged outside. I'm not proud to admit it, but I've always liked her helplessness. It made me feel powerful. In those small moments, I was the better one.

This is how my dream starts tonight. A dark storm rages outside my windows. I dream that I wake up in my bedchamber to find Violetta huddled beside me, under the blankets, her back turned to me, her body trembling, the curls of her dark hair spread against my pillow. I smile sleepily.

"It's all right, mi Violettina," I whisper. I put my arm around her shoulders and start to hum. "It's only a storm."

It will get worse, she whispers back. Her voice sounds strange, like a hiss. Inhuman.

I stop humming. My smile fades. "Violetta?" I murmur. I move my arm and roll her to face me.

Where Violetta's face should be, there is instead nothing.

The bed collapses beneath me—and suddenly I am falling. I fall down, down, down. I fall forever.

Splash.

I struggle to the surface, gasping, and wipe water from my eyelashes. Where am I? I'm surrounded on all sides by what looks like a still ocean, with no land in sight. Above, the sky is charcoal gray. The ocean is black.

I'm in the waters of the Underworld. The realm of the dead.

I know this immediately because the light here is not like the light of the living world, finished and whole, chasing the shadows away with its warmth. The light here is dead, faint enough to keep everything in a constant state of gray, no colors, no sounds, only a quiet sea. I look down into the dark water. The sight sends a coil of terror through my stomach. Deep, black, endless, filled with the gliding, ghostly silhouettes of monsters.

Adelina.

A whisper calls to me. I look to my side. A child walks on the surface of the ocean, her skin as pale as porcelain, her body skeletal under white silks, her long locks of black hair

spread out across the ocean like a web of endless strands, stretching as far as the eye can see. This is Formidite, the angel of Fear, the daughter of Death. I want to scream, but no sound comes out. She leans down toward me. Where her eyes and nose and mouth should be, I can see only skin, like someone has stretched cloth tightly across her face. It had been *her* curled in my bedchamber, not Violetta.

Fear is power, she whispers.

Then from beneath the water's surface, a bony hand grabs me and pulls me under.

I sit up in bed, trembling from head to toe. Everything vanishes, replaced with my empty chamber at the Fortunata Court. Rain slaps weakly against my windows.

After a few moments, I lean my head wearily against my arms. Images of my sister linger in my mind, fragments of ghosts. I wonder whether it's raining where Violetta is, and whether she is sleepless because of the thunder.

What am I going to do? I try, as I always do, to grasp the energy buried deep inside me and pull it to the surface, but nothing's there. What if I can never do it again? *Good,* a part of me thinks. Maybe I *shouldn't* use my powers again. Yet this thought makes my stomach flip.

What if I escape tonight? Run away from the Daggers? Raffaele's ominous words play over and over in my mind. He had mentioned nations in the cold Skylands that revere *malfettos* and Elites—I could flee Kenettra and sail far north.

But even as I consider it, I know it's dangerous and pointless. *Stay calm, Adelina, and think.* If I were to try running away from a group of Young Elites, how would I manage to stay ahead of them? They have finely honed powers—I don't. What I *do* have is the Inquisition Axis on my trail, probably combing their way through southern Kenettra at this very moment, waiting for me to make a wrong move. If I couldn't run from the Inquisition when I first tried to escape, how could I hope to evade the Daggers too? They would never rest until they caught me; they'd silence me before I could potentially give away their secrets. They might catch me before I even reached the harbor—and even if I could board a ship to the Skylands, they may simply tail me there. They're probably watching me right now. I will forever be watching my back. My chances are close to impossible.

So I contemplate my second option.

What if I *do* become one of them? What more do I have to lose? I'm no safer on my own than if I remain with them. But if I want to survive, I need to stay and prove myself. And in order to do that, I not only need to learn how to control my energy—I also need to make some allies. Some friends. Setting out alone hasn't exactly worked well for me. I shiver when I remember the reaction I had to the nightstone, how whatever Raffaele did had forced a darkness from within me and brought it to the surface.

What if that's who I am? *Be true to yourself,* Violetta once told me when I was trying in vain to win Father over. But

that's something everyone says and no one means. No one wants you to be yourself. They want you to be the version of yourself *that they like.*

Fine. If I need to be liked, *loved,* then that's what I'll do. I'll win Enzo's approval. Impress him.

By the time dawn finally creeps into my room and bathes it in pale gold, I'm exhausted. I stir when someone knocks faintly on my door. Probably the maid again. "Come in," I call out.

The door opens a little. It isn't the maid who has come to see me, but Raffaele. This time he's clad in a beautiful black robe trimmed with swirls of gold, his sleeves wide and billowing. Thin gold chains encircle both his forehead and his neck, hiding his throat from view, and his loose braid of hair cascades over one shoulder, strands of sapphire shimmering against the dark like a peacock's feather. His jewel-toned eyes are rimmed with bold lines of black powder. He looks even more stunning than I remember, and I turn away my stare in embarrassment.

"Good morning," he says, coming over to me and kissing me on both cheeks. He shows no signs of the hesitation he felt toward me after the gemstone incident. "Enzo and the others have returned." He gives me a serious look. "Let's not keep them waiting."

I dress hurriedly. Raffaele guides me down into the secret tunnel again, the same direction we went when he tested my energy. This time, though, we continue walking past the room's door and farther down the tunnel, until the darkness

swallows us. Our footsteps echo. As we go, the ceiling seems to rise higher and higher. A cold, damp smell fills the air.

"How far does this go?" I whisper.

Raffaele's smooth voice floats to me from up ahead. "Below the streets of Estenzia lie the catacombs of the dead."

The catacombs. I shiver.

"These tunnels lead all across the city," he continues. "They connect some of our safe houses, the homes and estates of our patrons. There are so many tunnels and tombs under the city that a great number have been forgotten over the ages."

"It's wet down here."

"Spring rains. Luckily, we're on high ground."

We finally reach a tall set of double doors. Gems embedded in the ancient wood gleam in the low light. I recognize them as the same types of gems Raffaele used to test me.

"I asked one of our Elites to embed them," he explains. "Only the heightened energy of an Elite's touch can bond with gems. Their energy, in turn, moves the switches inside the doors to open them." He nods at me. "Pay your respects, mi Adelinetta. We are in the realm of the dead now."

He murmurs a brief prayer to Moritas, the goddess of Death, for safe passage, and I follow his example. When we finish, he closes a hand over one of the doors' embedded gems.

The gems start to glow. As they do, an elaborate series of clicks sound out inside the wood, as if unlocking from within. I watch in wonder. An ingenious lock. Raffaele looks at me, and a spark of sympathy seems to light his eyes. "Be

brave," he whispers. Then he throws his weight against the doors. They open.

An enormous cavern the size of a ballroom looms before us. Lanterns on the walls illuminate pools of water that have collected along the floor. The walls are lined with stone archways and pillars that look like they were carved centuries ago, most standing tall, some collapsed and scattered on the ground. Glowing reflections of pale light on the water float, webbed and shifting, against the stone. Everything takes on a greenish cast in here. I can hear the drip of water coming from somewhere far away. Illuminated frescos of the gods decorate the walls, worn down from ancient receding water despite the artists' best efforts. I can tell immediately that the art is centuries old, a style from a different era. Along the walls are niches filled with dusty urns, holding the ashes of forgotten generations.

But what really catches my attention is the small half circle of people waiting down here for us. Aside from Enzo, there are four of them. Each is turned in our direction, wearing a dark blue cloak of the Dagger Society. Their expressions are hard to read, eerie in the dim light. I try to gauge their ages. They must be about my age; those who survived the blood fever were children, after all. One Dagger is enormous, his robes barely masking thick, muscular arms that seem like they could rip a man to pieces. Beside him is a girl who looks small and slight, with a hand resting easily on her hip. She's the only one who nods at me in greeting. An enormous golden eagle perches on her shoulder. I smile back

hesitantly, my stare fixed nervously on the eagle. Beside her stands a lean boy, and last is a broad-shouldered girl with long copper curls, her skin too pale to be Kenettran. A girl from the Skylands, perhaps? She crosses her arms and regards me with a slight tilt to her head, and her eyes seem cold and curious. My smile fades.

Front and center before them stands Enzo, his hair the color of blood, his hands folded behind his back, and his gaze fixed unwaveringly on me. Gone is the hint of mischief in him that I saw when we first talked in my chamber. Today, his expression is hard and unforgiving, the young prince replaced with a cold-blooded assassin. The cavern's strange lighting casts a shadow over his eyes.

We stop a few feet away from them. Raffaele addresses the group first. "This is Adelina Amouteru," he says, his voice clear and beautiful. "Our newest potential recruit. She has the power of illusion, the ability to trick one's perception of reality."

I feel I should speak, but I'm not sure what to say. So I simply face them with as much courage as I can muster.

Enzo looks at me. I don't know why, but I can feel myself drawn to him just like the first day we met. It is the straightness of his shoulders, the regal lift of his head. My alignment to ambition stirs at the sight. "Tell me, Adelina," he begins. His words echo in the cavern. "Have you ever heard the rhyme 'A newborn babe takes its first breath / and creates a storm that rains down death'?"

"Yes," I reply.

"Nothing is isolated. Do one thing, however small, and it will affect something else on the other side of the world. In a way, you are already connected to each of us."

He takes a step closer to me. The others remain still. "You are the first Elite to align so strongly with nightstone. There is a darkness in you, something that gives you immense strength." He narrows his eyes. "Today, I want to bring that to the surface and find a way for you to call upon it as you wish. Learn how to bend it to your will. Do you accept?"

Do I have a choice? After a moment's silence, I lift my chin. "Yes, Your Highness."

Enzo gives me an approving nod. "Then we shall use everything within our power to evoke yours."

Raffaele steps away from me. The fact that I'm now standing alone sends a spike of uncertainty through my chest, and I find myself wishing that he, the only person in here who doesn't frighten me, would stay by my side. The others talk in low voices among themselves. I look around the half circle of their faces, searching for help, but the only kindness I get comes from the girl with the eagle on her shoulder. She sees my anxiety and gives me a subtle, encouraging nod. I try to latch on to that.

Enzo raises one hand in the air. "Let's begin." Then he snaps his fingers—and every torchlight in the cavern flickers out at once.

The room goes dark.

For a second, I panic. I'm completely blind. The dizziness that I felt yesterday with the nightstone now floods my senses.

This is one of my worst fears, that I might someday lose my only good eye, and that I will then live in eternal darkness for the rest of my life. I look wildly around, blinking. Nothing but silence. Then, occasionally, a gust of cold wind—a murmur of breath—an echoing footstep. My heart pounds. *Please, let there be a little light.* I squint hard into the darkness, trying to force my sight to adjust.

Right as I'm able to make out the faint outlines of the cavern floor, I notice that all of the Daggers are gone.

Suddenly, Enzo's voice comes from somewhere in the darkness. "Spider. Star Thief." Its deepness now frightens me.

I tense. Nothing happens.

Then, out of nowhere, rushes of wind. The beating of wings. Suddenly there are thousands—millions—of them, squealing little creatures with fleshy wings beating against me, whirling around me in invisible circles in the blackness. I scream, then fall into a crouch as they swarm. My arms cover my head. Bats. They're bats. Their tiny claws cut at my skin. I squeeze my eye shut.

Someone large shoves me violently backward. I go flying, then fall hard to the ground. The blow knocks all the wind out of me. I gasp for air. A sharp metal edge slices across my upper arm—I cry out, my arms flying up in defense, but another cut slits open the skin of my other arm. Warm blood trickles out. I turn my head frantically from side to side. Where is my attacker? I can't see a thing. Someone kicks me in the back. I arch at the sharp pain. Another kick—and then the feeling of

rough hands grabbing me by my robe, hauling me up in the air. I grasp desperately for my power, wishing I could pull it from deep within. But nothing happens. As I struggle, a low growl of a voice comes from somewhere in front of my face.

"What *wolf*?" Spider snaps. "She's a little *lamb*."

I clench my teeth and struggle, kicking out with my legs. I strike only air, and collapse to the floor.

"She has a bite," someone says elsewhere in the cavern. It sounds like Raffaele.

One lantern flickers on in the cavern—its glow catches me off guard—and I squint in its direction. The millions of bats flutter fiercely in the new light, screaming, then they swarm into a cloud and disappear down one of the cavern's dark tunnels. As if they'd never been here in the first place. I glance around. A short distance away is the hulking boy, who must be Spider, and the girl with the eagle. Elsewhere, standing by pillars and walls in the shadows, I notice others. One of them snickers. Thin trickles of blood drip down my arms. The cuts look smaller than I expect, considering how much they sting. *They're not even trying,* I think feverishly. *They're toying with me.* How had Spider even been able to see me in the darkness?

The light vanishes. My vision adjusts faster this time— and in the darkness, I can see the faint silhouette of the Spider crouching. He attacks again. This time, he rushes at me with terrifying speed and disappears from view right before he can reach me. I look around for him, cursing my missing eye and poor peripheral vision.

He materializes on my weak side. Then he catches me around the neck before I can stop him. His arm tightens, choking me. I struggle. *Sight.* I realize abruptly that his powers must give him the ability to see where others cannot. "I'll have a sheepskin decorating my floor tonight," he says.

I throw an elbow as hard as I can. He must not have expected me to fight back, because I hit him hard in his throat. He gags, releasing me again. I fall to my knees, gasping. Spider whirls around, his eyes narrowed at me in rage, and I brace myself for another attack.

"Enough," Enzo says quietly. The word is a low, disapproving command that emerges from the shadows.

Spider steps away from me. I crumple in relief, sucking up air in the darkness. The torchlights all flicker on again. We stare at each other — the young Dagger's eyes green and gruff, mine wide and stricken. I don't feel anything in my chest except for the pounding of my heart.

Then Spider straightens and sheaths his blade. He doesn't bother helping me up. "One-eyed weakling," he says, his voice full of disdain. "Should've left you to the Inquisition and saved us all the trouble." He turns away from me.

A spark of anger shoots through me. I imagine what it would be like if I strangled him in return, my dark illusions flowing down his throat and blocking his air. Can my powers do that? The whispers hiding in my mind nod, hungry and eager. *Yes, yes.* "Coward," I whisper to his back. He doesn't hear me, but the girl with the eagle — Star Thief, I suppose — does. She blinks.

Enzo studies me with interest as Raffaele whispers something in his ear. Do they approve?

A moment later, Enzo raises his voice. "Windwalker."

Windwalker? I look around the cavern, searching for my next opponent. Finally, I catch a glimpse of her. She's the tall, pale girl, the one who doesn't look Kenettran. She chuckles as she steps toward me, sleek and menacing, and I take a step back. "With pleasure, Your Highness," she says to Enzo.

My breathing is too rapid. *Calm down. Focus.* But the force of the last attack has left me trembling, and the anticipation of what might come next sends prickles of terror down my skin. Spider has the power to see in complete darkness. What can the Windwalker do? Fly, perhaps?

Then—a piercing scream shatters my senses. I flinch. My hands fly to my ears in a vain attempt to shut out the sound, but it only grows worse. The sound destroys everything around me, turning the world into blinding streaks of red and piercing every corner of my mind. I can't see. I can't think. It goes on and on, a razor-sharp knife digging into my ears. I must be bleeding. I feel the dull sensation of cold stone against my skin. Tears stream down my cheeks. *I've fallen,* I realize dully.

Something stirs faintly in the depths of my body, but I reach out for it and miss. What kind of power is this? How do I fight it? *How do you shut out a scream that comes from inside your mind?* I try to struggle to my feet, but the scream overwhelms me. It ripples through the air again and again, threatening to drown me.

Somehow, through the chaos, I hear Windwalker's voice against my ear. It sounds like she's right beside me. When I jerk my head to the side, I see her.

She laughs. "Watch your step, little wolf," she taunts.

Suddenly I feel myself lifted off the ground by an invisible curtain of wind. Windwalker's arms are stretched out in my direction. She lifts me higher, then makes a cutting gesture with one hand. Wind rushes past my ears—I fly across the chamber. My back hits the wall hard. I crumple to the ground like a broken doll. All around me, the screaming continues.

I can't do this. I curl into a ball as Windwalker comes closer. She kneels before me—all I can make out of her now is her sly smile. The scream in my mind is shattering my soul, and the pain of being thrown makes my breath short. The scream sounds like my own. I see myself being dragged through the rain by my hair, my father's face staring straight into mine. Behind us, Violetta screams at him to stop. He ignores her.

I can't take it anymore. My anger rises—I reach for the energy just out of my grasp. My father's ghost hovers before me, and my sister's shrieks surround us. Disoriented, I let out a strangled cry and claw at the open air.

My hand strikes something. Suddenly the shrieks around me stop, and my father and sister vanish. This time, I don't hear any more snickers. To my shock, Windwalker is hunched several feet away, holding her neck. A thin trickle of blood runs down her hand where I'd raked her with my fingernails. With a start, I realize that I must have struck her when I thought I was striking at my father. The rage

inside me still churns, a black, seething fury, almost within my reach.

I grit my teeth at her. "Is that it?" I suddenly snap. "Attacking me while I'm defenseless?"

Windwalker stares at me in silence. Then she removes her hand to show me the gash I've caused. "You're far from defenseless." Several thin lines are scored into the skin of her throat. Without a word, she walks over and helps me onto my trembling feet. "Not too bad," she says, without a hint of malice in her voice. "You like being provoked. I can tell."

Gradually, my anger fades into bewilderment. Did she just compliment me? "What," I manage to say, "is your power, exactly?"

She laughs at my expression. She seems completely unconcerned about her scratched neck and is, somehow, friendlier to me. "Whatever the wind can do—whistle, scream, howl, uproot you from the earth—I can do too."

She leaves me. All around the cavern, the others whisper among themselves, their voices echoing in the empty space. Finally, Enzo steps forward, his hands folded calmly behind his back.

"Better." He tightens his lips. "But not enough."

I wait there, swaying on my feet, regaining my breath. His eyes sear me to the bone, bringing with them a wave of terror and excitement.

"The problem, Adelina," he says as he approaches me, "is that you simply aren't afraid."

My heartbeat quickens. "I *am* afraid," I whisper. But my words sound unconvincing. What is he going to do to me?

"You *know* your life is not at risk," he continues. "You don't embrace your darkness unless you are staring straight at death. Therefore, you cannot connect with your fear and your fury." He unfolds his hands from behind his back. "Let me see if we can correct that."

A ring of fire bursts to life around us, turning the dark cavern into an illuminated space. The flames stretch to the ceiling. I jump away in terror at the heat against my skin. A scream threatens to bubble up from my throat. *No. No, no.* Not fire. Anything but that. All I can see are Enzo's eyes locked on mine, dark and determined. So much fire.

I'm not tied to the stake. I'm okay. I'm okay. But I don't believe myself. We are back at my burning—the Inquisition is going to kill me in front of everyone, happy to watch fire consume me in punishment for my father's death. The gods save me. Suddenly, the attacks from the other Elites pale in comparison. The flames feel like they're closing in. They *are* closing in. I can't breathe.

He is forcing me to *relive the feeling* of staring straight at death.

Enzo reaches me. As flames roar all around us, he leans close enough for me to feel the heat of his body through his robes, the sheer power hidden underneath. The fear that has been building in my chest since Spider first attacked me now rushes through me in an unstoppable current, turning

my limbs numb. One of his hands touches the small of my back. A violent, irresistible wave of heat emanates from his touch and pulses through my body, scalding me. The flames around us lick at the edges of my sleeves—I watch in terror as the fabric curls, blackening. Everything about Enzo whispers of danger, of murder in the name of righteousness. I'm desperate to pull away. I ache for more. I tremble uncontrollably, caught in the middle.

"I know you crave the fear." His breath scorches the skin of my exposed neck. "Let it build. Nurture it, and it will give back all of your care tenfold."

I try to concentrate, but all I can feel is the heat. The stake, the pile of wood at my feet. The eyes of my dead father, forever haunting my dreams. *You are a killer,* his ghost whispers. But how many have the Inquisition killed? How many *more* will they kill? Wouldn't I have been one of the Inquisition's victims, had the Daggers not come to my rescue?

With the fire all around us, with Enzo's hand hot against my silks, with his words in my ears and my body still trembling from the others' attacks, the combination of my fear, hatred, anger, and desire finally fuse into one. I can feel the uncontrollable darkness growing inside me, millions of threads that connect everything in the world to everything else, the badness inside Enzo, the wickedness inside everyone around us, growing until I'm able to reach down and close my mind around a handful of those threads and *pull* on them. The darkness bows to me, eager for my embrace. I

close my eye, open my heart to the feeling, and soak in the delight of vengeance.

Show me what you can do, my father's ghost whispers.

Black silhouettes rise up out of the ground, their shapes demonic and their eyes scarlet red, their fangs dripping blood. They gather around us, growing taller and taller, until they reach the cavern's ceiling. They wait patiently for my command. I'm swept away, both giddy with joy at the feeling of power and terrified that I am completely helpless to it.

Enzo removes his hand.

The sudden lack of contact distracts me, and in a flash, my silhouettes disappear. The demons shrink into the ground. Enzo's columns of fire vanish. We're back in the heavy silence of the cavern, as if nothing had happened. My shoulders droop from the effort. Without the fire, the space has returned to its eerie green glow. The others aren't laughing anymore. I glance at Raffaele. He looks stricken, his brows furrowed in a tragic line.

Enzo steps away from me. I sway on weak legs. If I didn't know better, I'd say he seems surprised himself.

All I know is that I want to do it again. I want Enzo to touch me. I want to feel that flow of power, and I want to see the other Daggers' intimidation.

I want something *more.*

It is pointless to believe what you see,

if you only see what you believe.

–"*The Admiral*," *from* The Requiem of Gods Vol. XI,

translated by Chevalle

Adelina Amouteru

Two days after my testing, a mob of drunken gamblers burns a *malfetto* in the middle of a market square. Several days later, another murder. As if killing us will somehow make the city prosperous again. From the hidden courtyard that overlooks Estenzia, I glimpse the second victim dragged, sobbing, into a main street by a mob of shouting people. Inquisitors stand by and pretend not to notice.

I need to learn faster. The world is closing in on us.

"Both were *malfettos* accused of having powers, of being Elites," Raffaele tells me today, as we sit together before my bedchamber mirror. "Neither were, of course. But their families turned on them anyway. The Inquisition pays well for such information, and gold is hard to pass up in times like these."

I look at the array of creams and powders scattered on the dresser top, then glance at my reflection in the mirror. My maid took me this morning to a private bathhouse in the court and washed me until I gleamed and glistened. My skin now smells of rose and honey. I'm surprised at how quickly I've become used to such luxuries.

I turn my gaze back to Raffaele. "Why didn't the Daggers save them?" I ask.

Raffaele's reply is one that answers nothing. He picks up a tub of cream. "These hunts happen too often. We react when necessary."

I try not to look bothered by his answer, but secretly, I dwell on his real meaning. *We didn't risk saving them, because they were not Elites.*

"What are you going to do to me?" I ask.

"You stay at the Fortunata Court. You will need to look the part."

I recoil at the thought of transforming into a consort. Raffaele must have sensed the sudden shift in my energy, because he adds, "Would you prefer to be recognized by an Inquisitor?" He dabs a touch of the cold cream on my face. "No one will touch you, you have my word. But looking the part will give you some freedom."

The cream tingles. I watch, amazed, as it brings the warmth out in my olive skin. He runs an ivory comb through my hair. Occasionally his fingers brush the base of my neck, sending shivers of pleasure down my spine. There is a precision to his gestures that speaks volumes about his talents as

a consort. I have a fleeting thought of what being his client must be like, his skin warm against mine, his lips soft on my neck, his hands smooth and experienced, roaming.

Raffaele lifts an eyebrow at me through the mirror. "What you're thinking will cost you at least five thousand gold talents, mi Adelinetta," he teases gently, tilting his head in a subtle movement that sends blood rushing to my cheeks. Five *thousand* gold talents?

"A night?" I breathe.

"An hour," Raffaele replies, still working his way through my hair.

Five thousand gold talents *an hour*. In one night, Raffaele can fetch my father's annual salary.

"You must have singlehandedly turned the Fortunata Court into the wealthiest court in the country," I say.

He smiles shyly . . . but behind it, I sense something sad. My grin fades.

Raffaele rubs a fine oil into my scalp, and then finishes combing. He turns his attention to other details—touching my eyelid and lashes with a black, shimmering powder that hides the strands' silver color; rubbing an ointment on my nails that makes them gleam; smoothing my brows into perfect brushstrokes. I tremble again as his finger runs across my lips, painting them a color of rose that accents their fullness. I wonder if any of his clients are Dagger patrons, nobility enticed by the riches Enzo can reward them with once he's on the throne. Maybe all of them are. Or maybe they have no idea who the Daggers' leader is—only

that they are supporting an expert assassin who will dethrone the king.

"How did you learn so much about energy?" I decide to ask as he works.

Raffaele shrugs once. "Trial and error," he replies. "We are the first. There is no one before us to learn from. With each new Elite we recruit, I learn, experiment, and record. Someone needs to leave the knowledge behind for the generation after us. *If* there is another generation."

I listen in quiet fascination. He's a Messenger in more ways than one. "Do you know where it came from? I know it began with the blood fever, but . . ."

He reaches for a slender brush. "It did not begin with the blood fever. It began with energy, the link between the gods and the mortal world they created."

"Energy."

"Yes. It forms the land, air, sea, and all living things. It is what breathes life into us."

"And what gives us powers?"

Raffaele nods. He dips the brush in a shallow dish of sparkling powder, then touches it to the edge of my good eye. I frown as he works, trying to imagine this strange, invisible energy.

His brush pauses for a moment. "When you close your eye, you see sparks of colors, do you not?" he says.

I close my eye to test his theory. Yes. In the blackness float sparks of faint blues and greens, reds and golds, blinking in and out of existence. "Yes."

"You are actually seeing threads of energy." He touches my hand carefully, and a chill of delight runs up my arm. "The world is made of countless threads that connect all things. These threads give the world both its color and its life." He nods at the bedchamber around us. "Right now, in some small way, you're connected to everything in here. The mirror, the walls, the air. Everything. Even the gods."

His words stir my memory. I think back to the night of my father's death. When I suspended everything around me, the raindrops and the wind, the world had turned black and white, and translucent threads had glistened in the air. During my burning, I'd seen the color drain from my execution stand before it all came rushing back.

"Most people don't have enough energy to manipulate their connections to the world. We weren't meant to. But when the fevers affected you and me, something changed in us. Suddenly it linked us to the world in a way that our bodies were never meant to be linked." Raffaele turns my hand so that my palm faces upward, then runs his slender fingers along the inside of my wrist all the way to my fingertips. My skin tingles at his touch. I suck in my breath, blushing. "Every Elite is different, and pulling on threads in specific ways will do specific things. The Windwalker, for example, can pull on the threads in the air that create wind. Enzo pulls on threads of heat energy, from himself, from the sun, from fire, and from other living things. From the Sunlands come reports of an Elite who can change metal into gold. Another rumored Elite, Magiano, has escaped the Inquisition Axis so

often that the word *magic* evolved from his name. There are countless ways energy manifests in us. I can only imagine what undiscovered Elites out there can do, those beyond the Daggers and beyond who I know exist. There are even rumors of an Elite who can bring people back from the dead."

I wonder, for a moment, how many others exist outside of the Dagger Society. Are there rival societies? "And you?" I say.

"I can see and sense all the energy in the world," he replies. "Every single thread that connects everything to everything else. I can't do much, save to tug faintly on them—but I can feel them all."

Here, he pauses to look me in the eye. I feel a sudden tug at my heart, as if the sight of him had set butterflies loose in my chest. My eye widens in understanding. This is why his touch along my wrist left me tingling. "No wonder your clients fall so madly in love with you, if you look like this *and* can literally pull on their heartstrings."

Raffaele laughs his beautiful laugh. "Someday I'll teach you, if you like."

My heart thrills again at that, and I wonder if it has anything to do with Raffaele's energy this time. "What about me?" I ask after a pause. "My power?"

"Of all the Daggers, you and I are the most alike. We sense the intangible." Raffaele turns his eyes to me, and the sun catches the brilliant, shifting colors in his irises. "Think of the lesser gods—Formidite, the angel of Fear, or Caldora, the angel of Fury. Laetes, the angel of Joy. Denarius, the angel of

Greed. Threads of energy connect not only physical things, but also emotions, thoughts, and feelings—fear, hate, love, joy, sorrow. You have the ability to pull on threads of fear and hatred. A powerful talent, if you can tame it. The more fear and hate your environment has, therefore, the stronger you are. Fear creates the strongest illusions. Everyone has darkness inside them, however hidden." His eyes turn solemn, and I shiver, wondering what small darkness might lie within even *his* gentle soul.

"Was Enzo the first Elite you ever met?" I whisper.

"Yes."

I'm suddenly curious. "How did you meet him?"

Raffaele starts putting away the powders on the table. "He bought my virgin price."

I turn quickly in my chair to look at him. "Y-your virgin price? You mean, you and Enzo—"

"It's not what you think." He gives me a playful smile. "When I turned seventeen and came of age, I became an official consort of the Fortunata Court. So the court held a lavish bidding masquerade for my debut."

I try to imagine the scene: Raffaele at my age, young and innocent, more beautiful than anyone else in the world, standing before a sea of masked nobility and preparing to give himself away. "The entire city must have turned out for you."

Raffaele doesn't disagree, which is confirmation enough. "Enzo came to my debut night in secret, searching for others like himself." He hesitates for a moment, as if remembering.

"I sensed him the instant he arrived, even though he stayed hidden and out of sight. Never in my life had I met another with the type of energy I had. It was the first time I could see the threads of his energy around him like a halo, weaving together and apart. He must have noticed my strange interest in him. His manservant bid on me for him, and won."

"How much?" I ask curiously.

"An obscene amount." He lowers his eyes. "I was frightened, you know. I'd heard stories from the older consorts about their debut nights. But when he came to my chamber, all he wanted to do was talk. So we did. He demonstrated to me his abilities with fire. I confessed my ability to sense others. We both knew we risked our lives, talking openly about our powers."

I suddenly realize that there is only one person Raffaele never uses his talents on. Enzo. "Why do you trust him?"

My question sounds suspicious and scathing, and immediately I wish I could take it back. But Raffaele, ever graceful, simply meets my gaze with a level look. "If Enzo becomes king," he says, "I can step away from this life."

I dwell on the moment of sadness I'd seen from him before, then on the endless parade of aristocrats he is paid to entertain, both inside and outside the bedchamber. The lack of freedom. No one *chooses* the life of a consort, no matter how lavish.

"I'm sorry," I finally say.

Raffaele pauses to look over the broken side of my face. I tense. A hint of sympathy enters his gaze, and he touches

my cheek with one hand. I feel a slight tug on my heart. My anxiety calms, my chest warms in trust. Everything about his touch soothes and caresses. There is something oddly comforting about this moment. We're not so different, the two of us.

The maid returns with an armful of silks then, and our moment ends. Raffaele gives us privacy while she helps me change into the new garments—a beautiful gold dress cut in the Tamouran style. The loose silks feel delightfully cold against my skin. Clothing from the Sunlands has always felt more comfortable than the stiff corsets and lace that Kenettrans wear.

Before the maid leaves, she places a velvet box on top of the dresser. Raffaele returns. He nods in approval at the dress. "Amouteru," he says, lingering on the exotic accents of my family name. "I can see the Tamouran blood in you."

As I look on in wonder, Raffaele brushes my hair until it spills down my back like a silver curtain. He twists the strands into a smooth, glossy bun behind my head in traditional Tamouran fashion, picks up two long cloths of white and gold, and carefully wraps my head with them until all of my hair is hidden underneath an elaborate, intertwined series of gold and white silk, the cloth draping down behind me in a sheet of sun and snow. He pins jewels on the cloth. He ties the Tamouran headwrap so much more skillfully than I ever have. Finally, he places a thin silver chain on my head from which a single teardrop diamond suspends at my forehead.

"There," he says. "You will hide your markings like this from now on."

I stare at myself, stunned. My cheekbones and nose, the elegant sweep of my eye, all enhanced. I have never looked more Tamouran in my life. It's a convincing disguise.

Raffaele smiles at my expression. "I have a present for you," he says. He turns and opens the velvet box on the dresser.

My heart skips a beat.

It's a white half mask, made of porcelain and cold to the touch. Diamonds trace along its edges and twinkle in the light, and trails of bright glitter paint elaborate patterns across the mask's pale surface. Tiny white plumes arch at the point where it curves up toward the temple. I can only stare. Never in my life have I worn something so finely crafted.

"I commissioned this for you," Raffaele says. "Care to try it?"

I nod wordlessly.

Raffaele positions the half mask over my face. It fits snugly, like a long-lost possession, something that has always been a part of my body. Now snow-white porcelain and lines of shining light conceal the spot where my eye used to be. The mask covers it all. Without the distraction of my marking, the natural beauty of my face shines through.

"Mi Adelinetta," Raffaele breathes. He leans down close enough for his breath to warm the skin of my neck. "You are truly kissed by moon and water."

As I stare silently back, I feel something powerful stir

inside me—a buried fire, subdued during childhood and long forgotten. I have lived all my life in the shadow of my father and my sister. Now that I'm standing in the sun for the first time, I dare to think differently.

The broken butterfly has been made whole.

Faint voices come from the hallway outside. Before either of us can react, the door opens and Enzo strides in. I can't keep my cheeks from turning bright red, and I turn my face partly away, hoping he doesn't notice. His eyes settle first on Raffaele. "Is she ready?"

Then he notices me. Whatever words he meant to speak now halt on his tongue. For the first time since I met him, a strange emotion flickers across his face that hints at something underneath.

Raffaele studies him. "At a loss for words, Your Highness? I'll take that as a compliment."

Enzo recovers in an instant. He exchanges a quiet look with Raffaele. I look between them, uncertain what conversation has just passed. Finally, he turns away from us—and it seems as if he purposely avoids meeting my stare.

"She starts tomorrow," he says before he leaves.

Teren Santoro

As the sun sets over Estenzia, Teren locks himself inside his chambers. His jaw is tight with frustration.

Several weeks have already passed since Adelina's escape from her execution. He's not found a single trace of her. Rumor has it that she came here to Estenzia—at least, that was all his Inquisition patrols could gather. But Estenzia is a large city. He needs more information than that.

Teren undoes the gold buttons of his Inquisition uniform, strips off his robe, and removes the armor underneath. He pulls his thin linen undershirt up over his head, baring his torso to the air. The orange glow of sunset from his window highlights his shoulders, the hard, muscled contour of his back.

It also illuminates the maze of crisscrossing scars that cover his body.

Teren sighs, closes his eyes, and rolls his neck. His thoughts wander to the queen. The king had been dead drunk at his council meeting today, laughing off fears of his hungry people's rising anger at his taxes, impatient to return to his afternoon hunting trips and brothels. Throughout the whole meeting, Queen Giulietta looked on in silence. Her eyes were cool, calm, and dark. If her husband irritated her, she didn't show it. She certainly didn't show any signs that she had invited Teren to her bedchambers the night before.

Teren closes his eyes at the memory of her in his arms, and shivers in longing.

He looks down at the whip lying by his bed. He walks over to it. He had to have the weapon specially made: It consists of nine different tails, each tail equipped at the end with long blades—rare foreign platinum for weight, tipped with steel—honed so finely that their edges could slice open skin with the faintest whisper of a touch.

On any normal man, a weapon like this would shred his back into ribbons of meat with a single strike. Even on someone like Teren, with skin and flesh hardened by demonic magic, the metal whip wreaks havoc.

He kneels on the floor. Lifts the whip. Holds his breath. Then he snaps the whip over his head. The blades rake deep into the flesh of his back, ripping jagged lines across his skin. He lets out a strangled gasp as pain floods him, robbing him of his breath. Almost immediately, the cuts start to heal.

I am a deformed creature, he mouths silently, repeating the

words he once said as a twelve-year-old boy, an Inquisitor-in-training, kneeling before the sixteen-year-old Princess Giulietta.

He remembers that day so well. She was newly married to the powerful Duke of Estenzia. Young Enzo, still crown prince to the throne, lay in the infirmary, the lucky survivor of drinking poisoned soup. And the old king was already dying.

Giulietta bent down, studied Teren thoughtfully, and placed her finger under his chin. She gently tilted his head up until his pale, colorless eyes met her dark, cool ones. "Why are you afraid to look at me?" she asked.

"You are chosen by the gods, Your Highness," he said, ashamed. "And I am a *malfetto*, lower than a dog. I am unworthy of your presence." He hoped she couldn't guess his dark secret. That strange, demonic powers had appeared in him recently.

Giulietta smiled. "If I forgive you for being a *malfetto*, little boy, would you pledge your undying devotion to me? Would you do anything for me?"

Teren looked up into her eyes with desperation and desire. She was so pretty. Delicate, heart-shaped face framed with dark curls. Royal blood. Not a hint of a marking on her. Perfection. "I would pledge anything to you, Your Highness. My life. My sword. I am yours."

"Good." She tilted her head toward him. "Tell me. Who do you think should rule this country next?"

Teren leaned into her touch. The question confused him. "The crown prince," he said. "It is his birthright."

Her eyes hardened. Wrong answer. "You said you are a *malfetto*, and lower than a dog. Do you really want a *malfetto* as your king?"

Teren hadn't thought about it like that. He used to wrestle and spar with Enzo in the palace gardens, when Teren's father was busy leading the Inquisition Axis. They were friends, even, or at least *friendly*, always paired up in afternoon sword practice. Teren hesitated, torn between the idea of Enzo as pure-blooded royalty and the reality of him being tainted by the blood fever's markings. Finally, he shook his head. "No, Your Highness. I wouldn't want that."

Giulietta's eyes softened, and she smiled again. Right answer. "I am the firstborn. It is *my* birthright to rule."

For a fleeting moment, Teren wondered if she was the one who slipped poison into Enzo's soup.

She leaned closer. Then she said the words that would ensnare him forever. "Do as I say, little Teren. Help me rid this world of all *malfettos*. And I will make sure the gods forgive you for your abomination."

The memory fades. Teren raises the whip again and again.

To atone for my cursed magic, I devote myself to the Inquisition all the days of my life. I will serve the queen, rightful ruler of Kenettra. Not only will I rid this world of Young Elites, but I shall rid this world of malfettos.

Blood runs down the pulped flesh of his back as his body tries desperately to keep up in healing itself. He sways in

place, dizzy from the agony. Tears drip from his unnaturally pale eyes. His marking. But Teren only grits his teeth and smiles. His thoughts return to Adelina. She couldn't have just disappeared into thin air. She was *here*, somewhere. He would simply have to search harder. *Pay off every street urchin and beggar in the city. For the price of a cheap meal, they'll tell you anything.* His eyes pulse in anticipation. *Yes. Thousands of spies. I have plans for you, Adelina.* If Teren could have his own way, he would kill every Elite he could find. Then he would throw every *malfetto* in the city—in the *country*—into the dungeons. He would burn every single one of them at the stake. Abominations. If only he could make them understand.

I will find you all. I will use everything in my power to save your souls. I was born to destroy you.

In the good years, they wine and dine, laugh and love.

In the bad years, they draw their swords and

slit each other's throat.

—*Excerpt from* Relations between Kenettra and Beldain,

The Travels of Elaida Eleanore

Adelina Amouteru

My life at the Fortunata Court quickly falls into place. For two solid weeks, Raffaele teaches me the subtle graces of moving around the court. The art of walking. Of smiling. Of avoiding unwanted client advances as an under-age consort-in-training. Simple in theory—but Raffaele's effortless elegance is made up of a thousand tiny gestures that are shockingly difficult to imitate.

"You are comparing two weeks of training with many years," Raffaele tells me, laughing, when I complain about how clumsy my walk looks next to his own. "Do not worry so much. You know enough for a novice, and that will get you by."

And so it does. I become used to wrapping my hair in silks every morning, putting on my glittering mask, and

wandering the halls of the court. Few pay attention to me, as long as I follow Raffaele's advice. *You are underage. You have no name, as far as the court is concerned, and you are not permitted to speak to anyone who wants to be your client. This should give you protection if you ever feel you need to shake off unwanted advances.*

The freedom is nice. I spend my mornings down in the cavern, observing the other Elites whenever they gather. Gradually, I learn more about each of them. After Enzo and Raffaele, for instance, the Star Thief was their next recruit. Enzo named her after the scribe Tristan Chirsley's *Stories of the Star Thief,* a folk hero who could steal anything, because she could steal the minds of beasts. Her marking is a purple shape that stretches across part of her face.

After her came the Spider, who used to be a blacksmith apprentice. The dark, irregular markings on his neck extend down to his chest. The Windwalker was exiled here from the snowy Skyland nation of Beldain. I don't know the story behind that. One of her arms is covered in dark, swirling lines. The last one, the Architect, is a boy currently apprenticed at the University of Estenzia to a master painter. Capable of touching anything—a rock, a sword, a human—and unwinding it, then re-forming it in a different spot. Enzo gave him his Elite name after he designed the gem-locked door to the cavern. His fingernails have stripes of discoloration on them, lines of deep black and blue.

Altogether, there are six of them. I hope I survive to be the seventh.

I take lunches in my chambers alone, and wander the halls and courtyards when I feel restless. The others don't talk much to me yet. I rarely see Enzo. Even a banished prince must still have princely duties, I suppose, but whenever I don't see his face down in the cavern, I leave disappointed. Some days, I feel like the only one in the court's secret corridors.

I come to look forward to the performances that happen almost every night, elaborate dances put on by the consorts that draw potential clients from every corner of the city. Almost all of the other consorts are marked. They wear decorative masks like me — many with their hair also woven into elaborate headpieces. Works of art.

My only goal now is to master my power, to be included in the Daggers' missions, their secretive comings and goings. I start to forget that the Inquisition is hunting for me. I start to forget that I ever had a sister.

I only think of these things late at night, when everything is quiet. Perhaps she's moved on without me, anyway.

Teren Santoro

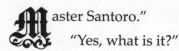aster Santoro."

"Yes, what is it?"

"This is a street urchin who begs near the edge of the Red Quarter. He says he saw something at the Fortunata Court that might interest you."

"Oh? Is that so? Speak up, boy—you'll have a hot supper and place to sleep if I like your answer."

"Y-yes, sir. Um. It was yesterday. I heard from other urchins that the Inquisition's—s-searching for a girl with a scar across her left eye."

"We are. And?"

"Well—I can't be sure—but I saw—"

"You're either sure or you're not. What did you see?"

"I'm sorry, Master Santoro. I—I'm *sure. Sure* I saw such

a girl, walking along the upper courtyards of the Fortunata Court. That fancy one—up on the hill—"

"Yes, I know the one. Get on with it."

"Y-yes, sorry, sir. The girl's hair was wrapped up in cloth, though, so I don't know what color it was."

"Wrapped, in a Tamouran fashion?"

"I don't know. I suppose so."

Teren sits back in his chair. He studies the filthy, shivering boy kneeling before him for a long moment. Finally, he smiles. "Thank you." He waves a hand at the Inquisitors who'd brought the boy in. "A gold talent, a hot meal, and a room at an inn." He nods once as the boy's face lights up. "Never let it be said that I'm not generous."

Once upon a winter
I met a man in the woods
The man beckoned me over
To see a satchel of goods
He offered three wishes
I asked for beauty, love, riches
And he froze me in stone where I stood.

—"The Greedy Ghost of Cypress Pass," common folk song

Adelina Amouteru

Another night at the Fortunata Court. Another night of glistening robes and sensual dances.

Raffaele helps me prepare until I am breathtaking in silks and jewels, and then leads me out of the secret halls and toward the main lounging chamber. The chamber is lavishly decorated tonight, dotted with velvet divans, plates of jasmine sitting on low, round tables, arching curtains of silks hanging across tall windows. Vases of night lilies stand in each corner of the room, their dark purple petals open, their rich, musky scent filling the air. Consorts dressed in their finest gather in clusters. Some already have clients with them, while others giggle among themselves.

In the center of the chamber is a low, raised circular

platform, ringed with thick scarlet cushions for guests to sit on. They are already half filled with people.

"I'll leave you here," Raffaele says as we stop behind the silk veil leading into the main chamber. "You know the routine."

"Are you performing tonight?" I ask.

Raffaele gives me a small smile. Then he kisses me on both cheeks. "Look for me." Then he leaves without another word.

The instant I step past the veil and into the chamber, I make my way toward where other consorts-in-training are already lounging on the cushions near the back. As I go, several clients catch sight of me, their eyes lingering before they glide on to available consorts. One man in particular, clad from head to toe in dark, glittering velvet, his face hidden entirely behind a black mask, watches me for a long moment, only half interested in his conversation with his companions. I keep my gaze determinedly forward. It always takes me a moment before I let down my guard at these events.

The other consorts-in-training exchange eye contact with me, but none of us speak. I choose a cushion at one end, then look on as more masked clients and consorts swirl in the room, until it fills to capacity.

Finally, servants extinguish several of the lanterns lining the walls. The room dims, and the conversation hushes. Other servants light the lanterns that circle the raised platform. I straighten, wondering what Raffaele will look like. After a few minutes, the court's madam sweeps through the crowd

and stops before the platform's edge. She is tall and regal, still beautiful in her golden years, with lines of gray in her hair. She spreads her arms wide. I'll have to ask Raffaele next time if she's a patron to the Daggers. She must be.

"Welcome to the Fortunata Court, my guests," she says. Her voice is rich and warm, and everyone in the audience leans forward, drawn in. "It is a cool, calm night, a lovely time for us to gather. And I know why you all have come." She pauses to smile. "You want to see our court's shining jewel perform."

A round of low applause answers her.

"I won't delay it any longer, then," she continues. "Abandon yourselves to an evening of desire, my guests, and dream of us tonight."

With that, the rest of the wall's lanterns go out, leaving only the platform illuminated. Deep drumbeats echo, one after another. They send a tremor through me, stirring my alignment to passion, and I feel my energy churn. A young consort glides through the darkness of the crowd. When he reaches the platform and steps into the light of the lanterns, I stifle a gasp.

Raffaele is dressed in pale silks that make him stand out, his chest is bared, and a glittering gold line is painted down the middle of his torso. He stops in the center of the raised platform, eyes lowered, and then kneels in a fluid gesture, his arms folded before him, wide sleeves trailing. His robes pool in a circle around him. He stays there for a moment as the drumbeats thicken, and then he rises back to his feet

and walks in a slow, hypnotic circle. I have never seen a composed, delicate dance like this, paired with a song that is nothing but drums—I may never see such a thing again. I glance at the clients filling the room. They are stunned into silence. Gradually, as the tempo increases, two other consorts join Raffaele on the platform, a girl and a boy, and together they glide in circles around one another, eyes both shy and piercing, movements flowing like water. The other two consorts are beautiful, but they pale next to Raffaele. There is no question whom the audience's eyes follow. I watch, mesmerized. Then Raffaele's moment of deep sadness comes back to me, and the performance chills me to the bone.

Someone new sits behind me. I don't think much of it at first—the room is crowded with patrons, at any rate, all focused on the platform. It is only when the person speaks that my heart stops.

"I won't hurt you, Adelina. Just listen."

The voice is very close to my ear, close enough that I can feel the speaker's breath, soft on my skin. He's so quiet, I barely hear him over the drums. But I do. I've heard this voice only once in my entire life, but I would recognize it anywhere.

Teren.

The energy in my heart spikes, and I have a sudden urge to scream in the middle of the performance. *He found me.* From the corner of my eye, I can see that he's not dressed in his Inquisitor armor and robes, but in black velvet, his face

hidden behind a mask just like everyone else here. He is the man I saw earlier, the one whose gaze lingered on me. How did he find me? *I've been too careless.* Did he spot me wandering around the court? Did he recognize me from the balconies? Is he alone? Are there other Inquisitors in the crowd? My heart beats frantically. Are they waiting to strike?

"You have no reason to trust me, I know," he murmurs as the performance continues. "But I did not track you down to arrest you. I've come to make a deal with you. This can work out strongly in your favor, if you want it."

I stay quiet. My hands are trembling violently in my lap, and I clutch them together harder so that no one will notice. My gaze stays fixed straight ahead at Raffaele's performance. Does anyone else notice him? Does Raffaele? *Someone help me,* I think, my eye darting around the room. If I make a commotion now, Teren will be revealed—but what will stop him from dragging me back to the Inquisition Tower, or killing me on the spot? The other Daggers aren't here to protect me, and Raffaele can't. I'm on my own.

"Tell me," Teren whispers. "Have the Young Elites taken you under their wing?"

Drumbeats pound in my ears. I stay frozen, unable to answer his question.

"Seeing as how you're alive and well, I'll assume yes." I don't even have to see Teren's face to know that he's smiling. "Are you so sure about their intentions? Do you trust your rescuers so easily?"

If I weren't terrified, I would laugh at his words. As if I had a reason to think the Inquisitors would be any more trustworthy.

"Speak, Adelina," Teren warns me. "I would hate to make a scene and arrest you."

My voice startles to life. I turn my head slightly, then whisper back in a tiny, choked voice drowned out by the drums. "What do you want?" I stammer.

The beat of the drums changes. Teren whispers to me through their thundering rhythm. "I know you are new to them. You probably don't know everything about their inner workings. But I suspect you will, and soon." He shifts closer as the drums grow steadily more frantic. "So here's how we can help each other out."

Why would I want to help you? I suck in my breath in a vain attempt to calm myself, and in the dark corners of the room I can see memories of my burning day, the way Teren's pale eyes had pulsed at me.

"Observe everything," he whispers in my ear. "Look, listen, and remember. I know where you are now. I will check in on you from time to time. And I expect you to share what you learn with me."

My heart keeps time with the frenzied drumbeats. I can't breathe.

"If you do, not only will I spare your life, but I will shower you with riches. I can grant you your every desire." He smiles. "Just think of it. You can redeem yourself, change from an

abomination in the gods' eyes to a savior." He pauses, and his voice deepens. On the platform stage, Raffaele pulls the young female consort to him. The two twirl. He spins away from her and does the same with the male consort. "If you don't, not only will I destroy you, but I will destroy everything you care about."

Tides of fear and anger rise in my chest, fusing into one, filling my mind with whispers. "What do you know of what I care about?" I murmur harshly.

"Have you already forgotten your little sister? What a cold heart."

Violetta. An icy claw grips my heart. Suddenly I'm back in my nightmare, putting my arm around my frail sister as a thunderstorm rages outside, then turning her around to find that she is not there at all.

No. He's just trying to bait you. "What could you possibly know about my sister?" I snap.

"Plenty enough. On the morning of your burning, she came to me to beg for your life. Did *you* know that? Now it's your turn to return her favor."

He's lying.

"You don't have her," I mutter.

Teren's reply is one full of amusement. "Do you really want to play that game with me?"

My resolve quivers. *She had gone to him?* What if Teren is telling the truth—what if she did, and he kept her? Whispers swirl in my mind, their words incomprehensible, filling

me with the buzz of terror. And I thought she had moved on, perhaps promised to marry some wealthy man. What if she'd instead been with the Inquisition for weeks?

Why would you do that for me, Violetta?

"I don't believe you," I whisper.

Teren doesn't answer, and for a long moment, we just listen to the drums. Just when I think he might have left altogether, he replies, "I have your sister, whether you want to believe it or not. And I will happily torture her until you can hear her screams from the Fortunata Court's beautiful balconies."

He is lying. He is lying. He must be. I imagine Violetta's terrified face, tears streaking her cheeks. I imagine blood.

"Give me time," I finally whisper. I don't know what else to say.

"Of course," Teren answers soothingly. "We are on the same side. You'll soon realize you're fighting for the right cause." His tone turns strangely reverential. Serious and grave. "You can help me fix this world, Adelina."

I'm caught in the middle of a tightening web.

"Next week," he whispers. "I want to see you at the Inquisition Tower. Bring me some information that I'll find useful."

"How do I know you won't simply seize me once I arrive?"

"Stupid girl," Teren snaps. "If I wanted you arrested, I'd do it right now. Why would I seize you when you can be my little helper?" He draws very close, his breath hot against my

ear. "If I like what you tell me when you arrive at the Tower, your sister gets to be pampered and fed until the next time I see you. If you don't come to me . . ." He pauses. I can see his subtle shrug out of the corner of my vision. "Then I don't keep up my end of the bargain."

Then he will kill her. I have no choice. I simply nod.

No answer. The brush of his breath against my ear vanishes, and cool air prickles my skin. The drumbeats finally come to a stop. Up on the platform, Raffaele and the other two consorts bow to the crowd. The roomful of clients leap to their feet, roaring their enthusiasm, their applause thunderous. In the midst of the chaos, I look around me in a frantic attempt to find Teren's face.

But he's already disappeared into the sea of masked faces, as if he were never there. Only his words remain, echoing in my mind, haunting me.

I have been turned into a spy against my will.

Let it be known, so the gods help me. I am not a traitor. I am not a spy.

—Inscription etched in stone on the wall of an Estenzian prison cell,
by an unnamed prisoner

Adelina Amouteru

retreat to my bedchamber that night without saying a word to anyone. Raffaele frowns at me as I leave, his eyes following my figure from across the main court, but I force a quick smile at him and hurry away. It isn't until he catches up with me in the secret halls that I finally turn around to face him.

Raffaele seems genuinely concerned for me, an emotion that tugs at my heart. He brushes my cheek with a brief touch of his fingers. His eyes are still bold with gold powder, his lashes long and black. "You seemed frightened during the performance," he murmurs. "Are you all right?"

I force back a smile and try to keep distance between us. The last thing I need is for him to sense how much I'm trembling. "Yes, I was," I lie, hoping he can't tell. "I felt too exposed in the

audience tonight. Perhaps just my nerves." I try to smile. "I've never seen you perform."

Raffaele watches me carefully. I try to comfort myself with the fact that he can only feel the shift of my energy, not read my actual thoughts. If he thinks I'm acting strange, let him think it's because of his performance, or from being out in public.

Or I could tell him what happened. I could let him know that Teren has hunted me down, confess the task he gave me. After all, Enzo saved my life. Didn't he?

But Raffaele's warning during my gemstone test haunts me. *What if the Daggers kill me?* They haven't known me long enough to trust me. What if this is enough to convince them that I am far too risky to keep around? *No.* I can't tell them. I might be dead by tomorrow if I do. And Violetta will stay in the Inquisition's clutches.

Finally, Raffaele decides to give in. He puts a hand on my shoulder. "Rest well tonight," he says. He kisses my cheeks in reassurance, then turns to leave down the hall.

I watch him go. Whether or not he actually believes me, I have no idea.

That night, I stare sleeplessly at the ceiling. I try to picture my sister shivering in the same dark Inquisition cell I stayed in. Had she really begged for my life? *Am I willing to risk myself to save her? How do I even know he has her? Do I dare doubt him?*

Next week. What am I going to do? How am I even going to sneak away?

The following day, when Raffaele asks me how I'm feeling, I only say that I feel much better. He gives me a sidelong glance, but doesn't force me to say more.

Another day passes. My initial panic settles into a steady undercurrent of unease. Maybe I had dreamed the whole thing, and Teren never came in the first place. This thought is so tempting that I almost let myself believe it.

By the third day, I'm able to think. In order to survive, I must play this game. And I must play it well.

⁂

Five days after the masquerade.

Raffaele and I are back in the cavern. He observes me as I study Enzo sparring with the Spider, trying to figure out how their energy works. Teren's words linger in my mind, reminders of what he expects from me. My week is almost up. How will I ever be able to sneak off to the Inquisition Tower?

I try to focus instead. "Where did he learn to fight like that?" I ask Raffaele as we watch Enzo circling the Spider.

"He was supposed to be king," Raffaele reminds me as he jots down notes on a sheet of paper. He pauses to dip his quill in an inkwell sitting on the floor. "He trained with the Inquisitors as a child."

Enzo waits for his opponent to strike first. For a long minute, nothing happens. The others call out jeers and encouragement from the edges of the circle. Then, suddenly—Spider lunges at Enzo, his wooden sword slashing forward

toward the prince's left side. My weak side. The move is so fast that I see nothing more than a blur through the air—but somehow, Enzo manages to predict the strike and darts out of the way at the last second. Fire sparks from his hands, engulfing him in a tight cylinder. Spider jumps back. Even with his speed, I can tell that the heat has singed the edges of his clothes. Enzo quells the flames at the same time as he dashes toward Spider, as if materializing from behind a veil of orange and gold. He strikes three times in rapid succession. Spider deflects the blows, one after another, then lunges back. The two of them rage on in a tense battle. The force of their hits echo in the cavern.

Finally, Enzo catches the tiring Spider off guard. He kicks Spider's sword out of his grasp, grabs the wooden hilt, and points it back at his opponent's neck. The other Daggers let out whoops, while Spider utters a growl of frustration. Duel's over. I let out a shaking breath as both of them lower their weapons and step away from each other.

Enzo is dripping with sweat, his hair tousled and loose, his lean muscles straining. As far as I can tell, Spider is the only one who seems capable of working the prince so thoroughly. Enzo's white linen shirt clings wet and translucent to his back. As he adjusts his gloves, he casts me a sideways glance and notices me watching. I try to avert my gaze. In my mind, I picture what Enzo might do to me if he finds out about my encounter with Teren. *He will engulf me in flames.*

Enzo gives me a polite nod without smiling, then approaches Spider to make sure he's unharmed. Star

Thief—accompanied today by two coyotes instead of an eagle—claps. The one called Architect runs gangly hands through his hair as he marvels at Enzo's speed. Windwalker asks Enzo how he made his last move. Even Spider defers to him now as they exchange words I can't hear.

I clear my throat and return my attention to Raffaele, who seems to be patiently finishing up his notes. "I hope you were concentrating during that duel," he says in a casual tone.

I blush at his teasing. This is Raffaele's way of introducing me to the concept of energy—trying to teach me how to *see* threads of energy in the air. I shake Enzo out of my head, focus on my center, and search for my alignments to darkness and ambition, curiosity and fear. I imagine myself leaving my body, rushing through the air, searching deep inside the souls of the sparring Daggers, practicing my analysis of their small, subtle movements, looking for glimpses of their energy in action, weaving my way through them to see the glittering threads of energy that make up their hearts and minds. My jaw tightens.

Nothing.

I sigh. I can't face Teren like this. Powerless. "First you tell me that I need to master my abilities before I'm a Dagger," I say, turning back to Raffaele. "How am I supposed to learn anything if I stay separate from everyone else?"

Behind Raffaele's serene face, I notice a flash of something calculating. "The ambition is restless in you today. But the surest way to slow your own progress is to rush yourself into

situations you're not yet ready for." A firm note enters his voice. "Patience."

Careful, Adelina. You don't want Raffaele suspecting you. "Why can I only call on my powers when threatened?" I whisper instead. From the corner of my vision, I see Enzo leave the cavern. My shoulders hunch slightly in disappointment.

"Think of this scenario," Raffaele says. "A hundred years ago, when the Beldish tried to invade our northern isles, a doomed army of forty Kenettran soldiers managed to fight off four hundred Beldish men, buying us time to get our reinforcements there. Sometimes, your body gives you strength that you ordinarily wouldn't have. Right?"

I nod. The Battle for Cordonna Isle is a well-known piece of history.

"Your specific power works the same way. When *you're* pushed to extreme fear or anger, your body magnifies your energy tenfold, sometimes a hundredfold. It isn't like this for everyone—certainly not for me, nor for our Star Thief, whose alignment with joy means that her strength scatters when she's frightened or angry. But you?" Raffaele leans back and regards me thoughtfully. "Now we just need to figure out how you can use that strength *without* death clawing at your throat. Enzo would rather you not risk your life every time you call on your abilities."

I lean back against the pillar. I almost want to laugh. If my life must be threatened in order to bring out my abilities, then I should be swimming in power by now.

Raffaele watches me with a small smile on his lips that sends my heart racing. Today he's dressed in robes of pale gold, and his smooth face is unadorned except for some shimmering powder lining his eyes. How is it possible for such small things to accent his beauty so much? There is no one immune to his charms, I've noticed. He makes even the sarcastic Windwalker blush with a tilt of his head, and when he teases Spider, the hulking boy coughs in embarrassment in spite of himself. Over the past few days, I've occasionally glimpsed Raffaele down at the court's entrance with clients. Yesterday, he was with a beautiful young lady. The day before, a handsome nobleman. It did not matter who the client was. I watched him ensnare them with nothing more than a smile and a sweep of his eyes. Every time, the client's face looked stricken with desire. Every time, I could believe wholeheartedly that he was in love with them.

Raffaele picks up several smooth pebbles from the floor. He places them in a line before me. "Let's start simple," he says. "Use the darkness inside you before seeking it out in the world around you." He nods down at the pebbles. "These stones are light gray. I want you to convince me that they are black."

I turn my attention to them. *Use the darkness inside you.* I tell myself to focus on my fear and hatred, dragging my darker thoughts and memories to the surface. Then I reach for the threads of energy inside me. I can feel them, but they stay just out of my grasp. Beside me, Raffaele takes some notes on his paper. Recording my progress and shifts in energy, no doubt.

I try for several minutes before I sigh and look up. Raffaele only nods at me. "Cheer up, mi Adelinetta," he says. "You were able to conjure your energy during your first test. Take your time and keep trying."

I concentrate on the rocks again. This time, I close my eye. In the darkness, I tune out the sounds of the others training, revisiting instead the night of my father's death. My thoughts turn from my father to my sister. A memory emerges of our early days, the way she would tuck my hair behind my ears, how she'd fall asleep against my shoulder in the warm slant of afternoon light. The image flashes away, replaced by one of her crouched in the corner of a dark prison cell. Teren stands behind me, whispering in my ear. Trapping me. Anger stirs painfully in the pit of my stomach, and I let it fester there, gathering weight and pulling my heart down until I feel the familiar lurch in my chest.

I open my eye and reach into myself. This time, I feel strings of energy pulled taut inside me, and my mind brushes past them like hands on a harp. I pull on them. My pull is unsteady, and I struggle to control the grasp. My brows furrow with the effort of hanging on to them. Before me, the rocks still stay as gray as ever . . . but a few feet away from them, a small ribbon of darkness creeps up from the ground. I gasp at the sight.

"Raffaele," I breathe. "Look!"

The instant I say it, my concentration breaks and the strings of energy slip out of my grasp. My illusion falls back into the ground. I let out my breath as the fear pooling in my

stomach trembles. Raffaele watches me quietly. I try again. My hand brushes past the strings of energy. I grab at them.

Suddenly a blade flashes silver before me. I duck on instinct. Someone laughs over me, and I realize that it's the Spider. He's rushed at me from the other side of the cavern. "A little dark ribbon," he says with disdain. "I'm terrified."

Raffaele gives the enormous boy a warning stare. "Don't," he says.

"Or what, consort?" Spider sneers at me as he sheathes his dagger. "Does it scare the little lamb?"

Raffaele arches an eyebrow. "Would you like to take this up with Enzo? I would not test his temper a few weeks before the Tournament of Storms."

The Tournament of Storms? What do they have planned for the biggest festival of the year?

A moment of doubt flickers across Spider's face, but he hides it immediately. "Tell Enzo whatever you like," he growls. Then he turns his back.

Irritation floods me, a release of all my pent-up fear and anxiety. Before I can think through what I'm doing, I stand up and reach out. This time, I see the energy threads connecting me to Spider. I pull on them. A dark silhouette bursts from the ground before him, stopping him dead in his tracks. It's thin and transparent, hardly threatening. But it's *there.* The shapeless phantom bares its teeth at him and lets out a hiss. Spider whips his dagger out.

I can't hang on—the illusion vanishes. I stand still, unable to believe that I just pulled it from the ground. The other

Elites stop to watch what's happening. Star Thief frowns at me in concern. "Leave her alone," she calls out to Spider, but he just ignores her.

Spider turns back in my direction and smiles. In an instant, he has a blade pointed at the base of my neck. Cold metal presses against my skin.

"Careful you don't take too big a step, little girl," he mutters. "You and your silhouettes."

"Soon I'll know more than just silhouettes," I murmur back. The illusion I created makes me suddenly bold, and I clench my teeth, eager for violence. "Wait and see." His lips curl at my challenge, but I just stare back, unafraid.

"No, you won't." He smiles, then leans close to whisper in my ear. "When that becomes obvious to everyone else, I'll enjoy watching Enzo slit your throat." His blade digs into my neck again. I fantasize about turning around his dagger, cutting him slowly from ear to ear, seeing his blood bubble from his mouth. The image flashes through my mind like lightning, leaving me swimming in a moment of terror and absolute delight. My father's delight. *Go ahead. I want to see you try it.* Maybe I should give Teren *his* name, when I go to the Inquisition Tower.

"*Enough,*" Raffaele snaps. The sharpness in his voice startles me. I don't think anyone has ever defended me so adamantly.

Spider pulls away with a laugh. "I was just playing around," he says in a nonchalant voice. "No harm done." I shiver. I don't think Raffaele heard what Spider whispered to me. I *hope* he didn't sense the image I fantasized about. At

the other end of the cavern, Star Thief casts me a sympathetic glance and then rolls her eyes at Spider.

"Are you okay?" Raffaele asks me. I manage to nod, and he sighs. "I apologize. He resents Enzo's interest in you. He has always considered himself Enzo's best fighter, and he dislikes that the prince's eye has now wandered. Give him time."

I silently thank him for his concern. My heart lurches embarrassingly at the thought that Enzo is interested in me. *In my potential powers*, I correct myself. Spider's words remain in my thoughts, taunting me, and I feel the ghost of his blade cold on my neck. Would Enzo really slit my throat?

As if on cue, the cavern doors swing open. I jerk my head in its direction.

Enzo comes back in, his long robes trailing behind him. He pauses for a moment at the door, looking quietly around the cavern. Then, he whistles at Star Thief. "It's time," he calls out. "How are you feeling today?"

Star Thief whispers at her two coyotes to stay, then hurries over and skids to a halt. She gives him a cheeky look. "Feeling pretty good," she replies with a quick bow. "As always."

A faint smile plays at the edge of Enzo's lips. "Excellent. Let's move."

Star Thief's face lights up, and I have no trouble believing Raffaele's words that she aligns with joy. She waves over the others. Raffaele rises to his feet in one fluid movement, then gives me a nod. "Stay a while longer, if you'd like to practice," he tells me. "We'll return tonight."

They leave the cavern without a word. I'm the only one remaining. Enzo doesn't even glance at me.

I realize I've been holding my breath. My darkness stirs in me, and I let it churn. I have no idea what they were talking about. Obviously they're off on another mission without me. *This is my chance to meet with Teren.*

The shock of that thought leaves me weak at the knees. My week is almost up. If the Daggers will be gone for a while, busy with whatever it is they have planned, then I need to take advantage of this moment. I suddenly look around the chamber, terrified that somehow one of them managed to overhear my silent thoughts. The *malfetto* murder I saw days earlier comes back to me. Then, Spider's threat.

Then, thoughts of my sister.

I'll just go near the tower. If it looks suspicious, I'll leave. I'm not going inside. I'll just. . . My thoughts fade away, drowned out by the beat of my heart.

I stand. I start to move. I'm not even sure if I'm in control of myself anymore, or if my body has decided to let my instincts take over. I ascend the stairs and make my way past the main courtyard. There, I glimpse the streets—and see them teeming with festivities. The sky overhead looks dark and menacing. Something important is going on in the city today.

The Daggers are on the move. So am I.

> Give a Kenettran gold, and he will do business with you.
> Give a Kenettran a purebred stallion, and he will kill for you.
> —Commission on the Prosecution of Maran and Accomplice,
> *High Court of Beldain*

Adelina Amouteru

he instant I sneak out of the Fortunata Court and into the main street, I sense that something's off.

Sure—people in colorful silks fill the road, and vendors selling masks are everywhere, clogging the street and hawking their wares like they would at a spring masquerade in Dalia. People laugh and cheer. Flowering vines grow thick and lush along the street's buildings, and horses pulling carriages and crates make their way up and down the wide roads. Gondolas line up in the river canals, heavy with passengers. A man pushing a cart of fruit tarts sings a folk song while a small cluster of children dance after him. The smell of butter and spices mixes with the pungent odor of crowds.

But black clouds blanket the sky, even darker than when I glimpsed it earlier from the courtyard. There's a dampness in

the air, a cold, tense stillness that contrasts sharply with the colorful banners hanging from balconies and the festivities on the street. The smiling people in masquerade masks look threatening to me. As if everyone knows what I'm about to do, and where I'm headed. I keep my face down.

There are reports posted by the Inquisition Axis at each main intersection, calling for the people to report any suspicious *malfettos*. I instinctively push myself into the crowd, trying to stay hidden. Everyone seems headed in the same direction, so I follow along, lost among their glittering outfits and bright masks. My slippers slap against the curve of cobblestone. *What Estenzian celebration is this?* I wonder as I pass through a narrow street with low-hanging vines dangling overhead.

"For the Red Quarter!" someone shouts beside me, waving a piece of red silk high over his head. It takes me a moment to realize that everyone in the crowd is waving colors of silk: red, green, gold, and blue.

Off in the distance and near the harbor, the roof of the Inquisition Tower shines under the sun.

The crowd jostles me. Finally, I manage to squeeze my way out of the main crowds and down a narrow, quieter alley. I'm careful to stay in the shadows. If I knew how to use my powers, I could probably use a dark silhouette to hide myself even further. I try to call on it again, but the threads stay just outside of my grasp, taunting me.

By the time I reach the Inquisition Tower, I'm drenched in sweat and trembling from head to toe. I'm lucky that few

people seem to be in this area of the city—everyone is off at the festivities. I stare at the entrance, where Inquisitors stand guard, and try to imagine Violetta inside the stone walls. I hesitate, wringing my hands.

What if Teren doesn't have Violetta at all? What kind of trap might this be? I bite my lip, dwelling on how Teren had not arrested me at the court, how he threatened to kill Violetta if I didn't come. I stare so long at the Tower that my vision starts to blur. Finally, when the street is clear, I hurry on silent feet to the tower's entrance.

The Inquisitors standing guard bar me. "What's this?" one of them grunts.

"Please," I manage to say in a hoarse whisper. Already, I feel exposed out here. If one of the Elites sees me . . . "I'm here to see Master Teren Santoro. He's expecting me."

The Inquisitor studies me suspiciously, then exchanges a look with the second Inquisitor at the entrance. He shakes his head at me.

"I'll pass the word to Master Santoro," he says to me. "Until then, you'll have to wait out here."

"No," I say in a rush, then look around me again at the streets. Sweat beads on my brow. "I have to see him now," I add in a lower, urgent voice. "I cannot be seen here. *Please*."

The Inquisitor shoves me away with an irritated look. "You *will* wait here," he snaps. "Until such time as—"

His words cut off as the door behind him shudders, then swings slowly open. There, standing casually at the entrance with his hands folded behind his back, is Teren. He smiles at

the sight of me. "What seems to be the problem?" he says to the guards.

The Inquisitor who shoved me whirls around, bewildered. All annoyance falls from his face. He bows hastily to Teren. "Sir," he begins, "this girl claims she is here to see you. We—"

"And so she is," Teren interrupts, his pale eyes focused on me. "I've been watching you make your way toward the tower." He gestures for me to come closer.

I swallow hard, then hurry past the two Inquisitors with my head down. When I step into the tower, Teren shuts the door behind me. I sag in relief at the knowledge that I'm no longer exposed outdoors.

Then I shudder at the sight of the tower's great hall, decorated with the same furs, tapestries, and symbols of the eternal sun as the tower in Dalia where I'd been imprisoned.

Teren leads me into a narrower hall, then into a chamber with a long table and chairs. There, he pulls a chair out for me and offers me the seat. I sit, shaking. My throat feels parched. Teren sits down beside me, then leans back in a relaxed posture.

"You kept your promise," he says after a while. "I appreciate that. It saves me a great deal of trouble."

I don't want to ask what he would have done if I hadn't shown up. Instead, I meet his gaze. "Is my sister safe?" I whisper.

Teren nods. "Safe and unharmed, for now."

"Let me see her."

He laughs a little at that. The amusement never reaches his eyes, though, and the ice in his stare chills me to the bone. "How about first you tell me something I want to know?" he says.

I stay quiet, unsure of what to say. My thoughts blur together into a frantic river. How little can I tell him, to keep Violetta safe? What will satisfy him? I take a deep breath, then gather all the courage I can muster. "I'll tell you nothing, if you can't prove you have her."

Teren's smile widens, and he regards me with a more interested look. "A bargainer," he murmurs. He waits a long moment before he leans back in his chair. He reaches into the space between his sleeve and his armguard. "I thought as much."

As I look on, he pulls something out and tosses it onto the table. It lands with a clink.

I peer closer. It's a sapphire necklace that Violetta likes to wear. But it is even more than that—tied to the necklace's silver chain is a long, thick lock of Violetta's dark hair.

My heart jumps into my throat.

"Before you begin," Teren says, cutting through my thoughts, "I want to make something very clear." He leans forward. His eyes pierce me. "My word is always good, so do not make a habit of testing it. You will want to tell me the truth. I have many, many eyes in this city. If you lie, I will find out. If you deny me what I want, I *will* hurt her. Do you understand?"

He has her here. I press my hands hard into my dress to

keep them from trembling. "Yes," I whisper. I don't dare question him further.

"Now. Since it seems like you are at a loss for where to begin, let me help you along with some questions." He leans on his knees with his elbows, and taps his hands together. "What have you been doing with the Elites, up until now?"

I take a deep breath. *I need to stall this for as long as I can.* "Resting, mostly," I reply. I'm surprised at how level my words are. "I was unconscious for many days."

"Yes, of course." Teren almost looks sympathetic. "You had many injuries."

I nod in silence. "They don't trust me yet," I decide to say. "They . . . they wear those silver masks. I don't know their names or identities."

Teren is not so easily fazed. "What *do* you know?"

I swallow. The air feels so heavy. *I must tell him something.* As if in a dream, I feel the words emerge. "They visit me occasionally at the Fortunata Court," I whisper.

Teren smiles. "Do they operate from there?"

"I'm not sure." I can hear my heartbeat. The darkness growing in my chest makes me dizzy. I sway in my seat, hungry to use the power. *I wish I had Enzo's abilities,* I suddenly think, and the wish makes the ambition in me surge. *I wish I had the power to burn this entire tower to the ground.*

"Tell me, Adelina," Teren says, watching me curiously. "What are they planning?"

With a great effort, I push the rising darkness down. I cannot use my powers on him. I'm too weak. Besides, what

would a bunch of shadows do? I clear my throat. What can I tell him, what will do the least harm? "They are planning something for the Tournament of Storms," I manage to say. "I don't know what."

Teren considers my words. Then, he claps his hands once, and a moment later, an Inquisitor opens the door. "Sir?"

Teren waves him over. He whispers something in the other man's ear that I cannot hear. The man casts me a wary look. Finally, Teren pulls away. "Tell the king immediately," he says.

The other Inquisitor bows low. "Of course, sir." He hurries off.

"Is that all?" Teren asks me.

Raffaele's gentle face appears in my thoughts, and with it comes a stab of guilt. I've given him so little. *Please, let this be enough to satisfy him.* "That's all I know," I whisper. "I need more time."

For a long moment, Teren doesn't move.

Just as I start to think that he'll demand more from me this visit, he relaxes and looks away. "You came to me today," he says. "And that is a useful start. Thank you for your information. For keeping your word, I shall keep mine. Your sister is safe."

Tears spring to my eye, and I slump in relief.

"She is safe—for as long as you continue to satisfy me." His eyes swivel back to me. "When will I see you again?"

"Two weeks," I say hoarsely. "Give me two more weeks." At his silence, I look down. "Please."

Finally, he nods. "Very well." He rises. "You may go."

And that is all.

Teren guides me out of the tower through a small back entrance hidden behind a gate and an alley. Before he lets me go, he takes my hands in his. He bends down to brush his lips against one of my cheeks. "You've done well," he whispers. He kisses my other cheek. "Keep it up."

Then he leaves me alone, and I wander back through the city's streets on trembling legs. *I am a traitor. What have I done?*

I wander, lost in a daze, until I realize that I've made my way back in the direction from where the earlier festivities had been going on. Here, silent streets make way for noisy revelers again, and before I know it, I turn a street corner and find myself engulfed by a cheering mob. My fear and exhaustion make way for a touch of curiosity. What's all the commotion? There's no way I can make it back to the Fortunata Court without going through all these people.

Then I turn another corner with the crowd, and we enter the largest public square I've ever seen.

The piazza is surrounded on three sides by water canals. People fill the space where they can, but most of it is completely fenced off with thick lengths of rope. Looping around the piazza is a dirt track, which several Inquisitors are inspecting. A line of people dressed in elaborate silk costumes and ornate masks parade along the edge of the track, standard-bearers and trumpeters and *arlecchinos*, aristocrats and their valets, all waving at the cheering onlookers. My eye wanders the crowd, which now looks roughly partitioned into segments

of people waving either red, blue, gold, or green silks in the air. People crowd onto the balconies lining the square. Each balcony has colorful flags hanging from it, muted by the dark sky.

A horse race. I'd witnessed several before in Dalia, although none were quite this big of a spectacle. I glance around the piazza, looking for a good route back to the court. The Daggers' mission today must have to do with this.

I look up to the balconies. Now I pick out the royal seats— on a building situated at the front of the racetrack is a balcony that gives a perfect view, its iron railings decorated with gold and white silks. But the king and queen aren't there. Maybe their royal seats are just for show.

A low rumble of thunder echoes through the city.

"Ladies and noblemen! Fellow spectators!" One of the costumed men on the racetrack holds both arms high in the air. The race's trumpeter, the official announcer. His booming voice hushes the roar of the crowd. The parade of colorful costumes pauses, and the scene changes from one of merry chaos to one of hushed anticipation. Inquisitors stand around the square, ready to keep order if needed. Thunder rumbles overhead, as if in warning.

"Welcome to the qualifying races for Estenzia!" the trumpeter calls out. He turns in a circle so that everyone can see him, and then stops to face the direction of the empty royal balconies. He bows low with an elaborate flourish. "Let this be a tribute to our royal majesties, and the prosperity they bring to Kenettra."

The response surprises me—no clapping or cheers from the crowd. Just a rumble of unrest and a few scattered *Long live the king* shouts uttered. Back home in Dalia, people complained about the king. Now I'm hearing that resentment firsthand. I imagine Enzo seated in the royal seats instead, the crown prince and rightful ruler. How natural he would look. How many of these spectators are loyal to Enzo? How many are Elite supporters?

For an instant, I dare to imagine myself up there on the balcony. The thought of such power leaves me trembling.

The announcer turns his attention back to the crowd. "Today, you will select from Estenzia the fastest riders to send to this summer's Tournament of Storms. Three racers have been chosen from each of our city's quarters. As tradition decrees, the top three racers from today's roster of those twelve will continue on." He grins widely, his teeth shining a brilliant white under his glittering half mask. He puts one hand to his ear in an exaggerated gesture. "Which quarter will come out on top?"

Here, the crowd's enthusiasm erupts. They roar with the names of their quarters. Colored silks wave furiously through the air.

"I'm hearing the Red Quarter!" the announcer taunts, causing a fresh round of cheering as the other three quarters scream themselves hoarse. "Wait—now I'm hearing the Blue Quarter. But the Green Quarter has a strong crop of three-year-old colts this year, as does the Gold Quarter. Who will it be?" He waves his hands in a flourish. "Shall we see our riders?"

The crowd shrieks. I stay frozen in place. *The Tournament of Storms.* This is what Raffaele had been talking about earlier. This is why the Daggers are here—*this* is their mission. They are trying to get one of their own to qualify for the Tournament of Storms' horse race, probably to get a shot at the king in a very public arena. My head feels fuzzy with the shock. *And now I've alerted Teren to it.*

Amid the chaos of cheers, the first three stallions parade out. Red Quarter citizens wave silks in the air, patting the horses' sides as they trot through the masses and onto the track. I'm momentarily distracted. It takes only one look to know that these stallions have superior blood to the horses I remember from my father's estate. These are Sunland purebreds, with perfectly arched necks and flared nostrils, their eyes still glowing with the wild temper that my horses had long ago lost. They toss their decorated manes adorned with red silks as their riders, similarly adorned, wave at their supporters.

Then, the Green Quarter's riders and their steeds come trotting out. This is when I let out a small gasp.

One of the Green Quarter's riders is Star Thief. The purple marking across her face is visible and prominent.

"Lady Gemma of House Salvatore, riding Master Aquino's glorious stallion Keepsake!"

He goes on to list out the stallion's past wins, but I'm no longer listening. In the midst of the roaring crowds, I realize that Gemma's family must be a wealthy and powerful one, for a *malfetto* like her to be allowed to compete like this.

I should head back to the Fortunata Court, before they find me missing. But the spectacle is too much to resist, and my feet stay chained to the ground, my stare fixed on the girl I know as the Star Thief.

Gemma's presence stirs a near riot in the crowd. I hear *"Malfetto!"* spat out in the air, mixing with a loud roar of boos, and when I take a good look at the crowd, I notice people who have put false markings on themselves, jeering and taunting Gemma with exaggerated purple patches painted on their own faces. One of them even flings rotten fruit at her. "Bastard child!" he screams, a cruel grimace twisting his face. Gemma ignores him, keeping her head high as her horse trots past. Other insults fly fast and thick.

A noble lady still gets insults like this? I bite my cheeks at the sharp twinge of anger that shoots through me—until I notice, with a start, that there are people defending her too. Loudly.

In fact, huge crowds of people are waving their flags in the air in her support, most from her Green Quarter, some even from the other quarters. I suck in my breath, and my anger changes to bewilderment—then to excitement. I look on in awe as Gemma nods in their direction. Never in my life have I seen such a sight. The tension between Gemma's supporters and enemies crackles in the air, an early taste of potential civil war, and I take in a deep breath, as if to inhale the power it gives me. *Not everyone hates* malfettos, Enzo had said. My eye darts nervously to the Inquisitors, who look poised to act.

Gemma soaks in the attention. She tosses her dark hair and grins back at the spectators, focusing on the ones who shout out their support for her. Then she hops up onto her stallion's back in one fluid motion. She balances there on both feet, nimble and petite, her arms crossed in satisfaction. Gemma waves, then jumps back down into a seated position. The entire time, her stallion stays perfectly calm. Of the competitors so far, she is the only *malfetto*.

The next two quarters' competitors finally trot out, and the twelve organize themselves into a staggered line at one end of the track. The crowd's roar is thunderous now. Gemma rubs her horse's neck, and the stallion paws the ground in anticipation.

"Riders, prepare your horses!" the announcer calls out. The crowd's roar dies down for a brief second as everyone hushes to watch the start.

The trumpeter lifts a bright yellow silk weighted down with a stone. He flings it skyward. "*Go!*" he screams.

The horses break. The crowd explodes.

A cloud of dust showers the track as the riders race their first lap around the track. I squint through the haze, then finally catch sight of Gemma's green silks flying in the pack. She's among the last half, but she wears a grin that could split her face.

First lap. A Red rider's ahead, and Gemma is ninth. I find myself cheering for her silently.

All around me is screaming and shouting as each person

calls out the names of their favorites. The chaos reminds me of my execution day, and with that, I feel darkness gathering within me. Raffaele had told me to watch the empty space, to look for threads of energy in the air.

The horses thunder around the bend and past me. Gemma has her head thrown back in a wild laugh, her dark hair streaming out behind her like a curtain. I focus on the space between her and the other riders. There's the flicker of something shining in the corner of my eye. It vanishes when I try to look directly at it.

The horses storm down the track again, nearing the end of the second lap. Only one more lap to go. Gemma is still in ninth. Then suddenly, she makes her move—she pulls on her stallion's mane, leans close to his neck, and whispers to him. At the same time, a gust of wind blows through the square. *Windwalker.* She must be watching from a vantage point.

Gemma starts moving up. Fast. Ninth to seventh, then seventh to sixth. Then fifth. Fifth to fourth, to third. The cheers of the Green Quarter's onlookers turn fever pitched. My heart thuds furiously. With Windwalker's help, and her own abilities, Gemma pulls gradually into second. I hold my breath. *Concentrate.* I stare hard at Gemma.

For a split second, I think I see threads glittering in the air, a thousand different colors, moving and shifting like strings on a loom.

The Red riders in first and third place try to block her, forcing her between them. But Gemma pushes harder—the

two other riders' horses toss their heads, startled, when dust kicks up near their hooves. Windwalker must've sent a curtain of wind to their legs, pushing them back.

A quarter of a lap to go. Gemma's horse suddenly pulls ahead in a burst of speed—right into first place. The others try to catch her, but it's too late. She crosses the finish line. The trumpeter flings the yellow silk in the air again, and shrieks fill the air. The Green Quarter is a sea of dancing silks.

She won.

I can't resist a smile of relief, even as I pretend to be as subdued as the rest of the Blue Quarter I'm standing with. Perhaps all Teren can do with the information I gave him is to post more Inquisitors to the Tournament when it happens. Perhaps I didn't affect the Daggers' plans. All around the square are boos, furious shouts of "Disqualify her!" and "*Malfetto,*" accusations that she is one of the Young Elites. Still, no one can argue. We saw her win the race.

The trumpeter approaches Gemma, who is taking a bow from where she's standing balanced on her stallion's back, and hands her the weighted yellow silk with a ceremonial flourish. Even though he stays festive, I notice him avoid contact with her, jerking his hand away so that he can't be dirtied by her touch. Gemma's smile wavers, the first sign that she's bothered by the treatment—but she still lifts her head high and masks her discomfort behind a widening grin. Then the trumpeter goes around to the other riders, handing each of them a length of green silk. The tradition is the same as it is in Dalia: The losing riders must wear the color of the

winner's quarters on their arms for the next three days, to show their good sport.

"Lady Gemma of House Salvatore!" the trumpeter shouts.

"Order! Order!" one of the Inquisitors calls out from where they're fencing in the people, but only a few seem willing to listen to him. The Green Quarter in particular is a frenzy of color and sound. The other quarters murmur indignantly among themselves. I start pushing my way out of the crowd, the way I'd come. If the races are over, then I should head back before anyone notices I'm gone.

"Order, I say!" the Inquisitor barks out.

I halt where I am. More Inquisitors block the square's exits, forcing me to stay put. One Inquisitor calls the trumpeter aside, says something to him that the crowd can't hear—and then, to my surprise, calls two other Inquisitors over to force Gemma to dismount from her horse. The other riders hurriedly make their way off the track and into the crowd. The crowd stirs as one Inquisitor rides his steed into the middle of the square.

He holds his hands up for quiet. "Ladies and noblemen," he begins, "I congratulate the Green District and their *malfetto* on her spectacular win."

Gemma stands uncomfortably alone in the square, suddenly unhappy with all the attention. *I have to get out of here. Now.*

"However, I bring news from the palace. His Majesty has decreed that *malfettos* are no longer eligible for the Tournament of Storms."

Immediately, the Red and Blue Districts cheer—while the Green erupts into angry shouts. Out in the square, Gemma remains on the track, uneasy and tense.

I swallow hard. A wave of guilt hits me. *This is my doing.*

The trumpeter exchanges a few more bewildered words with the Inquisitors. Then, he goes around to each of the other riders, collects their green sashes back, and hands them a red one instead, silently acknowledging the second place finisher's win. The Green Quarter roars their fury. Already, scuffles are breaking out in the crowd.

My gaze stays on Gemma's lone figure out in the square, bewildered and helpless, and for a moment I'm reminded of Violetta. The Inquisitors hold her there, as if they think she'd throw a fit. The trumpeter hands her a red sash. My hands grip the edges of my silks so tightly that I swear my nails are cutting open the skin of my palms. Threads of energy glitter in the air, signs of the crowd's—of my own—rising fear. My fingertips tingle, humming with the growing power. Through the masses, my father's ghost appears and disappears. He glides through the people, his haunting smile fixated on me.

Gemma's cheeks burn with shame. The crowd falls into complete silence. One of the Inquisitors holding her now wraps the red sash around her upper right arm. She bites her lip, keeping her eyes turned downward. The Inquisitor winds it three times, then yanks it viciously tight. Gemma gasps out loud and winces.

"Sir Barra of the Red Quarter!" the trumpeter calls out, as the new winner holds his arms up. Gemma's eyes stay

down. *Get out of there,* I suddenly think at her, wishing she could hear me. A million threads hang over the square.

Suddenly, someone in the crowd hurls a rock at the Inquisitor's head.

The Inquisitor blocks it with his sword before it can reach him, and it clatters off the metal and falls harmlessly to the ground. His eyes search the crowd for his attacker, but all he sees is a sea of stricken faces, suddenly silent and pale. I tense along with the crowd. In Dalia, attacking an Inquisitor is punishable by death.

The Inquisitor nods at his companions. Gemma lets out a cry of protest as they force her to her knees. The crowd gasps. Even the troublemakers, the ones who had insulted Gemma so freely earlier, now look uncertain. To my shame, excitement instead of horror wells up in my chest, and my fingertips tingle. My darkness is a building storm, black as the sky, the threads wound tight with tension and filling every crevice of my mind. The Daggers must be preparing to make a move. They *must* be ready to save her. Right? Raffaele said that Gemma's powers scatter when she's frightened.

"Perhaps we need a harsher reminder for this audience," the Inquisitor snaps, "on the etiquette of good sport." He presses his sword against her neck hard enough to draw blood.

Where are you, Enzo?

I can't hold back any longer. I have to do something. Before I can stop myself, I reach out with my mind and pull on the strings of energy inside me. The ease hits me with a thrill. There is so much tension to feed on here—so much

163

unease and ugliness, such dark feelings. Raffaele's words flash through my thoughts. I focus, gathering all my concentration on the specific threads I'm pulling, knowing what I want to make. The threads push back, protesting the change, but I force them to bend to my will.

Up on the roofs, shadowy silhouettes rise.

Sweat beads on my forehead, but I force myself to keep my focus. I struggle to hold on to the threads, but there are *so many* of them. Clenching my teeth, I force the shape of the silhouettes to change. And for the first time—they listen to me. The silhouettes take on the shapes of Daggers, their dark hoods and silver masks intact, crouching by the dozens on the rooftops like silent sentinels, black against the stormy sky. I hold them all in position there. My breaths turn ragged. I feel like I've been running for hours. Some of the silhouettes quiver, barely able to retain their shape. *Hold on.* They stabilize. I catch my breath at how real they look.

The Inquisitors glance up at the roofs. The sword falls away from Gemma.

"The Elites!" several in the crowd shriek, pointing up at my illusion. "They're here!"

The crowd bursts into screams. The horses startle. Gemma hops to her feet, her eyes wide, and seizes the moment to scamper back into the crowd. The rush of darkness through me is intoxicating and irresistible, and I find myself embracing it, letting it cover my insides like ink. *Such power over these little masses. I love it.*

I'm not strong enough to hold the illusion in place. The silhouettes scatter into nothingness as soon as I pull them back below the roofline. I shove my way frantically out of the square with the others. My sudden burst of bravado is replaced with anger at myself. Now Enzo will know for certain that I was here—they might find out why I was really in the streets. *They might find out about my meeting with Teren, and what I told him.* Nausea churns in me. I have to leave here.

All around me, people try to flood out of the square. Some Inquisitors are blocking the exits, but there are too many of us and not enough of them. I'm careful to stay close to the walls of the buildings as people shove past me. All around me is a blur of chaos and colors, masked faces and the sensation of others' fear. Threads of energy glitter in the air.

Then, out of nowhere—an arrow comes flying from the sky and hits an Inquisitor in the chest. It hits him so hard that it knocks him off his horse.

The people near him shriek, scattering in all directions. Another arrow comes flying, and then another. The Inquisitors turn their attention to their invisible attackers—and as they do, the people finally break past the blocked paths and free themselves from the square. My heart hammers in my chest at the sight of blood.

The Daggers.

I stumble out of the square, then retrace my steps as I rush along with others. Behind me, I hear Inquisitors shouting for order—the sounds of scuffles tell me that they're making

arrests as they go. I rush on. Energy courses through me in relentless waves, feeding me even as I try to ignore the flood of power in my veins. In spite of everything, I feel a strange sense of glee.

All this chaos is of my own creation.

By the time I reach the court, I'm soaked in sweat. My breaths come hard. I round a corner to the side wall of the court facing a narrow street, then climb on the ivy and hoist myself over the low ledge. I collapse inside the courtyard. Then I pick myself up, dust off my hands, and pull open a side gate that leads to the inner chambers. Finally, I reach the secret wall. I push on it, step through, and rush toward my room. *There. I've made it back before the others. I'll head to my room and—*

But someone's already waiting for me in the hall. It's Enzo.

The sudden sight of him catches me by surprise. Any hope of being spared his wrath is dashed when I see the expression on his face. His eyes are alight, the scarlet in them brighter than usual.

"You were to stay here," he says. His voice is deadly quiet. "Why did you leave?"

Panic rises in my throat. *He knows.*

Something stirs behind him. I glance over his shoulder to see Windwalker, her mask off. Spider lurks farther down the hall, his arms crossed as he leans against the wall. He looks smug, eager to see me punished. "Huh," he says. "Little lamb's in trouble."

I keep my focus on Enzo and try to think of some clever comeback. Anything to protect myself.

"I—" I start to say. "I wanted to help—"

"You caused a riot out there," Spider interrupts me. "Ever stop to think of what might happen if you lost control of your powers?"

"I stepped in for Gemma," I reply, suddenly angry. "I wasn't about to wait around and see her killed."

Spider's lips curl up. "Maybe it's time you keep your words locked inside that pretty little mouth, where they belong."

My voice flattens. "Careful. Lest I hurt you." I don't even know where the words come from until they've already left me.

Enzo hushes us both with a shake of his head. "Dante," he says, without bothering to glance over his shoulder. It takes me a second to realize that Enzo has revealed the Spider's real name to me. "You're dismissed."

The boy's rage changes to disbelief—at the use of his name in front of me, or at his dismissal, maybe both. "You'll let this girl have her way?" he spits out. "She could have gotten one of us killed. She could have ruined the entire mission—"

"The *Inquisition* ruined the mission," Enzo interrupts. His eyes stay on me, and I feel the familiar shudder pulse through my heart. "You're dismissed. Do not make me say it again."

Dante hesitates for a moment. Then he pushes away from the wall. "Watch your back, little lamb," he snaps at

me before stalking off down the hall. Windwalker watches him go, shrugs, and regards me with a suspicious look.

"Now what, Reaper?" she says. "A whole new plan for the Tournament of Storms?"

"No need."

She snorts. "But they've disqualified Gemma," she says. "She can't get close to the royals if she won't be able to race."

Enzo studies me with a gaze so intense that it leaves my cheeks red. "Not if someone disguises her," he replies.

I blink, my mind spinning with the new information they're feeding me. First, Spider's real name. Now, this. Is he . . . *pleased* with me? Permitting me to participate in the Daggers' plans? *I could learn to disguise Gemma. I could disguise any one of them to ride in the race.*

Enzo steps closer until he's now barely a foot away from me. The heat emanating from him burns my skin through the fabric of my clothes. He reaches out one hand and touches the clasp that pins my cloak at my neck. The metal turns white hot. When I look down, I see threads fraying on the cloak's cloth, their ends blackened and singed. My fear rises up into my throat.

"You want to train faster," he says.

I keep my chin up, refusing to let him see my anxiety. "Yes."

He's silent. A second later, he removes his hand from my cloak's clasp, and the heat is sucked out of the melting metal as if it were never there. I'm shocked it didn't burn straight through to my skin. When I look back up at Enzo, I notice

168

a tiny spark of something else behind his rage. Something in his eyes that sends a different kind of warmth tingling through me.

"So be it," he replies.

My heart jumps.

"But I warn you, Adelina. Dante is right. There is one line you do not cross with me." His eyes narrow as he folds his hands behind his back. "You do not recklessly endanger my Elites."

His words sting, labeling me as someone separate from them. *I am separate from them. I am a spy and a traitor.* Besides, what if things had gone horribly wrong when I used my powers? If I hadn't been there, the other Daggers would surely have made a move to protect her, and they are certainly more skilled than I am. What if Gemma had instead been harmed during my antics, because I didn't know what I was doing? What if the Inquisition had chosen to blame her for the false Elites on the roofs?

What if Teren had seen me out there?

"I'm sorry," I murmur at the ground, hoping he doesn't hear in my voice all the reasons why.

Enzo makes no indication that he has accepted my apology. His stare feels like it can burn straight through my skin. "This will be the last time you disobey me." He says it without a single hesitation, and I realize, with a horrible shudder, that he means exactly what he says. *If he finds out about Teren, he really will kill me.*

"Tomorrow." His voice is hard as diamond. "Be at the

cavern by dawn. Let's see how fast you can learn." Then he breaks the stare, steps away from me, and leaves down the hall.

Windwalker lingers for a moment. She gives me a small nudge and a grudging smile, then extends a hand. "I'm Lucent," she says.

I take her hand, unsure what to say in return. Another barrier between me and the Daggers breaks down. I don't know whether to feel joy or guilt.

"That's his way of showing thanks for your help, by the way," she says before she turns away. "Congratulations. He's going to train you himself."

Teren Santoro

Do you have any idea who Lady Gemma is?"

Teren stays bowed before the king. "Yes, Your Majesty."

"Do you realize that Baron Salvatore is her father?"

"I apologize, Your Majesty."

"You're a damn fool of a Lead Inquisitor. I cannot afford to anger a nobleman like Baron Salvatore. And he is *furious*. You do not allow your Inquisitors to threaten his daughter in public and make an embarrassment of me. Even if she is a *malfetto*. Do you understand?"

"But your decree, Your Majesty—"

The king makes a disgusted sound. "Carry out my decree *discreetly*." He leans back in his chair. "And the Young Elites attacked the qualifying races. You still haven't caught a single one."

Teren clamps down on his rising frustration. "No, Your Majesty."

"I should throw *you* in a dungeon cell."

Teren keeps his eyes cast down at the throne room's marble floor. His teeth are clenched. "Yes, Your Majesty," he says, but furious thoughts swarm in his mind. What a *fool* of a king. *He wants the Elites captured, but he's too cowardly to jeopardize his political relations. He's too cowardly to wage real war on* malfettos. Teren doesn't mention aloud that his Inquisitors threatened Lady Gemma on purpose. That it had been the queen's idea. That the game they play is tightening. *Turn the king's nobles against the king, and he weakens.*

And as soon as Adelina delivers her information . . .

Beside the king, Queen Giulietta leans over to whisper something in her husband's ear. The king just waves her off in annoyance. Teren's temper flares. Giulietta glances briefly at him.

Patience, my Teren, her eyes seem to say. *Everything will fall together.*

"The next time you embarrass me," the king goes on, "I will have your head."

Teren bows lower. "There won't be a next time, Your Majesty," he answers loudly.

The king looks smug and satisfied. He has not understood the double meaning in Teren's words.

I hereby pledge to serve the Dagger Society, to strike fear into
the hearts of those who rule Kenettra, to take by death
what belongs to us, and to make the power of our Elites known
to every man, woman, and child. Should I break my vow,
let the dagger take from me what I took from the dagger.
    —The Dagger Society Initiation Pledge, *by Enzo Valenciano*

Adelina Amouteru

The next morning, when I go to meet Enzo in the cavern, the sky churns with black clouds, and giant raindrops splatter on me as I hurry through the main courtyard toward the secret entrance. I head down the stairs alone, trying not to think about the last time I'd seen a storm like this.

No disguise on me today. My hair has taken on a dark blue-gray sheen under the stormy sky, the strands pulled tightly away from my face, and my lashes are a dull shade. I've even left my porcelain mask behind. My clothing is simple Kenettran garb instead of Tamouran silks, deep blue vest over white linen, dark trousers, dark boots lined with silver trim. I shake water from my hair as I go.

By the time I get to the cavern, Enzo's already waiting for me. The rest of the space is empty.

He's dressed in a dark doublet, and his Dagger hood is down, revealing his scarlet red hair. The anger that burned in his eyes last night is now replaced with cold sternness. I'm not entirely sure what he expects me to do, so I stop several feet in front of him and bow my head once. Here, alone, I suddenly feel small—I hadn't realized how much taller he is than I am.

"Good morning," I say. "You asked for me, Your Highness, so here I am."

Enzo watches me. I wonder if he'll comment on how I'd controlled my illusions yesterday. The memory makes me puff up a bit with pride. *Surely* he must be proud of that, regardless of the way I did it.

"You want a challenge," he replies after a pause. His voice reverberates in the empty space.

I lift my chin. "Yes." I make sure my answer sounds firm.

A faint spark of red shines in his eyes. "Does it excite you, feeling fear?"

I don't answer. But the words remind me of the chaos that had surrounded me at the races yesterday, and I can't help the rush of power the memory brings.

"What do you want to learn so badly, Adelina?" Enzo asks.

I give him a level stare. "Everything," I reply, surprised by my calmness.

He holds out his gloved hands. Tendrils of smoke rise from both of his palms. "I am not Raffaele," he warns. "Brace yourself."

Suddenly, two columns of fire explode to either side of

me—they roar to the ceiling and rush out in two long lines, imprisoning me in a corridor of fire. I stumble backward a step, then try to focus on Enzo. *You did this yesterday; you can do it again now.* I pull on the strings of energy I see. A hulking beast of a silhouette begins to rise from the ground.

But I haven't concentrated for two seconds when Enzo rushes at me. Metal shines in both hands—his daggers are drawn. He lunges for me. My concentration breaks—my illusion vanishes. I throw myself to the ground and roll out of his way. The edges of my boots hit the wall of fire. I wince at the heat, then scramble frantically away.

Enzo's on me again before I can blink. Metal flashes before my eye. I throw up a hand to protect myself, and the blade slashes a thin, shallow line into my palm. Pain blooms from the wound.

He's wasting no mercy on me. This is not just an accelerated training session, it's a lesson.

"Wait—" I call out.

"Get up, little wolf," he snaps. The heat of the fire reflects off his crimson hair.

I struggle to my feet. My hand leaves a bloody imprint on the ground. The pain and terror in me fuses, giving me the fuel I crave so badly. I pull on my energy, and this time I call forth a wolf of black mist, its eyes gold and its mouth pulled back in a snarl. It charges at Enzo.

Enzo rushes right through it, dispelling it and my concentration in a puff of dark smoke. The threads slip out of my hands and back into the world. I make a grab for them

again—the puff of dark smoke starts to shift into the shape of a hooded demon. Enzo makes a slashing motion at me with his hand. Fire erupts before my face. I lose my footing and fall, hitting my back hard on the ground. My lungs struggle for air.

Enzo's dark robes stop beside me. I look up to see his cold, ruthless expression. "Again," he commands.

Dante's words come back to me, but his voice sounds like my father's. *You'll never master your abilities.* Is a mess of black silhouettes and shapes resembling creatures all I can conjure? My anger and fear flood through me again. I drag myself to my feet. I'm past all pretense now—blindly I reach out for the darkness, then raise my hands over my head.

Enzo attacks me again before I can focus my powers. His daggers reflect the firelight. Another cut, this time a small nick on my arm. The sting of it blossoms against my flesh and sends stars bursting across my vision. I duck down and scramble indignantly out of his path. Fear clouds my mind—the threads of energy are all there, glistening strings hovering inside me and all around me—but I can't focus long enough to grab on to them.

I try again. Silhouettes appear in the air. Again, my concentration breaks. Enzo's assault is relentless—a blur of motion, knocking me down every single time I struggle to get back up. My hair falls out of its neat bun and strands of it stick against my face.

"Again," Enzo orders each time I fall.

Again.

Again.

Again.

I try, I really do. But each time, I fail.

Finally, I cry out and dart away from his blades, then turn around and run down the corridor of fire. My mind scatters. I give up trying to call my energy. Ahead of me, I see the cavern entrance, the doors shut tight. Before I can reach them, though, a wall of fire goes up in front of me. I trip, then collapse to the ground. I'm now blocked off on three sides by flames. I whirl around to see Enzo striding toward me, his robes billowing out behind him, his face a portrait of mercilessness. The heat around me burns the edges of my sleeves, blackening them. This time I curl up in a ball, shaking and bewildered. I can't focus enough to do anything. He stops me every time. How am I supposed to learn if I don't get a chance to concentrate?

But of course he's teaching me a lesson. *This isn't a game. This is reality.* And when I'm in the middle of a fight, this is what it'll be like. I whimper, shut my eye, curl up tighter, and try to shrink away from the columns of fire that roar around me. Tears run unbidden down my face.

I sense a figure nearby. When I open my eye, I see Enzo on one knee before me, studying my tear-streaked face with a look of bitter disappointment. It is this look, more than anything, that pains me.

"Broken so easily," he says with disdain. "You're not ready after all." The columns of fire vanish. He gets up and walks past me, his robes brushing over me.

I'm left alone on the cavern floor, crumpled in a heap, unable to control my tears. Strands of my hair fall across my face. *No. I'm not broken easily. I will never break.* I am going to find a way out of the mess I've gotten myself into—I *will* find a way to untangle myself from the Inquisition's grasp and finally be free. I look up at his retreating figure through a veil of teary anger. The anger fills me, seeping its blackness into my chest until I can feel it spilling out of every fiber of my body, every energy string pulled so tight, they might break. My strength begins to build. From the corner of my vision, I see my hair shift to a bright silver. I tremble; my hands flatten against the ground, then dig against it like claws. Pain shoots up my one crooked finger.

Vicious black lines start to crawl along the cavern floor. They turn into dozens, then hundreds, then millions of lines, until they fill the entire floor and snake up the walls. Between the dark lines drips blood, mimicking the red streaks on my injured palm. An enormous shadow blankets me. I don't need to look up to know what I created—black wings, ones so large that they seem to fill the entire length of the cavern, growing out from my back like a pair of phantoms. A low hiss fills the cavern, echoing off the walls.

Enzo stops and turns to look at me, his eyes still hard. I smile at him. My giant wings shatter into a million pieces— each piece morphs into a shard of dark glass. I send them hurtling at Enzo. They pass straight through him, hit the wall, and break into an explosion of glitter.

Enzo doesn't flinch, but he *does* blink. The shards had looked real enough to make him react. He folds his hands behind him, then regards me. "Better." He walks toward me again. Wherever he steps, the black lines on the ground creep upward, turn into skeletal hands, and try to grab at his legs. I drink in the exhilaration of it all, the millions of threads glistening before me, ready for my command.

"Weave the threads together," Enzo commands as he draws closer. Flames appear behind him. I pull myself to my feet and step away from him until my back touches the cavern wall. "Go ahead. Make something for me that is more than a dark silhouette. Make something with *color*."

Still drowning in my fury and fear, I take the threads I see and cross them, painting what appears in my mind. And just like that—slowly, painfully—a new creation emerges before me. Enzo has almost reached me. Between us, I paint something red, so crimson red that the color of it blinds me. The red changes into petals, each one layered on top of the other, covered in dark dewdrops. Beneath it spiral green stems covered in thorns. Enzo stops before the hovering illusion. He observes it for a moment, then reaches out to touch it. I pull on strings in the air. Blood blooms on his gloves, dripping from his palms to the ground, mimicking my own real blood on my injured palm. Reminding me of the day when I'd closed my hand around the rose thorns in my father's garden.

I *am* learning imitation from reality.

Enzo steps forward. He passes through the rose illusion,

then stops a foot away from me. The blood disappears from his gloves. I glare at him defiantly. I keep my heart wide open, relishing the flood of dark emotions that fill me to the brim. The heat of his fire turns my cheeks red.

Enzo nods once. "Very good," he murmurs. For the first time, he looks impressed.

"I *am* ready," I reply angrily. To my dismay, my tears are still wet on my face. "I'm not afraid of you. And if you give me a chance, I can show you what I'm capable of."

Enzo simply watches me. I search his eyes, seeing once again the odd expression lurking behind his cold features, something that goes beyond his desire to exploit my power. Something that almost looks like . . . familiarity. We gaze at each other for a long moment. Finally, he reaches up and gently wipes away one of my tears.

"Don't cry," he says, his voice firm. "You are stronger than that."

When the world was young, the gods and goddesses birthed the angels,

Joy and Greed, Beauty and Empathy and Sorrow, Fear and Fury,

sparks of humanity. To feel emotion, therefore, to be *human*,

is to be a child of the gods.

—The Birth of the Angels, *various authors*

Adelina Amouteru

The storm finally passes, leaving a devastated Estenzia in its path—broken roof shingles, flooded temples, wrecked ships, the dead and dying. As people flock to the temples, others gather in Estenzia's squares. Teren leads the largest of these gatherings. I can see it all the way from the Fortunata Court's balconies.

"We let a *malfetto* win the qualifying races," he calls out, "and look at how the gods have punished us. They are angry with the abominations that we allow to walk among us." People listen in grim silence. Others start to shout along, raising their fists in response. Behind Teren are three young *malfettos*—one of them barely out of childhood. Probably dug them out of the city's ghettos. They are tied together to a stake erected in the center of the square, and their mouths are

gagged. Their feet are hidden in the midst of a pile of wood. A pair of priests flank them, lending their silent approval.

Teren lifts the torch in his hands. The firelight casts an orange hue across his pale irises. "These *malfettos* are accused of being Elites, for being among those that attacked Inquisitors during the races. The Inquisition has found them guilty. It is our duty to send them back to the Underworld, to keep our city safe."

He throws the torch onto the pile of wood. The *malfettos* disappear, screaming, behind curtains of fire.

"From this day on," Teren calls out above the sound of the flames, "all *malfetto* families and shops will pay a double tax to the crown, as reparations for the bad fortune they bring upon our society. Refusal will be seen as reasonable cause for suspicion of working with the Young Elites. Offenders will be detained immediately."

I can't see the Daggers from here, but I know they are watching the burning from the roofs. I know that right now Dante is notching arrows to his bow, getting ready to put each of the *malfettos* out of their misery. I try not to dwell on why they don't risk saving them.

The next day, an angry mob tears down a *malfetto* family's shop. Broken glass litters the streets.

My lessons speed up.

Enzo takes me under his tutelage, coming to the court late at night or early in the morning. Not until Gemma whispers it to me do I learn that Enzo has never trained anyone like

this before. Her words are meant to be encouraging, but all I can do is lie awake at night, dreading the moment when I will have to see Teren again.

To hone my illusion skills, Enzo calls on Michel, the Architect. "Ridiculous," Michel says during our first session together. He brings the painter's eye, and his painter's eye critiques my work. "You call this a rose? The shadows are all wrong. The petals are too thick and the texture is too harsh. Where's the essence? The delicate touch of life?"

Michel forces me to create small illusions, as tiny as I can. This helps focus my concentration without draining my energy, requiring me to pay attention to everything on a minute scale, on details that I normally do not consider. I learn to make illusions of tiny flowers, keys, feathers, the texture of a wood splinter, the wrinkles of skin on a finger's joints. He reminds me that when I want to imitate a real object, I need to think like a painter: A smooth stone is not smooth at all, but covered in tiny imperfections; white is not white, but a dozen different shades of yellows, purples, grays, blues; skin color changes depending on what light shines on it; a face is never entirely still, but made up of tiny, endless flickers of movement we never think twice about. Faces are the hardest. The slightest mistake, and the face looks unnatural, eerie and false. Conjuring the spark of life in a person's eyes is nearly impossible.

Michel's words echo Raffaele's. I learn to *see*. I start to notice all the things that weren't there before. With this comes

another thought: If I can master my powers, perhaps I can face Teren next time with something other than traitorous information. Perhaps next time, I can actually attack him. The thought spurs me on with feverish intensity.

I spend every waking minute practicing. Sometimes I practice alone, and other times I'll watch as Enzo spars with Lucent and Dante. Occasionally Gemma takes me aside, working with me while the others duel. Gemma is the one who teaches me how to still my mind in order to better sense the minds of those around me.

"Why don't you duel with them?" I ask her. Today, she has a cat with her, a huge, feral one with a low growl.

Gemma grins at me, then looks down at the cat. It untangles itself from her legs and comes ambling over to me. I shrink away from its wild face, but it rubs its head against my leg and settles at my feet.

"I'm no fighter," Gemma replies, folding her arms. "Father thinks I have beautiful hands, and he doesn't want me to ruin them once I find myself a proper suitor." She holds up her hands for emphasis, and sure enough, they are indeed fine and delicate. I'd forgotten for a moment that Gemma, unlike Lucent and the ex-soldier Dante, is a proper-born lady. The only thing that had spared her the Inquisition's wrath after the horse race incident. I also feel a rush of jealousy that her family seems perfectly kind and encouraging. It'd never occurred to me that some might actually love their *malfetto* children.

The cat wound around my legs hisses at me before returning to Gemma. *Stupid creature,* I think grudgingly. I look

at Gemma. "Why do you always have different animals with you?"

"They follow me. Sometimes I have an easier time bonding to certain animals, to the point where I'll do it accidentally. This fellow tailed me all the way from my father's villa." She scratches the animal's head fondly, and it purrs back. "He won't stay forever. But I'll enjoy his company in the meantime."

I turn my attention back to the dueling. We watch the fight for a while, until Gemma clears her throat and I look back down at her again. This time, her carefree expression has given way to something more serious.

"I never properly thanked you for what you did in the racing square," she says. "That was reckless, and brave, and breathtaking. My father and I are both grateful."

Her father must be a patron of the Daggers, the way she talks about him. Her kind words stir warmth in me, and I find myself returning her smile. The darkness in me fades for a moment. "Glad to help," I reply. "You seemed a bit unhappy out there."

Gemma wrinkles her nose. "Not my best moment." Then she laughs. It is a bright, ringing sound, the laugh of someone who is loved. In spite of everything, I can't help laughing along with her.

"You've grown rather fond of Gemma," Raffaele tells me the next day, as we walk together in the underground catacombs. Today, his hair is tied high on his head in an elegant

dark knot, exposing his slender neck. He wears a bold blue robe trimmed in silver. I can only see the part of him illuminated by lantern light, and the sight unnerves me, making me feel like the darkness is trying to swallow us whole.

"She's easy to like," I say after a while. I don't like admitting it. I shouldn't be getting close to any of the Daggers at all.

Raffaele turns to give me a brief smile, then looks away again. "The tunnels branch once more here. Do you see?" He pauses to hold up the lantern, and in the gloom, I see the path before us split into two, the walls lined with endless rows of urns. Raffaele chooses the right-hand path. "We now walk underneath the Piazza of Twelve Deities, the city's largest marketplace. If you listen close, you can hear some of the bustle. It's a shallow spot."

We both pause to listen, and sure enough, eventually I make out the faint shouts of people hawking their goods: stockings and sweets, dental powders and bags of honey-roasted nuts. I nod. All my recent time with Raffaele has been spent learning the catacombs. It turns out that the main underground cavern is connected to a wider maze of tunnels. Much wider.

We continue walking, memorizing one branch after the next, a honeycomb of quiet paths that run parallel to the bustling surface world. I watch the frescos on the walls shift with the ages. The walls feel like they're closing in on me, ready to entomb me with the ashes of past generations. Without Raffaele's help, I know with absolute certainty that I would die down here, lost in the maze.

"This path leads to a hidden door under the temples," Raffaele says as we pass another branch. "The opposite path will take you to Enzo's northern villa." He nods to the dark tunnel up ahead. "There was even a path that used to run under the Inquisition Tower, although it has been sealed for many decades."

I fall silent at the mention of the tower. Raffaele notices my discomfort. We walk in the darkness for a long time without saying anything.

Finally, we stop before a dead end. Raffaele runs his fingers delicately along the edge of the wall. He finds a small groove in the stone, and then gives it a good push. The wall swings slowly to one side, and light streams in. I squint.

"And this," Raffaele says, taking my hand, "is my favorite path."

We step through the open wall and find ourselves standing at the entrance of a tunnel, the ancient stone steps sinking straight into the water of the canals, a quiet, hidden spot that looks out over the main harbor and the beginning of the Sun Sea. Distant gondolas glide by on golden water.

"Oh," I breathe. For an instant, I forget my troubles. "It's beautiful."

Raffaele sits on a step right above the water, and I follow his lead. For a while, we say nothing, listening instead to the water lapping gently against the stone.

"Do you come here often?" I ask him after a while.

He nods. His multicolored eyes focus on a faraway pier,

where the hazy silhouette of the palace rises. Light outlines his long lashes. "On quiet days. It helps me think."

We sit in comfortable silence. Off in the distance, the songs of gondoliers float toward us. I find myself humming along, the melody of my mother's lullaby coming instinctively to my lips.

Raffaele watches me with his small smile, his eyes bright with interest. "You sing that song often," he says after a moment. "'The River Maiden's Lullaby.' I know it. It's a lovely rhyme."

I nod. "My mother used to sing it to me when I was very little."

"I like it when you sing. It calms your energy."

I pause, embarrassed. He must be able to sense my heightened sense of unease for the past few days, as my next appointment with Teren draws near. "I'm not very good. I don't have her voice." I almost tell him about my sister, how Violetta's voice sounds closer to my mother's—but then I remember where my sister is right now. I swallow the words.

Raffaele doesn't comment on my energy this time. Maybe he thinks the thought of my mother saddens me. "Can you sing it for me?" I ask him, to distract myself. "I've never heard you before."

He tilts his head at me in the way that makes me blush. My alignment to passion stirs. His eyes go back to the water. He hums a little, then sings the first few verses of the lullaby. My lips part at the sound of his voice, the sweetness

of the melody, the way the lyrics hang in the air, light and clear and full of longing. When I sing it, the song comes out as individual notes, but when he sings, the notes change to *music*. I can hear my mother in the words. A memory comes back to me of a warm afternoon and our sun-drenched garden, when my mother danced with me to the lullaby. When she caught me, I turned around to hug her and buried myself in her dress.

Mama, Mama, I called up to her. *Will you be very sad when I grow up?*

My mother bent down and touched my face. Her cheeks were wet. *Yes, my darling,* she answered. *I will be very sad.*

The melody ends, and Raffaele lets the last note disappear in the air. He glances at me. I realize that tears are blurring my vision, and reach up to hurriedly wipe them away. "Thank you," I murmur.

"You're welcome." He smiles back, and there is genuine affection in his expression.

For a moment, I sense something I've never sensed outside of the Dagger Society. Something I'm finding only now, surrounded by young strangers that remind me of myself. Kindness. With no strings attached.

I can see a life for me here, as one of them.

It's a very, very dangerous way to think. How can I be their friend, with what I'm doing? The closer I get, the harder it will be the next time Teren expects me to deliver what I've promised him. But the longer he stays away and the stronger

I get, the bolder I grow. I return to watching the scenery with Raffaele, but my mind spins. *I need to find a way out, to find Violetta without giving Teren his information.* And the only way is to work up the courage to tell the Daggers the truth.

❦

Raffaele's sessions with me evoke gentle passion—but nothing I do with anyone comes close to my training sessions with Enzo himself.

Enzo pushes my emotions hard. He teaches me how to create a convincing illusion of fire, how a flame flickers, how the color of it changes from red to gold to blue to white. I weave and weave until I exhaust myself.

"Your strikes are unfocused," he snaps one night as he teaches me the basics of sparring with a wooden sword. "Concentrate." Our clashes echo in the empty cavern. He knocks the weapon out of my hand with one effortless blow, then kicks it up in the air and flings it back at me. I scramble to catch it, but my weak vision means I miss it by a good several inches. The wood hits my wrist. I wince. At this hour, all I want to do is go to bed.

"My apologies, Your Highness," I retort, ignoring the pain. Curse him to the Underworld—he always attacks on my blind side. I know he tries to anger me on purpose, to strengthen my power, but I don't care. "I'm a merchant's daughter. I haven't exactly trained for dueling."

"You're not dueling. You're learning basic defense. Young Elites have enemies." Enzo points his sword at me. "Again."

190

I strike. I conjure a dark silhouette of a wolf and fling it at him, hoping to throw him off. It doesn't. He dodges my blow with ease, then lunges back, clashing with me twice until we're close to the cavern's wall. He whirls and yanks a dagger straight out of his boot. This second blade stops a hairsbreadth from my neck.

My fury heightens. What's the point of pitting a lamb against an expert assassin? I conjure an illusion of smoke that explodes around us. Then I do a move he taught me—I grab his dagger and aim for his throat.

His hand clamps hard on my wrist before I can make contact. Heat rushes through me. Something sharp taps against my chest. When I look down, I see a sword point hovering over my ribs. "Don't forget one weapon just because of another," he says. A flicker of approval flashes in his eyes. "Or you'll find yourself skewered in no time."

"Then maybe you should know which weapons are real," I reply. The dagger I'm holding near his throat vanishes in a puff of smoke. The real dagger I'd taken from him is in my other hand, which I now press against his side.

Enzo studies me with a thoughtful expression. Then he smiles—a genuine smile, full of surprise and amusement. It warms his entire face. My fear is abruptly replaced by joy, the satisfaction of finally pleasing him. He carefully drops the wooden sword, pushes my hand away from his side, and fixes my grip on the dagger's handle. Heat rushes through me. His chest presses against my shoulder and side; his gloved hand covers mine. A surge of passion cuts through

my darkness, and the color of the smoke around us changes from black to red.

"Like this," he murmurs, molding my hand into the correct grip. He says nothing about the shifting color of the smoke.

I stay silent and do as he says. The warmth trickling from his fingers to mine feels as delicious as hot water over an aching body.

"Create a dagger again," he whispers. "I want a good look at it."

With my anger still churning and his touch sending shivers through me, I gather my concentration. The pull is easier now. Before our eyes, the outline of a dagger appears. It wavers and shimmers, not quite whole, and then I fill it with details, painting in the crimson handle, the grooves on the hilt, the smooth shine of the blade and the blood channel that cuts down its center. Solidifying it. The blade's edge sharpens to a severe point. I rotate it in midair until the point faces us.

There's hardly a difference between the illusion and the reality.

I look to my side to see Enzo's gaze fixated on the false dagger. His heart beats through the fabric of his robes, rhythmic against my skin. "Beautiful," he murmurs. Somehow, I think I hear two meanings behind the word.

He releases me, then sheathes his daggers with one flourish. The smile is gone. "Enough for today," he says. He doesn't bother meeting my gaze, but his voice is different now. Softer. "We'll continue tomorrow."

A sudden impulse hits me. Teren's face swims in my thoughts, then shifts to a vision of my sister. I don't know where this impulse comes from, whether it's my alignments with passion or ambition, but I reach out to him with my energy before I can stop myself. Enzo pauses, then glances back at me with a raised eyebrow. "Yes?" he says simply.

Silence. All of my pent-up tension from the past two weeks now comes to a head, and I find myself struggling to get the words out. *Tell him. This is your chance.*

Tell him the truth.

Enzo watches me with a patient, piercing look.

The words are right there, right on the tip of my tongue. *The Inquisition has forced me to spy on you. Master Teren Santoro is holding my sister hostage. You have to help me.*

And then, as I stare into Enzo's eyes, I remember the heat of his power. I try again to speak. Again, the words halt.

Finally, I manage to say something. But what comes out is, "When do I go on a mission?"

Enzo narrows his eyes at that. He takes several slow steps forward until we are separated by a couple of feet. My heart beats furiously. I'm a fool. *Why did I say that?*

"If you have to ask," Enzo replies, "then you're not ready."

"I—" The moment is lost. The truth that had sat so closely on my lips now shrinks away again, buried underneath my fears. My cheeks burn with shame. "I'd think you'd want me to come," I manage to finish.

"Why would I want you with me on a mission, little wolf?" he says quietly.

A surge of my passion courses through me, cutting through the tension warring inside my chest. "Because I impress you," I reply.

Enzo stays quiet. Then, one of his gloved hands touches my chin, tilting it gently up, while the other rests against the stone wall beside my head. I tremble in his grasp. What is this strange light in his eyes? He looks at me like he has known me before. I fight my urge to cover up the hideous, scarred side of my face.

"Is that so?" he whispers back. He leans closer, so close that his lips now hover right over mine, suspended in the space before a kiss, taunting me. Perhaps he's testing me again. If I move at all, we will touch. Heat rushes through me from his hand, flooding every vein in my body and filling my lungs with fire. My energy roars in my ears. I am in the middle of the ocean, buffeted on all sides by hot currents. At the same time, I feel a rush of something new, something I've only felt a hint of during my first test with the Daggers. The part of me that responded to the roseite gem, to passion and desire, awakens now. The energy from it rushes up into my chest, threatening to burst out of my skin, making my grasp on my powers unstable. Random illusions appear around us, flashes of forest and night and dark ocean. I'm grateful for the wall behind me. If I didn't have that to lean against, I'm sure I would crumple to my knees.

Is there something I need to know? I imagine Enzo asking.

And for a moment, I'm so convinced he says this aloud that I nearly confess everything.

Then Enzo steps away. The heat running through me dissipates as he pulls his energy back, leaving me cold and aching. My illusions vanish. For the first time since I've known him, he's not the cool, confident, deadly Reaper . . . There is a flicker of vulnerability in him, even guilt. I stare back with the same confusion. My cheeks are still hot. What happened between us? He's the leader of the Dagger Society, the crown prince, a notorious killer, the potential future king. And yet, I've somehow managed to unsettle him. He has unsettled *me*. The unspoken secret sits heavily between us, a dark abyss.

Then his moment of vulnerability fades, and he resumes the aloofness that I'm so familiar with. "We will see about your missions," he says, as if nothing has happened. Maybe nothing has—perhaps our little moment has been nothing more than an illusion I accidentally conjured, like everything else that popped up around us. Like my father's ghost.

My shoulders sag at the close call. I say nothing in return. Perhaps I've narrowly avoided certain death.

Enzo gives me a courteous nod, then turns his back and exits the cavern, leaving me alone with my pounding heart. When I look to my side, I notice that the wall where he had rested his hand is now blackened and charred with his handprint.

Raffaele Laurent Bessette

Any changes in opinion about her?" Enzo asks in a low voice.

Raffaele turns away from the prince. Today they both stand at the entrance of the caverns, looking on as several of the Daggers train. Both of their gazes are focused on the same thing: Adelina, who sits in a corner with Michel and practices weaving threads of her energy into small, familiar objects. A golden ring. A knife. A piece of lace. With each gesture, Raffaele feels her energy shift. Watching her learn to create illusions reminds him of the energy he feels when he watches Michel at work. Trying to imitate life. As she goes, Michel critiques her work with a string of halfhearted insults, but Raffaele can tell that the young painter is impressed with her. Nearby, Lucent stops training now and then to shout out challenges for Adelina. *Make a gold talent! Make a bird!*

Make a statue! Adelina obliges, her illusions growing in complexity. Lucent nods in admiration.

"Adelina was right," Raffaele finally replies, noting the growing friendships. Perhaps he had misjudged her in the beginning. "I was training her too slowly for her to work with her powers."

Enzo nods once in agreement. "She's learning at a pace I've never seen."

The words make Raffaele uneasy. He thinks back to the way she reacted to the amber and nightstone, how he warned Enzo that night to get rid of her. He thinks of the alarming shifts in her darkness lately, how the new speed of her training is affecting her energy, how frequently she seems anxious, scared, and alone. The emotions seep from her. Something about Adelina . . . there is a frailty underneath the dark shell she has started to build around herself, a small remaining light. A light that wavers precariously from day to day.

"There is a reason I trained her too slowly, you know," Raffaele says after a moment.

Enzo looks at him. "You were holding her back on purpose."

"I was holding her back to protect us." Raffaele chooses his next words carefully. "It's true, she may become the most powerful of us all. She can already create illusions that trick the eyes and ears. Eventually, she'll realize that she can also trick one's taste, smell, and touch." He casts Enzo a sideways glance. "You know what that means, don't you?"

"She will be able to fool a thirsty man into drinking liquid metal. She will be able to make someone feel pain that isn't there."

Raffaele shivers at the possibilities. "Make sure the control she learns doesn't eclipse her loyalties to you. Adelina may have aligned the strongest with fear and hatred, but she also aligned with passion and ambition. The combination drives her to recklessness, makes her unreliable and hungry for power."

Enzo looks on as Adelina slowly conjures a detailed illusion of a wolf, so realistic that it looks as if the animal were really standing there on the cavern floor. Michel claps his hands in approval. "She will be magnificent," he replies.

This time, Raffaele feels Enzo's energy shift at the mention of Adelina, flickers of an emotion not usually associated with the Reaper. Not for years. *Something happened between them,* he realizes. Something dangerous.

"She's not Daphne," Raffaele reminds him gently.

Enzo looks at him, and in that moment, Raffaele feels a pang of deep sympathy for the young prince. A memory comes back to him of the afternoon when he'd accompanied Enzo to the apothecary to see the shop's young assistant. When he'd witnessed Enzo's proposal. Even though quiet rain fell outside the shop, the sun still shone through, painting the world in a glittering haze of light. Daphne had laughed at the affection in Enzo's eyes, teased the gentleness in his voice, and he'd laughed with her. Raffaele had glimpsed her touching Enzo's cheek and pulling him close.

Marry me, Enzo had said to her. She'd kissed him in reply.

After she died, Raffaele never again sensed that emotion in Enzo's heart.

Until now.

Finally, Enzo nods a brief farewell and turns to leave. "Prepare her," he tells Raffaele before he goes. "She's coming with us to the Spring Moons."

I joined the Spring Moons festivities for the first time,
and it was as if I had come into a strange land. The people have
transformed into visions of faeries and ghouls. I cannot decide
if I want to stay or leave.
—Letter from Amendar of Orange to his sister,
on his second voyage to Estenzia

Adelina Amouteru

There was a time during my childhood, a brief time, when my father was kind to me. I dream of it tonight.

I am thirteen. My father wakes up in a cheery mood, then comes to my bedchambers and pulls my curtains open to let the light in. I watch him warily, uncertain what has brought about this sudden change. Did Violetta say something to him?

"Get dressed, Adelina," he says, smiling at me. "Today I am taking you to the port with me." Then he leaves, humming to himself.

My heart lurches in excitement. Can this be happening? Father always takes Violetta to the ports, to watch the ships and buy her presents. I have always stayed home. I sit in bed

for a moment longer, still unsure, and then I hop to the floor and rush to my dresser. I choose my favorite outfit, a blue-and-cream Tamouran silk dress, and tie two long strips of blue cloth around my hair, securing it high behind my head. Maybe Violetta is coming with us, I thought. I skip out of my room to hers, expecting her to be ready too.

Violetta is still in bed. When I tell her where we're going, she looks surprised, then worried. "Be careful," she says.

But I'm so happy that I just sneer at her. She *seems* kind here, but that is only because she's jealous that she isn't coming. I turn away. Violetta's warning fades from my thoughts.

The day is wonderful, full of bright colors. My father takes me on a canal ride. He helps me out of the gondola. The port is bustling with people, merchants calling for their wares to be shipped to the appropriate addresses, shopkeepers standing behind their stands, calling out at curious passersby, children chasing after dogs. My father *holds my hand.* I hurry alongside him, laughing at his jokes, smiling when I know I should smile. Deep inside, I am frightened. This is not normal. My father buys us each a bowl of sweet ice flavored with milk and honey, and together we sit to watch the woodmen and caulkers work on a new ship. He chats animatedly, telling me how strict Estenzia is about the quality of her ships, how every rope and sail and bobbin is tagged with labels and colors identifying the craftsman responsible. I don't understand everything he says, but I don't dare interrupt him. I wait for him to turn violent. But today

my father looks so carefree that I can't help but fall under the spell, letting myself believe entirely that he is finally happy with me.

Maybe things will be different from now on. Maybe I had just been making mistakes up until now.

Finally, when the sun begins making its way down the sky, we return to the gondolas and head for home. "Adelina," he says as we sit together, swaying and creaking with the current. He takes my face in his hands. "I know who you really are. You needn't be afraid."

My smile stays on, even though my heart wavers. What does he mean?

"Show me what you can do, Adelina. I know there must be something inside of you."

I stare back in confused silence, my foolish smile still planted on my lips. When I don't answer, my father's gentle expression starts to fade.

"Go on," he coaxes. "You needn't be afraid, child." His voice lowers. "Show me that you are no ordinary *malfetto*. Go on."

Slowly, I start to realize that he has been using kindness to coax my power out of me. Perhaps he's even made a wager with somebody already, somebody who would pay my father for me if I could demonstrate some strange ability. My smile trembles along with my heart. He has tried violence and failed to provoke a power in me. Now he wants to try affection. *Be careful,* Violetta had told me. Do you see what a fool I am?

Still, I try. I want so badly to please him.

The next day, we repeat the same routine. My father is curiously gentle and attentive, treating me as if he saw Violetta before him instead of me. Violetta says nothing more, and I'm relieved. I know what he wants from me. And I am so hungry to accept this false kindness that I try every day, as hard as I can, to conjure something to please my father.

It never happens.

Finally, weeks later, my father's good humor wanes. He takes my face into his hands one last time on that carriage ride home. He asks me to show him what I can do. And again, I fail. The carriage lurches along in an awkward, uncomfortable silence.

After a while, my father's hands leave my face. He edges away from me, sighs, and looks out the window at the moving landscape.

"Worthless," he mutters, his voice so quiet that I barely hear him.

The next morning, I lie in bed and anticipate my father coming in again with a smile on his face. *Today is the day*, I tell myself. This time, I am determined to please him, and his kindness will be able to coax something useful out of me. But he doesn't come. When I finally get out of bed and find him, he ignores me. He has given up his quest to find me useful. Violetta sees me in the hallway. The distance between us feels overwhelming. Her eyes are large and dark, pitying. Her face, as usual, is perfect. I look away from her in silence.

My two weeks have come and gone.

Throughout it all, I haven't found a single chance to visit Teren at the Inquisition Tower. Maybe I've been avoiding it on purpose. I don't know. All I know is that my time is now up, and he will be expecting me. I know what will happen if I don't show my face soon.

And tonight is my first official mission with the Daggers.

Their plan for tonight, as far as I understand, goes something like this:

The Spring Moons, Kenettra's annual celebration of the season, is made up of three nights of festivals and parties, one night in honor of each of our three moons. Each night, a huge masquerade ball will take place at the water's edge in Estenzia's largest harbor. At midnight, six ships laden with fireworks will put on a dazzling display of lights over the water.

But the Daggers are going to set fire to the ships before that can even happen, destroying the fleet in a spectacular explosion of fireworks. It will be a display of power, defiance against the king, to show his weakness. And I'm going to help them do it.

"The city is quickly turning into a powder keg," Raffaele explains to me as we head out from his chambers. Tonight he's a vision in green and gold robes, part of his face hidden behind an intricate gold half mask, his cheekbones and brows dusted with glitter. "If the king wants to burn us at the stake,

then the Daggers are going to respond." He smiles at me. It is an expert expression—secretive, shy, trained. "The people are tired of a weak king. When Enzo seizes the throne, they will be ready for the change."

I listen, distracted by my own thoughts. For a moment, I fantasize about myself in such a position—instead of being trapped by the whims of others, what would it be like to have others bowing to *me*, obeying *my* every command? What must it feel like to have that kind of power?

It's the first time I've stepped out into Estenzia at night. Soon, gondolas arrive on the canal that the court's street lines, and the court's consorts split into groups as we step into our individual boats. I join Raffaele and two others in the same boat, the seats creaking as I gently lower myself in. My movement sends ripples across the water. We pull away, gliding off to the harbor. I gape at the city.

No nights are as lovely as the nights of the Spring Moons, and no city is as breathtaking as Estenzia, which has transformed into a wonderland of light.

Lanterns hang along all the bridges, their glow bouncing off the water's surface in waves of orange and gold. Gondolas drift through the waterways, and music and laughter ripple through the masked crowds that have gathered out in the warm evening air. Overhead, the three moons hang large and luminous in a near-perfect triangle. Baliras glide past them, their glittering, translucent wings illuminated by moonlight. This close view of them is still a startling contrast

to the faraway figures I'd seen before I'd arrived in Estenzia, and the sight of their long, ray-like bodies passing before the moons takes my breath away.

Farther out at the harbor, the silhouettes of six ships with their fireworks sit on the water.

Inquisitors, some on horseback and some on foot, patrol the bridges. They are the only ones not adorned with bright, glittering colors and sparkling masks, and their white and gold figures look harsh against the festivities. They are everywhere tonight, adding to a uniform tension in the air. I turn my face carefully away from them. *The city is a powder keg,* Raffaele had said, and we are going to light it tonight.

By the time we arrive at the main harbor, the celebrations are in full swing. The statues of the angels and gods that line the square are all covered from head to toe in flowers. A few masked revelers, already drunk this early in the night, have climbed on top of the statues to wave at the cheering crowds. I inhale deeply, catching the scents of ocean, sweet and savory pastries, roasting pig and fish.

Raffaele waits until the others have left our gondola. Then he steps gracefully out and offers me a hand. I join him on land. The other consorts eventually scatter, each of them joining clients waiting for them along the edge of the harbor. Raffaele guides me through a section of the crowd. Then he squeezes my hand once. "Go," he whispers. "Remember the paths back down to the catacombs if you lose yourself during the mission."

Then he's gone, making his way through the crowd. For a

beat, I'm all alone, lost among swirling colors. I look around; my heart pounds. I've grown so dependent on Raffaele's guidance that his absence always leaves me short of breath.

A sudden hand on my waist makes me look to my side. It's Enzo.

If I didn't know to meet him here, I wouldn't have recognized him tonight. His hair is covered beneath a mask that transforms him from a young prince into a forest fae with glittering horns twisting up over his head, the structure adorned with dangling silver strings that gleam in the light. All I can see of his face are his lips and, if I look past the shadows the mask casts, his eyes. Even through his disguise, I can sense him taking in my new appearance, my elaborate Tamouran headwrap and my gold reveler's silks, the glittering white porcelain hiding the scarred side of my face. His lips part slightly, ready to say something.

Then he bows to me. "A lovely evening," he says. I return his smile as he kisses me gently on the cheek and offers his arm. I gasp at the brief flush of heat from the touch of his lips to my skin.

He leads us through the throngs. He keeps a respectful distance between us, our only contact being my arm looped through his . . . but even so, I can feel the warmth radiating from his robes, a soft, pleasing feeling, reaching for me. I force myself to stay calm. Through my mask, I focus on the silhouettes of ships at the harbor.

We enter an area full of dancers. Here and there are other consorts, swirling with their clients and patrons and other

onlookers in a sea of glitter, laughing uproariously as they move in time with the beat of drums and serenade of strings. I catch a glimpse of Raffaele with a richly dressed noblewoman on his arm, but neither he nor Enzo acknowledges each other. Inquisitors watch the scene from atop their steeds.

Enzo gives me a sidelong glance. Then he pulls me closer and puts one hand on the small of my back. Around us, the world turns into a frenzy of cheering and bright colors. He smiles his warm, genuine smile—it's a lovely expression he so rarely makes as the Reaper.

"Dance with me," he murmurs.

All part of our act. All part of the disguise. I tell myself this repeatedly, but it doesn't change the way I lean into his touch, how his words stir the longing in my chest. If he notices, he doesn't show it . . . but he does seem to stand closer than he needs to, and look at me with an intensity that I don't remember seeing before.

We spin with the others in a large circle. More join in, until we are all a tightly packed whirl of bodies. The minutes fly by. Enzo's movements are flawless, and somehow I find myself moving in sync with him, my steps as accurate as his. Enzo releases me as we dance into the arms of new partners, then switch off again and again in a widening circle. The drums keep time with my heartbeat. I spin until I'm paired once again with Enzo. He smiles at me from behind his mask. I want to reach up and touch his face. Then I remember that I'm disguised as his consort, and such a gesture wouldn't be

strange. So I do. I laugh, draw closer to him, and brush his cheek with my hand. It might be my imagination, but his eyes soften at my touch. He doesn't stop me. *He's just playing along.* I don't mind.

It takes me a moment to realize that the dance has ended. Around us, the others all give their dancing partners a quick kiss, the gesture of harmony between love and prosperity. Laughter and whistles go up from the crowd. *All part of the custom.* I glance at Enzo, suddenly shy—am I love, or am I prosperity?

He smiles, draws me close, and leans down. The elaborately carved grooves of his mask brush against my skin, and I wonder if it will leave a touch of glitter behind. I close my eye. A moment later, his lips touch my own. Only a touch.

It must have been brief—probably a second, no more—but to me, it seems like forever, like he let us stay this way for a beat longer than needed. The familiar bubbling of heat courses through me, the luxurious feeling of a hot bath on a cold night; I return his kiss, leaning into him, savoring his heat.

Then it's over. I find myself looking into his eyes, and there I see thin lines of scarlet slashed within his irises, glowing. His lips are still very, very close.

He steps away from me and guides us out of the dancing circle as a new song starts. We're now closer to the harbor than we were before, and a wooden railing separates us from the rocky pier near where the ships are waiting. Perfectly in position. I'm short of breath, still dizzy and giggling, and

Enzo laughs along, his low, velvet voice mixing with my higher one. I don't think I've ever heard him laugh before. It's a soothing sound, both tender and unsure, reminiscent of someone who used to laugh more. His arm stays wrapped securely around my waist. My lips tingle. Even if he's just trying to continue our disguise, he's doing an excellent job.

The crowds thin as we near the point that overlooks the beach; only a few scattered figures are out along the rocks and sand, admiring the trio of moons hanging suspended at the horizon. Several Inquisitors stand guard at each of the piers that lead out to the six ships. Long shadows shroud the piers in darkness.

My energy stirs restlessly. Almost time for my debut. I glance briefly up at the roofs of the closest buildings. I can't see anyone there, but I know that several Daggers are lying in wait, watching us for the first signal.

We head down to the piers. The lights from the festivities make way for the shadows cast by the buildings closest to shore, and I shiver as the cool night air surrounds us. Enzo pulls me close to whisper in my ear. I can feel his lips turned up into a small smile.

"The first pier," he murmurs. "Watch for me."

I giggle loudly in return, as if he'd just whispered some romantic nothings in my ear. One of the Inquisitors lounging along the first pier casts us a bored look and then turns away.

We edge steadily closer to the pier, continuing our little charade of romance the entire way. At least, it seems to be a

charade for Enzo. Far be it from me to complain—the laughs he coaxes out of me are real, and so is the flush on my cheeks. His hand is hot at my waist, the rivulets of warmth delicious on such a cool night.

Finally, I stumble over a rock and fall, giggling, into his arms. We're on the far end of the pier now, and the two Inquisitors guarding this pier are barely a few yards away. One of them holds up a gloved hand. "No one allowed past this point," he says, nodding in our direction.

Enzo gives them a disappointed sigh. He places a hand on the Inquisitor's shoulder. All pretense of lightheartedness vanishes from his face—in the blink of an eye, he has transformed from a smiling boy to a predator.

The Inquisitor looks at Enzo's hand in surprise. But before he can brush it off, his eyes widen. He shoots Enzo a stricken look. Beside him, his partner's stance wavers.

"Are you all right?" he asks the first Inquisitor. He draws his sword—but before he can do anything else, the sword unravels right before his horrified eyes. It reappears a dozen yards away, falling uselessly to the sand. *Michel is here in the darkness.*

Enzo touches his other hand to the second Inquisitor's arm. Both of them open their mouths in silent screams.

He's melting them from the inside. Even knowing that this was the plan, the sight catches me off guard. I look on in horror as their faces turn red and contort in agony. Blood leaks from one's mouth. They shudder.

"Now," Enzo whispers to me.

I reach within and pull on my energy right as the two Inquisitors' knees buckle, sending them collapsing to the pier's deck. All around us, I conjure a vision of an empty pier—planks of wood appear over where the Inquisitors lie—and Enzo and I both disappear behind an illusion of waves and night air, rendering both us and the dead men invisible. The darkness and unease in me soars, thrilling my heart, and I embrace the ecstasy. On top of this illusion, I weave an image of two white-cloaked Inquisitors standing as if nothing had happened. Up close, it's easy to tell that the two fake Inquisitors are nothing more than smoke and air, their faces too simple to be real. But from the point of view of anyone who might look in this direction from afar, it's a convincing cover.

The whole scene looks as if we were never here. As if I'm not standing in front of two corpses.

Such power. I swirl in the midst of it all, my jaw clenched, my lips curving into a triumphant smile even as another part of me recoils at what we just did. I feel numb—in control and yet completely helpless.

Through my invisibility shield, I sense Enzo give me a single nod. I nod back, letting him know that I'm ready. He leaps down from the pier. Fire erupts from both of his hands—he holds them out, and in the shadows, I see a masked figure that must be Michel lift his arms. He unravels Enzo's flames, then reforms them far down the pier onto the deck of the first ship, near its crates of fireworks. The two

vanish into the darkness. Seconds later, I hear the sound of startled shouts from the ship.

My hands tremble. Flashbacks of the night when I killed my father come rushing back to me, clouding my illusions. Suddenly my father's ghost smiles at me in my thoughts. I think I can even see him standing on the pier. *You're a murderer, Adelina. Nice to see you coming into your own.*

Seeing him disrupts my concentration—the shroud I'd put over the two dead Inquisitors at my feet suddenly vanishes, revealing them to the world. I start running to the second pier. My mind is completely numb; the image of the dead men is seared into my vision. *Keep going. You can't afford to stop.* My attention turns to the buildings lining the harbor, and to the other Inquisitors patrolling the other five piers. Taking a deep breath, I call forth more of my energy. The threads pull taut in my mind, protesting.

I force them to bend, then to weave together.

Against the walls of the buildings, silhouettes of people run by. Illusions of dark blue hoods. Suddenly, Daggers seem to be everywhere on the piers. Inquisitors on the other piers raise the alarm—I conjure Daggers all around them, then run toward the second pier. My fear heightens, and as it does, so do the illusions closest to me. Inquisitors call for help as they strike out against my phantom Daggers. I reach the second pier under cover of invisibility just as flames ignite onboard the second ship.

"They're all fake!" one of the Inquisitors cries as his sword

slashes straight through one of my illusions. He calls on the other soldiers to stop, but they're all too distracted, blinded with fear from my apparitions. "Stop—find the culprit who's—"

He never finishes his sentence. One of the Daggers lunges for him with the speed of a striking viper—he twists the man's arm around and stabs him straight through his chest with his own sword. A real Dagger. Dante. The other Inquisitors turn at his shriek, then attack the Spider, but he's far too quick for them. He cuts them down in quick succession. His movements blur in the night, so that even after I erase the false Daggers, it looks as if there were more than one of him. The last Inquisitor at this pier tries to run for his life. Dante catches him before he can, and runs a dagger across his throat.

Up at the festivities, some revelers finally notice what's going on.

Screams go up—then complete chaos.

My mind races. I move on to the third pier, then the fourth. We slaughter the Inquisitors as more patrols rush from the festivities in our direction. So much death.

My eye goes again to the roofs closest to the piers—and this time, I see figures stir. The other Daggers, flesh and blood, their faces hidden behind masks and hooded sapphire robes. One of them rises up from her crouch, carefully notches an arrow to her bow, and aims at the Inquisitors. Gemma. Above her swirls a circle of ravens—when she lets

the arrow fly, the ravens plummet down, aiming in unison for the enemy. My illusion of phantom Daggers moving along the walls flickers for a moment, but I grit my teeth and sharpen my concentration. The phantom Daggers turn solid again. More Inquisitors run in their direction.

The Inquisitors are now within firing range. Suddenly, one of them is yanked straight up into the air. He lets out a strangled shriek as he's thrown up as high as the top of the buildings, then plummets to his death. I wince—my illusions shudder again. That was Lucent's work. Up above, more arrows rain down, one piercing the throat of a second Inquisitor.

Hurry, Enzo. As the other Daggers kill the Inquisitors with ruthless efficiency, I clench my teeth in desperation. *I want to leave this place.* I glance over to the ship docked at the first pier.

And there I see him—Enzo, this time with his face entirely covered by a hood and silver mask. He flashes through the inky blackness of the night. There one moment, gone the next. My cue to get out of here.

Dante grabs my arm, then breaks into a sprint. The wind rushes past us. In a matter of seconds, we've crossed the sand and grass and run into the shadows of the festivities overlooking the harbor. Screams everywhere. I drop the illusions I've been holding. The threads of energy all snap back into place, and I gasp at the sudden emptiness.

The first ship explodes.

The blast knocks me right off my feet. The earth shudders; screams burst from everyone around me. I cover my eye from the blinding glow, and when I squint through my hand at the inferno, I see a rainbow of fireworks light up the night sky in a terrifying display of glory. Fire and fireworks consume the ship's deck. I picture Enzo setting each of the ships ablaze, his figure a shadow in the night.

Rough hands yank me up onto my feet. "Get to the Messenger," Dante hisses at me. Then he vanishes into the crowd, his eyes fixed on other Inquisitors.

I fight my way through the crowd, remembering my next step. *Meet Raffaele at the end of the square. He'll usher you to safety.* The energy in the air is like lightning—I can practically *smell* the terror—the power crackling all around me in a glittering shower of energy threads. The darkness inside me hungers for it, yearning to break free, and I have to force down the irresistible urge to flood this entire square with illusions of Underworld monsters. So much power around me, *going to waste.* For a moment, I attempt to shroud myself in invisibility—but too many people are jostling past me, and every time I start to throw the illusion over myself, I'm jolted out of it. Finally I just give up and continue running.

It takes me a moment to realize that some in the crowd are cheering. They raise their fists to the sky at the fireworks and flames. They watch the dazzling display with smiles on their faces. I recall what Raffaele had told me earlier. *Let the Inquisition Axis see what happens when they force us to humiliate*

ourselves. The people here are *cheering on* the Young Elites. Applauding the strike.

At the piers, a second ship explodes. Then, a third. An unstoppable chain reaction continues along the water's edge, each ship's demise causing the next, until flames and exploding fireworks consume the entire harbor, transforming the night into day, orange and yellow everywhere I look, the earth trembling from the sheer energy released into the sky. Explosions, the roar of flames, the shouts of thousands of people—it all swirls together into deafening chaos. Never could I have imagined panic like this. Their fear pools in me, a black and powerful current.

I have to find Raffaele. I turn a corner into a narrower alley in an attempt to get away from the frenzied crowds. For a moment, I'm alone. Almost there. My slippers hit a puddle, and cold water splashes against my ankles.

Something white flashes before my face.

Before I can react, a hand catches me around my neck and shoves me against the wall. I see spots exploding before me. Blindly, I strike out.

A voice chuckles at my antics. I freeze. I recognize that voice. The white blur that flashed past my eye now stills into the unmistakable look of an Inquisitor's cloak. "Well, well, well," the voice says. "A Tamouran girl."

I stare into Teren's face.

No. Not here. Not tonight.

The sight is enough to unleash my energy. I bare my teeth

at him as a red-eyed demon lunges out from the wall behind me and throws itself at Teren with a shriek. Teren flinches for a split second, but his grip never lightens. His eyes widen in surprise.

"What's this?" he says with a smile. "Have you grown defiant since the last time we talked?" He hoists a cross-bow. "Any more moves like that, and I might decide to kill off your sister. I gave you your two weeks." His smile turns hard. "And you are late."

"I'm sorry," I say urgently. My mind spins. "Don't—please don't hurt her. I couldn't find a time to get away and see you. They've been training me relentlessly." I glance at the main square. "If the Elites see me talking to you, they will kill me, and you won't get your—"

Teren only ignores me and keeps me pinned in place. His grip is unnaturally strong, his face too close. "In that case, you had better start talking. You owe me some information."

I swallow hard. The Daggers can't be that far away. They knew I would be heading down this way, and if I don't show my face soon, they will search for me. And they will see me here.

Teren's grip tightens so much that it starts to hurt. My hands fly up to where he holds my neck. He narrows his colorless eyes. "Give me their names."

"I—" *What can I tell him, without destroying the Daggers?* My mind scrambles frantically for a solution.

"I saw you arrive at the festival with a Fortunata Court

consort," Teren adds. "He has been with you before, too. Is he one of them?"

No. I shake my head automatically, letting the lie come. "He was just my escort."

Teren's stare wanders across my face. "Just your escort," he muses.

Tears well up in my eye. *No. Please don't hurt Raffaele.* "Yes, just my escort."

Teren makes an annoyed sound in his throat. "*Talk.* Lady Gemma—does that name sound familiar to you? Any idea why she was a rider at the qualifying races?"

I shake my head dumbly.

"*Who leads them?*"

No, no, I can't. "I don't know. Truly, I don't!"

Teren narrows his eyes again. He hoists his crossbow with one arm and points it right in front of my good eye. "You're lying."

"No, I'm not," I whisper through his tight grip.

"Violetta will pay for this, you know. Not you. *Violetta.*" He leans close, his voice like honey. "Do you want to hear all the things I will do to her?"

He whispers them into my ear, one by one, and I start to cry in earnest. I don't know what to do. My thoughts are too tangled. Violetta. I glance again to the chaotic square. Where is he keeping her? Energy lurches through me, feeding on my terror. It begs for release, but I clamp down hard on it.

"I beg you—" I start to say. My mind spins. "I'll tell you

what you want. Just give me one more week. *Please.* You can't be seen here with me, it won't help either of us." I scan the alley. "There's no time. They're here too. They can't—"

Before I can utter anything else, Teren's eyes flicker up. I do the same—and see a flash of dark robes high up on the rooftops. A jolt of terror leaps up my spine. *The Daggers, they're coming. They're going to see us.* All around us, the other Inquisitors are consumed with containing the chaos. *He doesn't have enough men with him.* I can feel him weighing his options, deciding whether or not he has time to force answers out of me right now before the Daggers catch up to me.

Please. Please let me go.

His instant of hesitation vanishes. He grabs me by my collar and pulls me close. "You have three days," he says in a low voice. "If you go back on your word again, I will shoot an arrow through your sister's neck and out the back of her skull. She'll be lucky if that's the first thing I do." He smiles, his teeth flashing in the night. "We can be enemies, Adelina, or we can be the best of friends. Understood?"

That's all he has time to say. I look up to the roofs. And I see Dante crouched there, arrow nocked, staring at both of us through his mask.

A rush of sapphire robes strikes Teren, knocking him to the ground and releasing me from his clutches. I stumble against the wall. Before me is a tangle of white and blue—Teren shoves a Dagger off him and rolls up onto his feet. The two face each other. It's Enzo, face hidden behind his silver mask, daggers in hand.

"The Reaper!" Teren exclaims, pointing his crossbow straight at Enzo and pulling out his sword. "Always coming to the rescue of *malfettos*, aren't you?"

Enzo's blades turn bright red, then white hot. He lunges at Teren before he can fire his crossbow, then strikes, seeking out his eyes. Teren dodges him with a fluidity that shocks me. He swings his sword in an arc—it almost catches Enzo in the chest before he darts out of the way. Fire bursts from Enzo's hands and consumes the two of them in a haze of light. Through the inferno, I can see Teren locked blade on blade with Enzo.

The flames don't harm him. His skin seems to burn for an instant, then return back to normal, smooth and untouched. I freeze at the sight. It is not just a trick of the light—the flames *do not harm him at all.*

How is that possible? Unless—

"Go!" Enzo snaps at me. Their blades clash with a ring of steel. Again and again. Overhead, an arrow sails down and strikes Teren near his neck. He grunts in pain—but then, to my horror, he reaches up and yanks it out unceremoniously. He tosses it away. His skin stitches itself together, healing in seconds, until I see nothing but a smear of blood on his neck.

Teren is a Young Elite.

I find my feet and make a run for it. When I glance up, I catch sight of Lucent with her bow and arrow locked on Teren, trying to find a good shot.

A rough hand clamps down on my arm. I turn and stare right into the silver mask of a Dagger.

Dante. "How about you cloak *us* in invisibility and get us out of here." There is something in his voice that chills me. Something in his eyes that tells me he saw more tonight than I wanted him to see.

All around us is screaming, panic, people, the roar of a firework-fueled inferno raging at the harbor. I force myself to do as Dante says. I cloak us in a hurried illusion of invisibility, and he leads us away in the direction of the closest catacomb entrance. Behind us, Enzo has already vanished, disappearing as quickly as he'd come. Teren's voice rings in my ears.

Three days.

They were the best of friends as long as they did not know
they were supposed to be enemies. The truth would do its
damage soon enough.
—Brothers in Fire, *by Jedtare*

Adelina Amouteru

I rest alone in my room.

Out in the streets, people chant for and against the king, for and against the Elites.

Maids come in to check on me, making sure I'm unharmed from the previous night, but I send them away and stay under my blankets. Every time I hear one of them approaching, I jump—it is Dante, who has figured out my betrayal and is coming to kill me. Once, I hear Enzo's voice out in the hallway, asking a servant whether I'm all right. Gemma tries to get me to come out, but I refuse her. I lie here until the shafts of light have shifted to the other side of the room. Memories of Violetta run through my mind, tangled with all the ways Teren has promised to torture her.

I have three days. Three days of time, before I either tell the Daggers the truth or betray them entirely.

I linger on the way Teren's skin stitched itself together after Dante's arrow tore through his shoulder. Teren is an Elite hell-bent on killing other Elites, on killing *malfettos* altogether. I turn the thought over and over in my head, unable to make sense of it. No wonder Enzo didn't even try attacking Teren on my execution day. No wonder they have not targeted Teren earlier. How can an Elite turn on his own kind?

Through my shock, I feel a sinking despair. If even the Daggers cannot hurt Teren, then what chance do I have?

Raffaele is the only one who finally pulls me out of my thoughts. He comes to my door at sunset. "You're awake," he says gently. "Come. Get dressed and follow me."

I have a sudden urge to tell Raffaele everything—Teren's threats, his stranglehold on my sister, what he has offered. *You could get the others to help me right now. We could do a mission together, to save my sister.* But each time I think this, I hesitate. They are intent on seizing the throne. An attempt to free Violetta from the Inquisition's clutches is a significant and dangerous detour. Do they care enough about me already to risk their entire mission? Besides, I have no idea where my sister is. Teren could kill Violetta before any of us gets to her in time.

Raffaele watches me carefully. I hope he can't predict why my energy is shifting so much. I open my mouth, and out comes a harmless phrase. "Is it time?"

At my expression, he nods. "Yes, it's time."

A lump lodges in my throat. I'd looked forward to this day. Now I'm not so sure.

He starts to turn away, then pauses and looks back at me.

"I know last night was frightening for you," he says. "It's all right, mi Adelinetta. No one will hold it against you."

He thinks I feel this way because of yesterday's killings, because Teren attacked me. He doesn't know what Teren *said* to me. I nod in silence beside him, then keep my gaze turned down.

We make our way through the now-familiar corridors, then head out into the courtyard and down toward the cavern. Neither of us says a word.

Finally, we step into the cavern. For only the second time, I see all the Daggers gathered. The only one missing is Enzo. His absence sends a spike of panic through me. He's probably at his royal estates, or gathering his patrons. *Or . . . what if Teren has discovered his identity? What if the Inquisition is after him right now?*

Raffaele nods for me to come forward. I do as he says, until I'm only a few feet away from him. The other Daggers look on without a word. Gemma flashes me a smile, and so does Michel. I smile faintly back. At the other end, Dante watches me with a dark, ominous look. I try to ignore him, but his expression sends nausea through me, reminding me of Teren's words. *What is he thinking? What did he see?* I look at the others again, searching for anything I might have missed. Do any of them know?

Raffaele steps toward me and hands me a neatly folded bundle of cloth. When he steps aside, I see that within the cloth is a silver mask. In the silence, I take it and hold it out solemnly before me. *They don't know yet.*

My hands are shaking uncontrollably now. In spite of everything, my heart still leaps in a moment of excitement. This is *my* silver mask, *my* dark robe. From this day forward, I am supposed to be one of them. For the first time in my life, I have been accepted by a group.

The excitement fades quickly, replaced by dread.

"Repeat after me," Raffaele says. I nod wordlessly, my throat dry. His words echo all around us.

"I, Adelina Amouteru—"

Violetta will pay for this, you know. Not you. Violetta.

"—hereby pledge to serve the Dagger Society, to strike fear into the hearts of those who rule Kenettra—"

I'll tell you what you want. Just give me one more week. Please.

"—to take by death what belongs to us, and to make the power of our Elites known to every man, woman, and child."

Three days. If you go back on your word again, I will shoot an arrow through your sister's neck and out the back of her skull.

"Should I break my vow, let the dagger take from me what I took from the dagger."

I repeat the words. Every single one. Darkness swims inside me. *Should I break my vow, let the dagger take from me what I took from the dagger.*

Raffaele bows his head to me when we finish. "Welcome to the Dagger Society." He smiles. "White Wolf."

꧁꧂

Afterward, I dress in a flowing length of red robes and head down to the cavern with Gemma. The others are already there

by the time I arrive, along with several strangers dressed in aristocratic clothing. Patrons? Around them swirl a few consorts from the Fortunata Court. The Daggers have donned formal Kenettran robes tonight, and now they lounge in a circle on pillowed divans in the underground sitting room, ignoring the trays of cold grapes and spiced wine. Despite the intense conversations they seem to be having with the richly dressed strangers, there's a noticeable sense of celebration in the air, the nearing of their end goal. It contrasts oddly with the urns and ashes lining the walls. Their voices sound low, excited. I watch it all like it's a dream of colors moving around me. None of it seems real. Somewhere beyond these walls, the Inquisition Tower looms.

How will I ever find a chance to get away?

I pick out Enzo's figure in the midst of the group. Raffaele is nowhere to be seen. Perhaps he's not attending this meeting, or perhaps he's occupied. I try to explain away his absence.

"Adelina." Gemma's voice cuts through my maelstrom of thoughts. She smiles at me, then leads me over to the group. The strangers cast me curious glances. I look back at them. Only one looks familiar—the madam of the Fortunata Court, dressed tonight in an elaborate silk gown of blue and gold. "These are our noble patrons," Gemma whispers as we take a seat on a divan. "They're eager to meet you."

So, these are the people who support Enzo's claim to the throne. Gemma introduces me around the circle with her animated chatter, stopping to point out her father in particular.

I smile and play along as the patrons each greet me in turn, their eyes lingering. At the other end of the circle, Enzo leans back on a divan with a glass of wine in one hand, his boots crossed on a low table and his face partially hidden behind a mask. He glances briefly at me and returns to his conversation.

"I've heard the king cannot cancel the Tournament," one of the patrons says to Enzo. "It would make him look like a fool and a weakling to the people. He and the queen must appear by tradition."

"Exactly the corner we wanted him backed into," another replies.

"Can your illusion worker get us into the palace?" says a third. His eyes flicker to me, and I feel a jolt of anxiety. "The people are ripe for an overthrow now, especially after last night's display. We could try making a move before the Tournament, even tonight."

Enzo shakes his head. "My sister will not be with the king. Their apartments are on opposite ends of the palace. Adelina's skills are not strong enough to hold an illusion for that long, at such close quarters. The Tournament is our best chance."

The others break into frustrated murmurs. Michel sits back and holds up a glass of wine in apology to Enzo. "If only I could unravel living things. I'd happily march into the palace and unravel the royals off a cliff for you." Scattered laughter.

Lucent rolls her eyes as she twirls a curly blonde lock of

hair around her finger. "And *I* still say we all forget about saving this damned country, ship off to Beldain, and live like kings. *Some* nations know how to treat *malfettos*." More laughter, while Michel affectionately mocks Lucent's Beldish accent.

I just look on numbly, trying to play along.

"He will, someday," Gemma whispers to me. I startle at her voice, then realize she must think I'm confused by the conversation. "Michel, I mean. He'll figure out how to unravel living creatures. He says the energy of the soul gets in the way."

The energy of the soul. If Michel were to see the energy of my own soul, what would he see?

The conversation filters back to me as I hear myself mentioned again. "And can she work her illusions well enough for the Tournament?" one patron asks Enzo.

"Yes, Your Highness—can she uphold her end of the mission?"

"We want a demonstration."

"Adelina," Enzo suddenly says, looking in my direction. The nobles turn to look at me too.

I blink, taken off guard. "Yes?"

"Create an illusion of a person for us."

I hesitate, then suck in my breath and concentrate on the darkness in my chest. Gradually, I weave in midair a face that resembles Enzo, the same eyes and nose and mouth and hair, the thin scar prominent on the cheek. The nobles murmur among themselves. It's still not quite right—there

is a lack of refinement in the details, the glassy-eyed look of something that doesn't seem quite human, the amateur texture of the skin. It wavers a little. Now and then, it looks translucent. It would not work for us at close quarters. But it will be enough. I hold the illusion there for a moment, then release it.

Enzo smiles at me. "When the Tournament of Storms comes," he says, "the king and queen will announce the horse races, then watch from a close vantage point. If you can disguise Gemma, no one will notice her when she's moving on the back of a horse. Can you get her close enough to strike?"

He's announcing before all his patrons that I'm included in their final mission. My heart jumps at the thrill, then squeezes painfully at the memory of Teren's words. "I can do it," I reply.

The nobles look thrilled with me. Enzo smiles pleasantly with them and clinks glasses—but even here, in the safety of the cavern and surrounded by supporters, he has a wariness about him, the lingering unease of someone preoccupied with other problems.

I wonder if he can sense anything suspicious about *me*. Thank the gods that Raffaele isn't here to notice the dark shifts in my energy. He must have a client tonight. The spiced wine eases some of the anxiety stirring in me, and I find myself holding my glass out again for the consorts to refill it.

"You seem less cheerful than you should be," I say to

Enzo in a low voice, when there's a lull in his conversation with the nobles.

He glances back at me, seems to think about answering, and then glides around my comment. "Feeling festive, mi Adelinetta?" He nods as a consort fills my glass for the second time. My heart flutters fiercely at the way he says the affectionate version of my name. "Careful. It's a strong wine."

It's true; the wine makes me bold, helps me forget. "I'm the White Wolf," I reply. "Surely that deserves a second helping."

Enzo's lips tilt up in amusement, and I feel the roar of attraction rising in me. How will I tell him about the Inquisition? His eyes wander back to the other Daggers. "So it does." He raises his glass in the air, and the nobles join him. "To the White Wolf," he says, glancing at me. "And the beginning of a new era."

Gemma leans over to me as I take a sip of my wine. "You like him," she teases, jabbing me hard in the ribs.

I wince and shove her with my elbow. "Quiet," I hiss. Gemma laughs with mischief at the expression on my face, then pushes away from me and hops up, barefoot, onto the divan. I let my breath out again, but I can't help smiling. *Of course she's just messing around with me.*

Enzo glances at her. She crosses her arms. "I've been practicing, Reaper," she declares. "Watch this."

She points at Enzo, then narrows her eyes. I watch curiously. "You!" she commands. "Fetch me a slice of melon."

Enzo raises an eyebrow at her. "No," he answers flatly,

and the patrons let out a round of laughter. Her father smiles indulgently.

Gemma laughs along, then rolls her eyes and slumps back down on the divan. "Well, just you wait," she says. "Men aren't so much more complicated than animals. I'll figure it out."

Her antics coax an affectionate smile out of Enzo, cutting briefly through his tension. "I don't doubt it, my Star Thief," he says, and she beams at him in the midst of more chuckles from the Daggers and nobles. I look on, trying to fight down my envy as Gemma laughs with her father.

One of the consorts claps her hands. "A game!" she exclaims. She passes out long golden necklaces to us. I'm not familiar with this, but apparently the others are—because they let out whoops and whistles. The consort notices my puzzled look. "Loop your necklace around the person you're most fond of," she explains with a smile. "The one with the most necklaces wins."

The shouts and laughter fly fast and thick. Gemma attempts to steal everyone's necklaces for herself, only to have Lucent toss them up into the air and knock Gemma onto a divan with a playful gust of wind. The aristocrats clap, applauding their powers and murmuring about how they will show them off during the Tournament. Several consorts loop their necklaces over Michel's neck, making his grin as wide as his face. Even Dante, with his permanent scowl, lets a consort give him a necklace and wraps his arm around her waist.

Gemma offers me her necklace, as does one of the other

male consorts. I blush, laughing along. Enzo watches us all with a calm expression. He twines his gold necklace around his fingers, deep in thought.

"Come, Your Highness," Michel calls out at him, twirling his trio of necklaces around his hand. He grins. "Unless you're most fond of *yourself.*"

More carefree laughter. Enzo gives him a small smile, then tosses his necklace up in the air. "For you, then," he replies. Michel gestures at the necklace, and it vanishes in midair and reappears wrapped around his hand. He throws it around his neck with a triumphant grin. Enzo waves off the consorts attempting to give him a necklace and looks on as the others fight over the prizes, each one more enthusiastic than the last.

None of them know what's going through my mind. None of them know that even as they celebrate, I am thinking about what to do with Teren, how to get to the Inquisition Tower to save my sister. How I will betray everyone in here.

I sway in my seat. The others don't notice, but Enzo does — he turns to look at me. I put down my glass of wine and take a deep breath, but it's no use. Darkness pools in the pit of my stomach, feeding ravenously on my fear. I can't stay here.

It takes me a moment to realize that Enzo has risen to his feet. He strides over to me, offers me his gloved hand, and helps me up. I lean unsteadily against him. The others pause for a moment to look over at us, and some of the laughter fades.

"Are you all right, Adelina?" Gemma calls out.

I start to say something, but it's hard to focus. Enzo wraps an arm around me and guides me away from the circle. "Carry on," he tells the others. "I'll return shortly." Then he lowers his voice to me and leads me back inside the court. "You look like you need to rest," he murmurs.

I don't argue. As the noise of the others fades away, leaving only the echo of our footsteps up the stone path to the surface, I slowly come back to life. The darkness fades a little, replaced with the pulse of Enzo's heart. His hand is hot against my side. My legs feel weak, but he keeps me steady. My head reaches to his shoulder and I'm reminded again of how tall he is, how small I am.

"I don't think I've quite gotten over last night," I murmur as we walk, trying to think of a good excuse.

"Don't apologize," Enzo replies. "Teren is not an Inquisitor to take lightly."

I look at him. My curiosity rises. "Your fire didn't hurt him," I decide to say. "Have you . . . always known?"

Enzo hesitates. "I knew him when we were children." There's something strange about the way he says this, as if he feels a certain sympathy for Teren. "He's the only Elite that Raffaele cannot sense."

Raffaele. "Where is he tonight?"

"The madam informed me that Raffaele was called to a client's home," Enzo says after a moment. "I'm sure all is well." But something about his tone tells me that Raffaele should have returned by now. I look back down, trying not to think the worst.

We reach the wall that opens to the courtyard fountains. A light drizzle has started, chilling the night air. By now, I'm able to walk on my own again, and I pause here for a moment to savor the quiet dance of rain on my skin. Enzo waits patiently. I tilt my face up and close my eye. The drizzle is cold, clearing my senses. The damp grass soaks the hem of my robes. "I feel better now," I say. Partly true, at least.

He gazes out at the courtyard too, as if taking in the shine that the rain gives to the night scene. There's a faraway look in his eyes. Finally, he turns back to me. He looks like he wants to ask what's troubling me, as if he knows it extends deeper than what I'd claimed, but he doesn't. *Can I tell you? Would you turn on me?*

Enzo watches me silently. The lanterns on the courtyard wall outline his face in a halo of damp, golden light, and the beads of water in his hair glitter in the darkness. He is such a startlingly different beauty from Raffaele—dark, intense, wary, perhaps even menacing—but I see a softness in him, a stirring desire. Something mysterious flickers in his eyes.

The spiced wine from earlier now gives me a sudden rush of courage. On impulse, I take my gold necklace off, then lift my arms and drape it over his neck. My hands brush past his crimson hair, the skin of his neck. I half expect Enzo to push me away. But he doesn't stop me. His eyes are liquid dark and beautiful, slashed with scarlet, ringed with long lashes, full of an emotion deep and wanting. I swallow, suddenly aware of the attention I've stirred. Then I lean up on my toes, gently tug the necklace toward me, and bring his lips to mine.

I hover there for a second, heady with the rush of courage. He doesn't move a muscle. To my surprise and dismay, warmth doesn't surge through me at the connection between us. Not the way it had when he'd kissed me at the Spring Moons. *There's fear in his heart. He's holding back his energy.* This thought brings me back to reality, and suddenly I feel stupid. Our last kiss had been one of necessity, part of blending into the festivities. That was all. I pull away. Rain dances cold against my face. *Stupid.* I'm in no state to act appropriately right now—there are too many thoughts racing through my mind, and I am so exhausted from them. I'm too embarrassed to look him in the eyes, so I just start to step away.

He places a gloved hand against the small of my back and stops me. I stand still for a moment, trembling in his grasp. Rain shines on his lashes. His other hand tilts my chin up. I only have time to glance once at his face before he brings his lips down to mine. Then he's kissing me, *really* kissing, reaching deep down for more.

Heat explodes inside me, flooding every vein in my body, a fire so intense that I can't catch my breath. My mouth opens, gasping for air until he seizes my kiss back. The hand he uses to lift my chin now runs along the naked line of my jaw, careful and caressing, but even as he restrains his deadly abilities, I can sense the raw power churning under the surface. He pins me to the damp wall so that his body is pressed solidly against mine. In this moment, I can't seem to

remember anything. I push myself up on my toes and wrap my arms around his neck. I can feel the contour of his chest through his doublet and linen, the body hidden beneath the Reaper that makes him human.

His kiss goes on and on—I have trouble keeping my thoughts straight now. My hand slides from the back of his neck to the part of his throat exposed by his shirt. I push the linen farther aside, revealing bare skin, then the smooth line of his collarbone, then the curve of his brown shoulder. My fingers run across a scar there. He takes my hand, pulls it away from his skin, and pins it firmly to the wall over my head. His kisses wander down to my neck. Heat ripples in rings across my skin each time his lips make contact. My toes curl. I'm going to fall, I'm sure of it—but he holds me steady. The edges of my skirts are sliding higher, leaving wet streaks on my legs. His gloved hands. Soft leather against my skin. Then another wave of liquid fire bubbles through my body, and I can think of nothing else. The tiny raindrops landing on my lips and skin are pinpricks of ice against the heat coursing through me. I delight in the contrast. When I squint into the drizzle, I see the steam of my breath curling up into the night sky. A strange tingle runs through my toes. *I cannot think—I'm losing control over my powers.* Threads of my energy start to snake out of my chest, searching for Enzo's heart, wrapping its strings around his own, clouding them with darkness.

This is dangerous. A small light of warning flashes inside

me, and with all my strength, I force my illusions back under control. "Stop," I whisper, pushing away.

He pulls back immediately, taking the heat of his energy with him. My body cools. He looks confused, as if he can't quite remember what's just happened. His eyes search my face. The moment ends, and all of my dark thoughts return in a rush, leaving me weak and nauseous. My skin tingles. What had my energy been trying to do? I can still feel the remnants of its dark threads, still eager to seek out Enzo, to overwhelm him.

"I'm not seventeen yet," I decide to say. "I cannot give myself away."

Enzo nods. "Of course." He suddenly seems to recognize me again, the familiarity returning to his eyes, and the expression puzzles me. He gives me a small smile that seems tinged with apology. "Let's not anger the gods, then."

He guides us out of the courtyard and back into the hall. We walk in silence, my heartbeat keeping time with our footsteps. Finally, we reach my chamber door. Enzo doesn't linger. Instead, he gives me a courteous bow and bids me good night. I watch him go until he turns a corner and disappears. Then I enter my chamber.

The room is dark, the reflections of rain on the windows painting moving shadows against the walls. I stand against the door for a while, replaying our kiss in my mind. My cheeks stay hot. Long minutes drag by, until I have no idea how long I've been here like this. Had I run my hand along the naked skin of his throat, the line of his collarbone, his

exposed shoulder? Had my energy surged out of control, seeking to wrap itself around him?

I have to tell him.

I'm an official Elite now; I should be able to tell the Daggers everything. Enzo had confided in me that he had some sort of history with Teren—if I should tell anyone about what Teren whispered to me, I should be able to tell *him*. Suddenly, I find myself moving toward the door again. I step out, then follow the corridor the way I'd come. I will never have another chance like this.

The sky is completely dark by the time I make my way back down the corridor, the candles lining the hall are already lit, and the sound of rain beats steadily against the roofs. I head down to the cavern. Laughter and conversation drift from the space. Everyone must still be down here, and by the sound of it, the wine's still flowing freely. My hands tremble as I walk.

I reach the hall leading into the cavern, then pause behind the final pillar that overlooks the room. Here and there, I catch a glimpse of Enzo's crimson hair. The sight of him sends my heart pounding. *I'm one of them now. They are my friends and allies. They deserve to know.* I start to step out.

Then I stop.

Dante has pulled Enzo aside. They exchange a few words, and then Dante nods toward my hallway. They walk in my direction, seeking out the corridor for a private chat. I tense. They'll discover me here. For some reason, fear or curiosity or suspicion, I shrink back into the shadows and conjure a

curtain of invisibility around myself. I paint the illusion of an empty hall over me, blending myself in with the shadows of the wall and pillar. Then I hold my breath.

What are they talking about? Beside me, my father's ghost appears without warning, his shattered chest heaving, his mouth twisted into a dark smile. He places a skeletal hand on my shoulder and points at their approaching figures. *Do you see that?* he whispers in my ear, turning my insides to ice. *Let's listen to what your enemy has to say to your love.*

I want to ignore his voice, but when Enzo and Dante finally reach the hall and come to a stop barely a dozen feet away from me, I catch their conversation. They're talking about me.

And Moritas rose out of the Underworld with such fury in her eyes
that all who saw her fell to their knees, and all wept,
begging her forgiveness. But Moritas had no desire to forgive.
She called on the earth, the earth trembled, and the mountains
buried the village in ash and stone.

—An account of the destruction of Teaza Island, by Captain Ikazara Terune

Adelina Amouteru

y heart hammers loudly against my ribs. I pray to the gods that they can't hear it.

"—but the point is, she was recognized," Dante says. The mere sound of his voice sends a tremor of anger through me, bringing back with it the memory of his threats during my training. "And not only was she recognized, I saw them *talking* to each other." He scowls. "Has she told you what words she exchanged with him?"

"He had her pinned against a wall. She tried to attack him."

Dante grits his teeth. "They talked for longer than that. Where is she now?"

"She's resting," Enzo replies.

Dante waits for him to say more. When Enzo doesn't, he

continues in a growl. "You've killed your own before, when they've endangered the safety of our entire group."

Enzo stays quiet, as if reminded of something he would rather forget. My hands clench together.

"Her presence here now endangers us all," Dante goes on. "We still have some days to go before the Tournament of Storms, and Adelina can't be recognized again."

"She may be the only way for us to get close enough to the king and queen."

"She may be the one *sabotaging* us. Is it strange that the Inquisition banned *malfettos* from entering the Tournament on the same day Adelina left to watch the qualifying races against your wishes?"

"If she wanted to turn us in, there would be Inquisitors swarming all over us right now." Enzo folds his arms behind his back. "It would have happened already."

Dante looks at him sideways. "Is that all, Your Highness?"

Enzo narrows his eyes. "What are you suggesting?"

"I saw you escorting her away. All the other Elites suspect it. I've known you for years—I can see the truth on your face."

"There's nothing to see."

"She reminds you of Daphne, doesn't she? That little Tamouran face?"

A cloud of numbness sweeps over me. *Daphne. Who is Daphne?*

Through the fog that envelops me, I sense an overwhelming tide of anger rising in Enzo's heart, pushing and straining

to lash out. The energy makes me gasp—I clamp a hand over my mouth to silence it. My heart pounds a frantic warning.

"You're on dangerous ground," Enzo says to him in a quiet voice.

Dante hesitates, wavering for a moment, but then scowls and plunges on. His voice takes on a surprising switch, a transition from his arrogant, bullying condescension to something with genuine concern in it. "Listen. We all liked Daphne. Best non-*malfetto* I ever knew. She nursed me back to health—I'd have died if it wasn't for her. You think I didn't notice all the times you abandoned your estates or the Fortunata Court in order to go find her? Think we didn't know you wanted to marry her?"

To marry her.

Dante's voice stills. "You think I didn't mourn her too? That I didn't want to murder every Inquisitor in the city for her?"

Enzo listens in silence, his face a portrait of stone. There are walls around his energy now, barring me from his emotions. I fight to concentrate on my illusion of invisibility. *Why aren't you calling him a liar, Enzo?* Because it's all the truth, of course. No wonder Enzo sometimes looks at me as if I were someone else. It's because he *is* seeing someone else. Another girl who once lived, whom he once loved, whom he loves still.

Dante leans over. The anger in him swells. "Adelina *is not her.* She's got the fire, I'll give her that, and—markings aside— the face. But they are completely different people, Reaper.

243

And I can tell you that while everyone trusted Daphne, *nobody* trusts your new girl. We all tolerate her, at best." Dante pauses to hold up two fingers. "She's gone against your orders, and she's been spotted talking to the enemy. You've killed for less than that. You've given her advantages that you don't give others. You've softened to her. *I* don't like taking orders—but I still take them from *you*. I haven't taken them for years just to see you fall all over yourself for a girl who reminds you of a dead sweetheart."

The look that Enzo now gives Dante is enough to make the latter take a careful step back. "I'm quite aware of who Adelina is," the prince says in a low voice. "And who she's not."

"Not if you think you're in love with her, Your Highness."

"My affairs are not your business."

"They are if she's a distraction from our goals."

Enzo narrows his eyes. "She is *nothing* to me," he snaps with a careless gesture of one hand. "Nothing more than a Dagger recruit. Just part of our plans." The ice in his voice hits me hard. *Nothing more.* A rip appears on my heart.

Dante snorts at his words. "If that's the truth, then you should have no trouble taking some advice from another one of your Daggers." He gestures at himself.

"And you're suggesting?" Enzo says.

"On my honor, I will tolerate her so long as *you* tolerate her. Use her as you will. But after you're on the throne and finished with your fun, you should get rid of her. She won't stay loyal to you long."

I tremble at the darkness awakening in Enzo's heart, a fury that blacks out all the excitement drifting over from the other Daggers and patrons, a rage that envelops the cavern.

"I appreciate your concern," he says after a moment, emphasizing the words in slow, ominous notes. "But our conversation here is done."

"Suit yourself, Your Highness," Dante says in disgust. "You may have sentenced us all." He turns away to head back to the group. Enzo stays where he is, his expression guarded, his eyes trained on the Spider's back, thinking. It occurs to me, with all the agony of a twisting knife, that he might be *considering* Dante's words.

Finally, Enzo also returns to the others. I don't. I stay where I am, crouched in a shuddering heap at the entrance of the chamber, shrouded in invisibility, alone as the gathering continues. The words I prepared to say to the Daggers have withered on my tongue. The memory of the kiss I shared with Enzo so recently now leaves me cold and shivering.

I feel no anger. No jealousy. Just . . . emptiness. A bone-deep sense of loss. Somehow, the echoes of Gemma's wise-cracks and the patrons' laughter sound menacing to me now. *Gemma has treated you well. Raffaele took you under his wing.* I hang on to these thoughts in desperation, searching for comfort, trying to convince myself that Dante's lying. I can't.

They are only good to me because they need me. Just like Enzo. *Kindness with strings attached.* Would they have befriended me if I were worthless?

Finally, I rise to my feet and head back to my chamber. My

illusion ripples around me. If someone were here in the hall, they would see a current of movement in the air, a strange shadow gliding along the corridor.

I reach my chamber, lock my door, release the illusion, and crouch against the foot of my bed. Here, I finally unleash my emotions. Tears run down my face. So much for thinking that I can tell them everything. Time passes. Minutes, an hour. Who knows? The moonlight shifts its slant through my windows. I am back again in my childhood bedchamber, running away from my father. I am back against the railings of my old home's stairway, listening to my father sell me to his guest. Or maybe I'm listening to Dante denouncing me before Enzo. They're talking about me. *They are always talking about me.* I have made a full circle and I have not escaped my fate at all.

My father's ghost appears through the wall beside me. He kneels before me and cups my face in his hands. I can almost feel the whisper of his touch, the cold shiver of death. He smiles. *Don't you see, Adelina?* he says gently. *Don't you see how I have always looked out for you? Everything I've ever taught you is true. Who will ever love a malfetto like you?*

I clutch my head and squeeze my eye shut. *Enzo is not like them. He believed in me. He took me in and stood up for me.* I recall the way he had danced with me at the Spring Moons, the way he protected me from Teren. All our days training together, the gentleness in his kiss, his affectionate laugh. I repeat this to myself until the words blur together into something unrecognizable.

But did he really do those things for you? my father whispers. *Or for himself?*

I have no idea how late the night has turned. For all I know, dawn could be arriving soon. Or perhaps only a few minutes have passed. All I know is that, as the time drags on, the true part of me is slowly but surely giving way to something bitter. What was once sadness is making way for anger. The darkness creeps in. Exhausted, I welcome it.

I rise from my crouch. My feet move toward the door. I head out into the hallway again, but this time I don't go in the direction of the others. My feet point instead toward the opposite path, the one that leads me out of the court, into the streets, and down to the canals.

Toward the Inquisition Tower.

Teren Santoro

The lights in the palace burn low tonight. Teren makes his way down the empty halls, tracing a very familiar path. His boots echo faintly against the floors, but he steps lightly, and the sound is almost imperceptible. At the end of the hall is the king's private bedchambers. But guards are always posted outside of the doors. Teren takes a detour instead, wandering down a narrower hall and pushing through an invisible panel in the wall that will take him directly into the bedroom.

The secret door swings open without a sound. Teren's eyes go immediately to the bed. By the light of the moons, he can see the king's snoring figure rising and falling under the blankets. Beside him, Queen Giulietta sits upright in bed. She so rarely visits the king's chambers that the sight of her in here feels foreign to Teren. She meets his eyes and motions him closer.

The smell of wine is a pungent cloud around the king.

Teren steps closer. He gives the queen a questioning look. She stares at him levelly in return.

Teren removes a knife tucked at his waist. It is an unusual weapon—so small and thin that it looks like something a doctor would use in surgery. He hoists it in one hand. With his other hand, he produces a heavy wooden mallet from within his cloaks.

Teren learned this as a child, when his father lay on his deathbed and he stood by, crying, while a doctor put his dying father out of his misery. It had been quick and painless. Most important, it had been free of blood or obvious wounds. When the Inquisition buried his father, it was as if he simply died in his sleep, his body intact and seemingly untouched.

Now, Teren positions the needlelike knife over the inside corner of the king's right eye. He hoists the wooden mallet over the end of the knife, then pulls the mallet back. Giulietta watches him in silence.

Giulietta is the rightful ruler of Kenettra. The gods ordained it by marking Prince Enzo, cursing him as a *malfetto*. The gods gave Kenettra this weak king, the Duke of Estenzia, a nobleman not even of the royal bloodline. *But Giulietta is pure.* She should rule Kenettra. With Adelina's help, Teren will destroy the Young Elites. And with Giulietta's support, they will rid the entire country of *malfettos*. Teren smiles at the thought. Tonight, Giulietta will cry out for her guards and tell them the king has stopped breathing beside her.

They will pronounce the king dead of natural causes, of excessive wine or of heart attack. And tonight, Teren will begin a true purge of the city's *malfettos*.

He gathers his strength. Then he slams the mallet down on the knife's handle. The knife strikes true. The body goes rigid, twitching. Then, gradually, the movements fade.

The king is dead. Long live the queen.

To love is to be afraid. You are frightened, deathly terrified, that something will happen to those you love. Think of the possibilities. Does your heart clench with each thought? That, my friend, is love. And love enslaves us all, for you cannot have love without fear.
    –A Private Thesis on the Romancing of Three Kings,
        by *Baroness Sammarco*

Adelina Amouteru

I haven't been out in Estenzia often enough to know, but I would have guessed that at such a late hour, the city would be quieter. No such luck tonight. The streets are teeming with Inquisition guards. In fact, I can't turn a single corner without seeing a patrol making its way down the street. Their presence forces me to slow down. Something has happened. *What is going on?*

I pass through the shadows, my silver mask tucked neatly under my arm. I cloak myself in an illusion of invisibility, but the act exhausts me quickly, allowing me to do it only for a few moments at a time. I pause frequently in dark alleys to gather my strength. Invisibility is hard, as hard as disguising myself as another person. With each step, my surroundings change, and I have to shift my illusion to change with

it. If I don't shift quickly or accurately enough, I look like a ripple moving through air. The consequence of invisibility, therefore, is constant concentration, to the point where I can barely remember what my real self looks like. At least it's nighttime. A more forgiving hour.

I hide again as more Inquisition patrols hurry past. Somewhere distant in the night, a few shouts go up. I listen intently. At first, I can't make out what they're saying. Then, moments later, the words become clear.

"The king is dead!"

The distant cry freezes me in place. The king . . . is dead?

A moment later, another voice joins in, repeating the phrase. Then another. Among them, I hear another phrase. *Long live the queen!*

The king is dead. Long live the queen. I steady myself against the wall. Did the Daggers make their move tonight? No, they wouldn't have. They didn't plan for it. The king had died before they could get to him.

What happened?

Teren, a whisper in my head suggests. But that doesn't seem right. Why would he want the king dead?

Without risking a gondola ride, it takes me a full hour before I can even sight the Inquisition Axis's tower looming in the distance. Beyond it lies the palace—and if I'm not mistaken, the clusters of Inquisitors seem to be heading in that general direction.

By the time I'm in the same square as the tower, a cold sheen of sweat has broken out on my brow. I stop in the

shadows of a nearby shop, then let down my invisibility illusion, remove my mask for a moment, and take a deep breath. This is easily the longest I've ever held an illusion in place, and the result is a wave of dizziness that leaves me swaying in place. When I was nine, I went into my father's study and ripped apart a letter he had been writing to a local doctor, asking advice on medicines to subdue my temper. My father found out what I'd done, of course. He told Violetta to lock me in my bedchamber for three days without food or water. When Violetta found me nearly unconscious at the end of the second day, she begged him to release me. He did. Then he smiled and asked me if I'd enjoyed the rush of thirst and hunger. If it had woken anything in me.

The dizziness I felt back then, leaning against my locked door and shouting myself hoarse for my sister to release me, is not unlike how I feel now. The memory gives me some strength, though. After a few minutes, I swallow and straighten myself. My gaze focuses on the tower.

A short walkway leads from the main square up to the tower's looming doors, and Inquisitors line this path. A large, round lantern hangs at the tower's entrance, illuminating the door's dark wood. I start to cover myself up again—then stop. Why should I drain my energy now? If I get to the door successfully with an invisibility illusion, I will still need to pull it open in order to enter. No way for me to disguise *that*.

So, instead, I walk up to the guards. The memory of the last time I did this, in a city gone wild with the qualifying races, comes back to me.

Two of them immediately draw their swords. I force myself to stare straight back at them. "I'm here to see Master Santoro," I reply. "He asked for me personally."

A flicker of doubt appears on one of the men's faces at the mention of Teren's name. My energy stirs at the emotion, strengthening. I frown at them. This time, I take advantage of their obvious unease. From my cloak, I produce the silver mask. "I have information for him on the Young Elites." My voice is surprisingly smooth. "Do you really want to risk turning me away?"

The guard's eyes widen in recognition at the sight of the mask, and my energy strengthens again as I feel myself winning control over this soldier, forcing him to do something against his will.

Finally, the first Inquisitor gestures for two of the others to seize me. "Let her in." Then he growls at me. "You'll wait until he returns."

Teren's not in the tower tonight. Their hands on my arms remind me of my execution day in Dalia. As they lead me away, I look over my shoulder as more Inquisitors run by on the streets. The energy of fear seems high tonight. It pulses through me, stimulating my senses.

We step inside the tower. They usher me into a small chamber branching off from the main hall, and here they seat me on the floor. Then they surround me in a circle, each of their spears pointed straight at me. Outside the door, more wait. I stare back at them, determined not to show them any hint of emotion. The dungeons should be somewhere below

us, if this tower is anything like the one I was once kept in. Where is Teren keeping Violetta . . . if he has her at all?

I don't know how long I'm in here, counting the minutes away. The Inquisitors stay unmoving. Is this what they go through in training—standing motionless for hours at a time? I can sense their unease around me, a persistent, underlying emotion that peeks through from the stern, unfeeling shell they try to pull over it. I smile at them. Their fear grows. My excitement grows with it.

Suddenly, from outside the windows comes the sound of shattering glass. Then, screams. I turn in the direction of the sound. The guards all hoist their swords at my movement, but I continue to look toward the windows. The sound of running feet, hundreds of them, then more voices, then chaos. A faint glow of yellow and orange flickers against the windows' dark glass. *The king's death.* Is this related? Do the Daggers know what happened? Does Enzo know I've run away yet?

The door bursts open. A new Inquisitor comes hurrying in, then whispers something in the ear of the closest guard. I try in vain to catch what he's saying. Outside, more shouts and shrieks ring out in the night.

And then I hear it—a familiar voice from down the hall. My head jerks in its direction. Teren has returned.

He strides into my room, a swagger in his step, his head held high, and a cold smile on his lips. He pauses at the sight of me. I suck my breath in sharply. Suddenly my entire mission—all my powers—seem to pale in his presence.

"You came," he finally says, stopping before me. "It's

about time. I was sure I'd have to kill you tonight." He crosses his arms over his chest. "You saved me the trouble."

"I hear the king has died," I whisper.

Teren bows his head once, but his words are stripped of empathy. "A sudden illness. We are all in mourning."

I shiver. *Are you, Teren?* His matter-of-fact answer is confirmation enough that the Daggers weren't the ones responsible. But just because the Daggers didn't assassinate the king . . . doesn't mean he wasn't assassinated. *A sudden illness* sounds suspicious.

"You promised me my sister," I say, my eye focused on his bloody cloak. "And her safety." For a moment, I consider using my powers on him. But then what? All I can create are illusions. I can't hurt him. Not even Enzo can hurt him.

"My word is as good as yours," he replies, eyeing me pointedly. "But it may not be good for long."

Whatever it is that Teren has ordered done to the city tonight, it has brought with it a cloud of terror. I study him, sensing the swirling darkness in his heart, the madness glinting in his eyes.

Collect yourself. Concentrate. I steel my heart, sharpening my fear into a razor-sharp blade. "Take me to my sister. Or I'll tell you nothing."

Teren tilts his head. "Demanding, aren't we?" His eyes narrow. "Something has happened to you since the last time we crossed paths."

In my chest, my alignment with ambition surges. "Are you interested in capturing the Young Elites, or not?"

My answer coaxes a single laugh out of him. His smile wavers for a moment, diminishing his madness, and he gives me a more serious look. "What made you turn your back on them?"

I withdraw. I don't want to revisit what I heard. "Isn't it enough that you threatened my sister's life? That you threw me against a wall?"

His eyes pulse with curiosity. "There's more."

The heat of Enzo's kiss springs unbidden to my mind, the way his eyes had softened at the sight of me, the way he'd pushed me against the wall . . . the conversation between him and Dante. I push the emotion away and shake my head at Teren. "Let me see my sister first," I repeat.

"What if I tell my men to kill her now, unless you give me what I want?"

My jaw tightens. *Stay brave.* "Then I'll never talk." I meet his stare with my own, refusing to back down. The last time we met, he had taken me by surprise and I cowered before him. This time, I can't afford to do the same thing.

Finally, Teren nods at me to follow him. "Come, then," he says, gesturing to the Inquisitors. "Let's play your game."

Success. The Inquisitors lower their swords and drag me to my feet. Gradually, I start to gather energy in my chest. I'm going to need everything I have, or there is no hope of escaping this place with Violetta.

He leads us farther down into the dungeons, down, down, until I stop counting the number of stony steps we've covered. How far does this go? As we continue, I hear the cries

of prisoners ringing from other floors, a chorus of haunted wails. I have to hold my breath down here. Never in my life have I felt so much fear and anger concentrated in a single place. The emotions swim around me, hungering for me to do something with them. My own anger and fear threaten to overwhelm my senses. I grit my teeth, hanging on to my powers. I could do so much down here. I could conjure an illusion like none of them have ever seen.

But I continue to hold back. Not until I see Violetta myself.

Finally, Teren guides us down to a floor quieter than the rest. Small wooden doors covered with iron bars line the walls. We walk through a narrowly lit corridor until we stand before a lone door at the very end. I nearly stagger, so powerful is my darkness here. I was in a place like this once.

"Your sister," he says to me, giving me a mock bow. One of the other Inquisitors unlocks the door, and it groans open.

I blink. Behind the heavy door is a tiny, cramped cell. Candles burn along small ledges on the wall. A bed of hay is piled in one corner, and on it sits a girl with a sweet, fragile face and a head of dark locks that now look tangled and dull. She is thin and frail, shaking from the cold. Her wide eyes find me. I'm ashamed by my rush of mixed emotions at the sight of her—joy, love, hate, envy.

"Adelina?" my sister says. And suddenly I remember the night I ran away from home, when she stood in my bed-chamber's doorway and rubbed sleep from her eyes.

Inquisitors immediately file in and surround her. She shrinks away from them on the bed, tucking her knees up

to her chin. As she does, I notice the heavy shackles on her wrists and ankles that keep her chained to the bed.

Darkness roars inside me. What illusion can I perform that could get us out before they can hurt her? I gauge the distance between us, the number of steps that separate the Inquisitors and me, me and Teren. All of Raffaele's and Enzo's lessons run through my mind.

Teren waits for me to step inside the room, and then closes the door behind him. He strolls closer to Violetta. As he does, I feel her fear spike—and with that, mine does too. Teren looks her over with a critical gaze, then turns back to me with a sweep of his cloak.

He studies me. "Tell me, Adelina—what are their names?"

I open my mouth.

Tell him about the horrible Spider, the little whispers say gleefully in my head. *Go on. He deserves it. Give him Enzo, and Michel, and Lucent. Give him Gemma. You're doing so well.* In my head, I imagine confessing everything I know to Teren.

"Where are the Young Elites?" he'll say.

"The Fortunata Court," I'll reply.

"Where?"

"It has many secret passages. They use the catacombs underneath the court. You can find the entrance in the smallest garden."

"Tell me their names."

I do.

The vision in my head vanishes, and I once again see Teren standing before me. Somehow, the confessions don't come out.

Despite my silence, Teren seems calm. "Adelina, I'm impressed. Something *did* happen to you."

A faint warning buzzes in my head. "You want their names," I say, prolonging the game.

Teren observes me with an interested stare. His lips twitch. "Still hesitant, aren't you?" He walks in a slow circle around me, close enough that I can feel the brush of his cloak against my skin. With a chill, I realize that it reminds me of when Raffaele circled me during my test with the gemstones, sizing me up, studying my potential.

Finally, Teren stops before me. He draws his sword and points it at Violetta. My heart twists. "Why do you protect them so loyally, Adelina? What did they promise you, once you were part of their circle? Did they make you believe that they're a band of noble heroes? That they recruited you for some honorable cause, instead of the murder they *actually* commit? Do you think their Spring Moons stunt didn't claim any innocent lives?" He fixes his pale, pulsing eyes on me. "I've seen what you can do. I know of the darkness in your soul. You were willing to run from them—I'd wager that you don't trust them. There's something . . . different about you. They don't like you, do they?"

How could he possibly know that? "What are you trying to say?" I ask through clenched teeth.

"You're here because you know you don't belong," he replies coolly. "Let me tell you something, Adelina. There's no shame in turning your back on a group of criminals who want nothing more than to burn this entire nation to the

ground. Do you think they'd protect you if you were in danger?" He turns, his gaze sidelong.

I think back to how *malfettos* have burned at the stake, and how the Daggers chose not to save them. Because they weren't Elites.

"They came for you that day because you had something they wanted," Teren says, as if he knows what I'm thinking. "No one throws away something useful to them—that is, until it's no longer useful."

He's right.

"I've grown fond of you, in the time we've spent together," he continues. "Do you ever think on the myth of the angel of Joy and his brother, the angel of Greed? Do you remember the story of Denarius casting Laetes from the heavens, condemning him to walk the world as a man until his death sent him back among the gods? *Curing* the angel of Joy of his arrogance in thinking that he was the gods' most beloved child?" He leans closer. "There is an imbalance in the world, just as there was when Joy left the heavens—warning signs of demons walking with us, defying the natural order. Sometimes, the only way to set things right is to do what is difficult. It is the only way to love them back." All pretense of amusement is now gone from his face. "That's why I was sent by the gods. And I feel, too, that perhaps *you* were sent for the same reason. There is a yearning in you to set things right, little *malfetto*—you are smarter than the others, because you *know* there is something wrong with you. It tears at your conscience, doesn't it? You have hatred for yourself, and I admire that. It's why you keep

261

coming back to me. The only way to cure yourself of this guilt is to atone for it by saving your fellow abominations. Help them return to the Underworld, where they belong. Do this with me. You and I can set the world right again, and when we do, the gods will deem us forgiven." His voice has taken on a strange, gentle tone. "It doesn't *seem* right or kind, I know—it *seems* cruel. But it *must* be done. Do you understand?"

Something about his words makes sense. They twist around my head and my heart until they seem logical. I *am* an abomination—even to the other Daggers. Perhaps it really *is* my duty to set the world right again. *I do this because I love you,* my father's ghost whispers. *You may not understand it right now, but it is for your own good. You are a monster. I still love you. I will set you right.*

Teren's serious look shifts to a sympathetic one, an expression I recognize from my execution day. "If you pledge yourself to the Inquisition, to *me,* and swear to use your powers and your knowledge to send *malfettos* back to the Underworld, I will give you everything you've ever wanted. I can grant your every desire. Money? Power? Respect? Done." He smiles. "You can redeem yourself, change from an abomination in the gods' eyes to a savior. You can help me fix this world. Wouldn't it be nice, not having to run anymore?" He pauses, and for a moment, a note of real, painful tragedy enters his voice. "We are not supposed to exist, Adelina. We were never meant to be."

We are mistakes.

"Now, Adelina," he says, soft and coaxing. "Tell me."

I want to—oh, how I want to—in this moment. Teren can offer Violetta and me such an easy life if I only give him what he wants. The Daggers' plans are ruined anyway, aren't they? The king has died of his own accord. I have no reason to stay loyal to them anymore. I open my mouth. Dante's words are fresh in my mind, and a surge of bitterness rises in me, eager for release. I could destroy them all right now, with just a few choice words.

But the words still don't come. I am thinking instead of Enzo's gentle expression, of Gemma's quick smile. Lucent's casual friendship, Michel's art lessons. I am thinking of Raffaele most of all, with his patience and grace, his kind, calm faithfulness that has earned my trust. If he had been at the court tonight, I might have confided in him. He would have helped me. Things could have gone differently if he were there. I have something when I'm with the Daggers, something beyond an unwritten business contract to do what they tell me.

Some spark of clarity emerges through the net Teren's words have cast over me, a trickle of logic that brings me out of the fog. He says the Daggers are using me. But he is using me too. This is the real reason why I cannot seem to give him what he wants. It is not so much that I am protecting the Daggers.

It is that I am tired of being used.

Teren sighs, then shakes his head. He nods at one of his men. The Inquisitor draws his sword and moves toward Violetta.

I glance at my sister. She realizes I'm about to make a move. I gather my strength. Then I reach out and *pull*.

A sheet of invisibility shoots up around me, mimicking the wall behind me and the floor beneath my feet. I weave the same around my sister. To the naked eye, it seems as if my sister had suddenly been replaced by empty space.

For the first time, Teren looks surprised. "You've improved," he snaps. He draws his sword, then shouts at the other Inquisitors, "Enough of this. Find her."

They start in my general direction, but I'm already on the move. I pull again, wrapping each one of them in a vision of nightmares—shrieking demons, their piercing wails the sound of metal ripping against metal, their mouths pulled all the way back. Several Inquisitors fall to their knees, their hands pressed over their faces and ears. Their terror makes me gasp. It feels so good.

Teren and I reach my sister at the same time. He gropes blindly, grabbing at her arm. He yanks her to him and presses his sword against her throat. "Don't," he shouts to the air. Even through his anger, he seems to see something in me that fascinates him. I turn my concentration onto him, then seek out his senses, aiming to drown him in illusions with his men.

I hit a wall.

I've never felt this in anyone else before—like a block of ice, something hard and impenetrable that shields his energy from my own. I grit my teeth and push harder, but his own energy pushes back. A smile spreads across his face as he

senses me struggling. I'd witnessed how Enzo's fire barely affected him, and heard Enzo talk about how Teren cannot be injured like a normal person. Now, for the first time, I'm feeling it for myself.

"Try that again, and I'll cut her," he says.

Violetta squeezes her eyes shut. She takes a deep breath.

And the strangest thing happens. Teren stops cold in the middle of his attack. He shudders. I feel the wall of ice shielding his energy from me crack—then shatter. He lets out a terrible gasp, releases Violetta, and falls to his knees. Suddenly, just like that, I see his energy threads, his fear and his darkness, the threads that tie to his senses that I can now seek out and twist like I did to the others. What happened?

Someone tampered with his abilities.

I glance at Violetta, stunned. She returns my stricken look. That's when I know. I know it immediately.

My sister is an Elite.

And she just took away Teren's powers.

While my illusion holds, I hurry over to him and yank the key from around his neck. Then I rush over to my sister and remove her invisibility for a moment. She's shaking all over, a sheen of sweat on her delicate brow, and her eyes stay fixed on Teren as he crouches on the ground. My trembling fingers attempt to position the key at her iron cuffs. I wince as I force my one crooked finger to work with the others. Gods help me, but I'm so exhausted. I hadn't even realized how much of my energy I'd used, but now I feel it weighing me down. My fear is the only thing that keeps me going.

Finally, Violetta's chains fall away and she springs to her feet. She swings one of my arms over her shoulder, steadying me, and together we make for the door. I strengthen our invisibility. I pause right before the door, then glance at Teren over my shoulder. He grins; the wall of ice around him is gradually piecing itself back together.

"Adelina," he exclaims. "You constantly surprise me." He laughs again, the sound of a madman. We stagger out into the corridor as Teren shouts for more guards.

We climb the steps in silence, our breaths turning into hoarse gasps. My energy weakens—even my own fear isn't enough to keep the illusion going. Our invisibility flickers in and out. Inquisitors dash past us. I try to save my strength for when they near us. But by the time we've reached the main level of the tower, we appear as ripples moving against the walls.

"Hang on, Adelina," my sister coaxes. We hurry onto the street and into chaos.

Shattered glass everywhere. Screams in the night. More Inquisitors than I've ever seen in my entire life, swarming the streets and dragging *malfettos* out of their homes—still in their nightgowns—and into the square, beating them senseless, clamping chains on them. I stumble to a halt in a nearby alley. There, I finally release the last of my energy and slide down the wall into a fetal position. Violetta collapses beside me. Together, we look on in horror at the scene unfolding before us. One Inquisitor runs a sword straight through the body of a young *malfetto* woman with a streak of gold in her

black hair. She lets out a broken shriek—her blood spills onto the cobblestones. Cries ring out across the square.

The king is dead! The king is dead!

This is all wrong. I watch as the Inquisitors kill other *malfettos*. I am numb. Something has gone terribly wrong.

I pull Violetta close. "Think of something else," I whisper into her ear, feeling her trembling uncontrollably against me. I force myself to take in the terror and evil that swirls around us, letting it strengthen the darkness in me so that I can weave an illusion of calm around my sister. I block out the screams for her. I weave a blanket of darkness around her, shielding her from the sight of the crying *malfettos* gathered in the square. This must be happening all across Estenzia—across Kenettra, even. As Violetta weeps against my shoulder, I stare at the horrific scene in her stead.

How ironic, that I should embrace such evil in order to protect my sister from evil.

Through my fog of terror, I remember the catacombs under the city. I touch my sister's face. "We have to go," I say firmly. Then I take her hand and begin to lead us away—

—until we turn the corner and run straight into Dante. He stares down at me, his face swathed in shadows. "Well," he growls. "I knew I'd find you out here."

> He could feel the storm's energy in the breeze, as if it were
> some sort of living creature, breathing life and fear into his body.
> —Tales of Lord Dunre, *by Ephare*

Adelina Amouteru

My first, feverish thought: *Dante followed me.*

He'd somehow seen me leave the Fortunata Court. He'd tracked me to the Inquisition Tower. And now he knows I must have visited the Inquisition. A flurry of thoughts flash through my mind in the span of a second. If he goes back to the other Daggers, he will tell them about everything. *No— they cannot find out in this way.* I open my mouth, trying to think of something to say.

He doesn't give me a chance. Instead, he lunges at me with an outstretched hand, trying to grab my arm. Violetta cries out—my energy roars in my ears.

I fling an illusion of invisibility desperately over us and throw myself to the ground. My powers are fading fast, and we blink in and out of sight. I scramble to my feet right as Dante lunges for me again. This time he attacks with a dagger.

My illusion manages to throw off his aim, but the blade still catches the edge of my thigh, slicing through my clothes. I wince at the bite against my skin. Darkness roars inside me, feeding on Dante's own fury. My strength grows again.

"You *traitor*." He points the dagger at me. "Enzo should've done away with you the instant you came to us."

How dare you. I protected you all. "I didn't do anything," I shout back. "I told them nothing."

"You expect me to believe you?" Dante twirls his blade.

"Let me explain," I say, holding my hands out. "I didn't give anything to them. What you saw happen at the Spring Moons—"

Dante's lips curl into a snarl. "I know what I saw. How long have you been working with Teren?"

"I wasn't working with him! He found me—months ago, at the court—" I don't know how to tell Dante this, without making it sound like everything is my fault. *It is my fault.*

"And yet, you told us none of this. Why keep it a secret?"

"I didn't mean to! I was afraid of getting hurt. My sister—"

Dante sneers. "I knew you were no good. I should carve your mouth right off your face, because it spits out nothing but lies."

I'm starting to have trouble breathing. My words come in gasps. "You have to believe me. I didn't tell him anything."

"Did you tell him about the Tournament of Storms?"

"I—" I hesitate.

Dante catches my pause. He narrows his eyes. "And you betrayed Raffaele to the palace, didn't you?"

I blink. What? Raffaele? "Raffaele hasn't returned?"

Dante doesn't need to speak for me to know the answer. *Raffaele was absent at the last meeting, he never returned from his client visit. No, not him.* The thought of Raffaele being the first to suffer—

Dante lashes out again. He knocks me to the ground and holds me down. I can't find my energy to pull on. Violetta lets out a choked scream.

"I'm taking you back to Enzo," he growls, narrowing his eyes at me. His hand presses down on my neck, choking me. *No, you can't. I should be the one telling him, not you.* "You'll answer to him, you pathetic little coward."

I'll kill you before you can ruin this deal.

My father's words from that fateful night suddenly echo all around me, filling my ears and taking me back to the rain-soaked marketplace where he'd died. Dante's words to Enzo run through my mind. The darkness that has risen in me ever since I left the Daggers now claws eagerly for freedom—it builds and builds, feeding off the fears and hatred of Dante, the Inquisitors, the terror of the people in the streets, the darkness all around us. Above me, I no longer see Dante . . . instead, I see my father, his lips twisted in a dark smile.

Enough. I twine the glittering threads of energy around myself—there is suddenly so much of it that I feel light-headed from the power, as if I'd left my body. Raffaele once showed me how to create illusions of *touch.* Can I do that now?

I bare my teeth. And I unleash my anger.

For a single, terrible moment, I can see every single one of the energy threads connecting Dante to myself. From myself to his pain senses. On instinct, I reach out and pull hard.

Dante suddenly scrambles away from me. His hand leaves my neck—I gasp desperately for air. His eyes bulge. Then he drops his weapons and lets out a bloodcurdling scream. The sound sends a flood of excitement through me so intense that I tremble from head to toe. *The illusion of touch; the illusion of pain.* Oh, I've wanted to do this for so long. I pull harder, twisting, increasing his belief that he is in agony— that his limbs are being ripped off one by one, that someone is peeling the skin off his back. He collapses to the ground and writhes. Scream after scream.

At first, all I feel from him is rage. He glares at me with murder in his eyes. "I'm going to kill you," he spits out amid his pain. "You've attacked the wrong Elite."

I harden my expression. *No, you* have.

His rage changes to fear. Terror pours from him—it only makes me stronger, and I throw all the extra power back into torturing him. A part of me is horrified at what I'm doing. But the other part of me, the part that is my father's daughter, delights in it. I'm heady with pleasure—it washes over me until I feel like I am a completely different person. I walk closer to where he writhes and look on patiently with a curious tilt of my head. I open my mouth to speak, and my father's words spill out of me.

"Show me what you can do," I whisper in Dante's ear.

Somewhere in the midst of swirling darkness, I catch sight

of Violetta cowering in the corner, her terrified eyes fixed on me. *She has the power to stop me,* I realize through my haze of exhilaration. But she's not.

Stop? Why should I stop? This is the boy who told Enzo to kill me. He has threatened my life from the moment I joined the Daggers—he tried to kill me *right now.* Just like everyone else. I have every right to torture him. He deserves to die at my hands, and I will make sure he feels every last moment of it. All the rage and bitterness I've held in my heart for *everything* now reaches a peak. My father's image replaces Dante again, his body bent backward in agony. My smile turns dark and I twist harder, harder, harder.

I will destroy you.

"Stop, *please!*" At first I think it's Violetta screaming this at me, but then I realize that it's my father. He has resorted to begging. His heartbeat increases to a violent pace.

Something inside me screams that this is going too far—I can feel the darkness taking over my senses. My father—Dante—gasps. His scream cuts off as his face freezes into a trembling picture of shock. *Harder.* I try in vain to shove it away, to regain control. I can't. A real trickle of blood runs from his lips. My heart trembles at the sight. That isn't supposed to happen. I am a conjurer of *illusions.* Can even the illusion of pain eventually trigger something real? Again, I reach out to stop myself. But my father's ghost only laughs, mingling with the gleeful whispers in my head.

Keep going, Adelina, and no one will ever command you again.

I feel something snap in Dante's heart, a breaking of strings.

He freezes. His mouth stays open in a silent scream; his lips are stained red. His fingers twitch, but his eyes are glazed. The darkness in me that took over my mind now vanishes in a rush—I collapse to my knees, suddenly unable to catch my breath, and lean against the wall in exhaustion. I feel like I've returned to my body. My energy shrinks away into nothingness, just like that—my father's ghostly presence disappears, and his voice melts into the night. Violetta stays where she is, staring in stunned silence at Dante's body. I do the same. The chaos out in the streets rings in my ears like an underwater scream.

I wanted to hurt him. To defend myself. To get revenge. To escape. *But I didn't just hurt him.* I made sure that he will never again lift a finger against me.

In my fury, I killed him.

Baliras are violent when provoked. But be silent and still,
and you may yet see the frailness under their enormous size,
the way they wrap their fins around their young.
—Creatures of the Underworld, *by Sir Alamour Kerana*

Adelina Amouteru

'm not sure how long we stay in the alley. Maybe a minute. Maybe hours. Time loses meaning for a while. I only remember leaving that narrow street in a stupor, my hand clenched tightly around Violetta's. There is a corpse lying on the ground behind us that I don't dare look at again.

Somehow, we manage to stay hidden in the shadows, the chaos in the city working to our advantage. In the heart of Estenzia, the steady presence of Inquisition patrols has quickly turned into teeming numbers, more white cloaks than I've ever seen in my life. Broken glass litters the streets. Shops owned by *malfettos* are smashed, burned, and destroyed — their owners dragged from their beds, still in their shifts, and thrown into the street to be arrested. The palace is taking its revenge for what we did at the piers.

I am taking my own revenge.

We continue on. It seems like the night sky has started to lighten . . . dawn already? *We must have stayed in the alley for some time,* I think as we go. Sheer exhaustion suddenly hits me, and I lean into a wall to steady myself against the wave of dizziness. *Something happened in that alley. What was it?* Why does everything feel so out of focus? A memory comes to me clouded and half formed, as if I had witnessed it through another's eyes. *Someone had been there. A boy. He'd tried to hurt us. I can't remember beyond that. Something happened. But what?* I look at Violetta, who returns my stare with wide, frightened eyes. It takes me a moment to realize that she is frightened of *me.*

Perhaps I do remember. Perhaps I'm forgetting on purpose.

"Hurry, Adelina," she whispers as she hesitantly takes my hand. I follow numbly. "Where should we go?"

Through the fog in my head, I murmur back, "The Fortunata Court. This way." If I can just talk to Raffaele, I can explain everything. Enzo will listen to him. I shouldn't have left them behind—this has all been a terrible mistake.

I lead us through the waning dark, past burning buildings and wailing people, the air filled with the smell of terror. I stop again when the darkness in my stomach becomes too much for me to handle.

"Wait," I gasp out to Violetta. Before she can reply, I lean forward and heave. What little is in my stomach comes spilling out. I cough and retch until I have nothing left. Still, the

darkness churns in me, relentless, bringing with it tides of both nausea and comfort. I teeter between revulsion and joy.

Through my dizziness, I feel Violetta wrapping her arm around my shoulder. She steadies me. When I look up, I meet her solemn eyes. "Who was he?" she whispers.

Her question sounds like an accusation. It confuses me. "Who?"

Violetta's eyes turn stricken. "You mean, you don't—"

This must be what it feels like to lose your mind. I shake off her arm and turn my attention back to the streets. "I don't want to talk about it," I snap. I wait for Violetta to say something in return, but she stays quiet, and we don't exchange another word until we near the arches of the Fortunata Court.

By the time we arrive, the city is full of the sound of screams, and the faint dawn is broken by bursts of orange. We pause in an alley to catch our breath. All of my strength has been sapped, and I don't even try to conjure an illusion to protect us. Violetta keeps her eyes turned away from me, her expression stricken.

"Get back," she suddenly whispers.

We shrink into the shadows as Inquisitors come running past the main street and into a nearby shop. Moments later, they drag a *malfetto* woman out, throwing her down with such force that she falls onto her hands and knees. She's sobbing. Behind her, white cloaks flutter inside her shop, and the first signs of fire flicker at the windows. We watch in silence, hearts in our throats, as the woman begs them for mercy. One of the Inquisitors prepares to strike her. Up in the windows

of nearby homes, neighbors look on. Their faces are pictures of horror. But they stay silent, and do not help.

Suddenly, the Inquisitor who is about to strike the woman tilts backward. As if a curtain of wind swept him off his feet. Then he's yanked, shrieking, high into the air, past the roofline of the buildings. My eye widens. *Windwalker.* The Elites are here. The Inquisitor hovers in the sky for a moment—and then plummets to the street with a sickening crunch. Violetta flinches and turns into my shoulder. At the same time, the flames in the shop vanish without a trace, leaving nothing but black smoke curling from the building. Other Inquisitors shout in alarm. But wherever the Daggers were, they're already gone. I shrink farther into the shadows, suddenly terrified that they will find me.

In the distance, we hear several *malfettos* in the street call out, "The Young Elites!" The woman on her knees screams, "They're here! Save us!"

Others chant the same. The desperation in their voices raises the hairs on my neck. But nothing else happens. The Inquisitors sweep the streets, looking for them, but they are nowhere to be found.

"We have to get out of here," I whisper. "Follow me. We're going underground."

And with that, Violetta and I backtrack out of our alley and flee down a quieter path, away from the carnage.

By the time the sun finally rises, we arrive at the streets in front of the Fortunata Court. I freeze, unwilling to believe what I see. The place, once a crown jewel, is now charred and

destroyed, ransacked by Inquisitors. Blood stains the street at its entrance. The Daggers must be gone too—all their plans, their mission to assassinate the king, their safe house, destroyed. In one night.

There's nothing left.

When the Aristans conquered the Salans, they took everything
with them, their jewels, their honor, and their children,
sometimes straight from the womb.
—*Journal chronicling Amadera's First Civil War, 758–762,
by Mireina the Great*

Adelina Amouteru

I didn't dare step back inside the Fortunata Court. I didn't
know if there were still Inquisitors combing through
the rooms there . . . and I didn't know if I'd be ready to see
whether or not the Inquisitors found the Daggers' secret
chambers. Whether or not there are any bodies inside that I'd
recognize. I didn't *want* to know.

Instead, I took Violetta's hand and led us down to the only
place where I thought we'd be safe. The catacombs.

From deep within the tunnels underneath the city, the
roar of people aboveground sounds like a strange, muted
echo, whispers of the ghosts that must haunt these dark, narrow corridors. Faint shafts of light come from small gratings
at the top of the corridor, and the dimness of a rainy morning paints everything in a haze. I don't know where else to

go. We've been down here for a full day since we fled the Fortunata Court's ashes, hiding in the midst of death. From here, we heard Teren's voice ringing out across the palace square, saw Inquisitors swarming through the city streets. The memory of last night leaves a nauseating, aching feeling in my stomach. I should've stopped and helped the people in the streets. But I had no strength.

What has happened to Enzo, now that the court is ruined and the king is dead? What will they do now?

We can't stay here long. Maybe the Inquisition has discovered the Fortunata Court's secret passageways and uncovered the Daggers' access to the catacombs. Maybe they are searching through the tunnels now, hunting for us. For now, though, we rest here, too exhausted to continue.

"Are you all right?" I ask my sister as we both lean wearily against the wall. My throat's parched, and my words come out weak and hoarse. Above, the sound of gentle rain muffles my words.

Violetta nods once. Her eyes are distant, studying the new white mask that covers my missing eye.

I sigh, then push stray hair away from my face and start braiding the strands. Long minutes of silence pass between us. I braid, then unbraid, then braid again. The silence between us drags on, but somehow it's a comfortable one that reminds me of the days we used to spend in the garden. Finally, I look at her. "How long did Teren have you imprisoned like that?"

"Since the day you escaped your execution," she whispers back. It takes her a while to continue. "The Inquisition in Dalia searched for you for days. They scoured the city for other *malfettos* with silver hair. They killed two other girls." She looks down. "They were already stationed in our home, so I couldn't leave. Then Teren came and fetched me. He told me he was taking me to the port capital."

"Did he . . . hurt you?"

She shakes her head. "No. Not physically."

"Did he have any idea that you have powers?"

"No," Violetta whispers.

I struggle up to a better sitting position, then firmly fix my gaze on her. She props herself up on her elbow. "Did *you*?"

Violetta's silent for a moment. In her eyes, I see the truth. "You *did* know," I whisper back. "When? How long?"

Violetta hesitates and pulls her knees up to her chin. "I've known since we were little."

I'm numb. I can't breathe.

"I found out by accident one day. I didn't think it was real, at first," she said, meeting my gaze timidly. "After all, I had no markings. How could I possibly be a *malfetto* with demonic"—she pauses—"with unusual powers?"

I try to ignore the buzzing in my ears. "When?"

"The day Father broke your finger." Her voice turns quieter. "Do you remember when you pulled away from him? You wanted to hide behind a dark veil, *literally*. I could feel it."

Only Raffaele can do that. "You could *sense* me?"

Violetta nods. "That day, I knew instinctively that I didn't want you to do something to anger Father even more. I knew that if you were to do something extraordinary, he'd have you killed, or sold, or worse. So I reached out . . ." She pauses for a moment, as if trying to figure out a good way of explaining herself. "And I *pushed back* on you. I stopped you."

In a flash, Raffaele's words come back to me. *There is something dark and bitter inside you.* Is this where all of my terrifying thoughts come from? Do they originate from so many years of pent-up energy, yearning to break free?

It all makes sense now. Raffaele wondered why my powers didn't surface earlier in life. They did. I just never knew it, because Violetta always suppressed them. She came down with a fever the day after that first incident, I recall.

And hadn't I used my powers for the first time on the *one* night that we were separated? Hadn't I felt like a mantle was lifted from me when I said my good-byes to Violetta? Hadn't I used my powers during my execution?

And *Raffaele*. I start to shake my head. "No. No, there must be something you're not telling me. We—the Daggers—had a Messenger, someone who could sense other Elites. He never sensed you. How could he have missed you?"

Violetta has no answer to this, of course. I'm not sure why I expect her to give me one. She only stares back helplessly. *Raffaele couldn't sense her,* I suddenly think, *because she must have unconsciously suppressed his power too.* It is the only explanation. To Raffaele, Violetta's power is invisible.

"When did you let me go?" I whisper.

Violetta's voice sounds hollow now. "When the Inquisition first arrested you, I reached out and pushed your powers away. I didn't want to think about you unleashing on the Inquisitors while you were in prison. I thought maybe they would pardon you if they couldn't prove that you did anything out of the ordinary. But then I heard about your pending execution—I saw them drag you out to the square. I didn't know what else to do . . . so I released your power. And you called on it." She lowers her eyes. "I don't know what else happened to you after the Young Elites took you away."

My heart hammers against my ribs. Away from my sister, I learned for the first time how to grasp on to that energy after training with the Daggers. Suddenly, I reach out for her hand and press it to my heart. "I want to see you do it," I say quietly.

Violetta hesitates. Then she takes a deep breath, closes her eyes, and *pushes*. I gasp. I feel it this time—as if someone were squeezing the air from my lungs, taking my lifeblood and pushing it down until it is invisible. Unreachable. I slump against the wall, dizzy. A strange emptiness hollows my chest. Odd. I don't remember ever feeling this in the past. Perhaps it's impossible to miss something you didn't know existed. Now I know, though, and now I feel its absence. I reach out tentatively for my energy, searching for the darkness that pools in my chest. A jolt of panic hits me when I can't feel it at all. I look back at my sister. "Give it back," I whisper.

Violetta does as I say. I suck in my breath as the air comes rushing back through me, life and darkness, addictive and sweet, and suddenly I can see the threads of energy again, I can feel the hum through my body and I know where to reach out in order to grasp at the strings. I sigh in relief at the feeling, relishing the pleasure it brings me. I test my powers, forming a small rose before our eyes and spinning it in a slow circle. Violetta watches me with wide eyes. Her shoulders slump a little more, as if using her power has taken all of her strength.

She can suppress an Elite's ability, and then release it again. All this time, my little sister has been sitting on a power that might dominate all others. A thousand possibilities rush through my mind. "You're a *malfetto,* just like me," I whisper, staring absently at the rose hovering between us. "An Elite *malfetto.*"

Violetta looks away. She's ashamed, I realize.

"How could you keep that a secret from me?" My voice is raspy with anger. "How could you let me suffer alone?"

"Because I was afraid too," Violetta shoots back. "I didn't want to encourage you, and I knew how things would go for me if Father knew about my powers. You had your ways of protecting yourself. I had mine."

All of a sudden, I understand my sister better. I always thought of her as the sweet, naïve one. But perhaps she wore her sweetness and naïvety as a shield. Perhaps she always knew exactly what she was doing. Unlike me, who pushed

people away, she protected herself by making people like her. *When people like you, they treat you well.* So she stayed quiet at my expense.

"I saw how Father treated you," she says in a small voice. Another pause. "I was afraid, Adelina. Father seemed to love me . . . so how could I tell him? Sometimes I imagined myself saying, 'Father, I am a *malfetto*. I have powers that don't belong in this world, because I can give and take away Adelina's powers.' I was a child, and I was terrified. I didn't want to lose him. So I convinced myself that I wasn't like that, that my lack of markings made me better. How could I tell *you*? You would have wanted to experiment, and Father might've discovered us both."

"You left me to fend for myself," I whisper.

She can't look at me. "I'm sorry, Adelina."

Sorry, always sorry. What in the world can you buy with an apology?

I close my eye and bow my head. Darkness swirls inside me, washing at the shores of my consciousness, hungry for release. All those years, I'd suffered alone, looking on as our father lavished attention on the one daughter he thought was pure and untainted, suffering his tantrums by myself, thinking my sister was unlike me, that she was pristine. And she had let it go on.

"I'm glad you killed him," she adds quietly. There is something hard about her expression now. "Father, I mean. I'm glad you did it."

I don't know what to say to that. I never thought I would hear such a thing from my sister's lips. It is this that softens the tight knot in my chest. I try to remember that she went to Teren to beg for my life. That she risked everything. I try to remember the way she used to braid my hair, the way she'd sleep in my chambers during a thunderstorm.

I can only nod.

The sound of commotion in the streets above us breaks through my thoughts. The bells at the Inquisition Tower are tolling. Teren must be getting ready to deliver a speech. We both listen for a while, trying to catch words from above-ground, but we can't hear anything properly. Only the bells and the sounds of hundreds of muffled footsteps.

"Something big is happening," I say. Then I motion for us to get up. We have to get to higher ground if we want to find out what's going on. "This way."

I lead us farther down the catacomb tunnel, until it branches off into three narrow corridors. I pick the left one. When we've walked fifteen paces, I stop and search for the small door embedded into the stone. My hand finds the rough gem in the wood. My energy activates it, and the door opens. We make our way up a tiny flight of stairs, until finally we find ourselves emerging through the wall that borders a dark alley at the edge of the main market square. We wander until the alley meets a side street, then peer out from the shadows at where the main square begins.

The square is crowded with people. Inquisitors line the

streets, funneling the people down, and in the canals, gondolas sit idle. No water traffic allowed this morning.

"What's happening?" Violetta asks.

"I don't know," I reply as I look from the crowd to the Inquisitors. We'll have to wait—with my powers sapped, we can't be out in the open with so many people around and risk being recognized by a guard. I hold my breath as a group of Inquisitors march past our narrow street. My back is pressed so hard against the wall that I feel like I can melt into it.

They pass by without noticing us. I let out my breath again.

I grab Violetta's hand and pull us through the shadows. We make our way forward, slowly and laboriously, through winding streets until we finally reach the space where the main square opens up. Here, we crouch in the shadows of a canal bridge entrance and look on as more people file into the square.

The space is crowded this morning, as if it were a market day, but the people are all eerily quiet, waiting in fearful anticipation for an announcement from the Inquisition Tower. My eye wanders up to the rooftops, where statues of the gods line the ledges. They are crowded with Inquisitors today, but even now—somehow, hidden behind tile and chimney, the Daggers must be waiting in silence.

I'm still weak, but the square's energy crackles with fear, vibrant and dark, and it feeds me.

A faint flicker of movement appears on the Inquisition

Tower's main balcony. A flash of gold robes flanked by white, the glimmer of a leader walking among his men. I tense. Moments later, Teren appears.

He wears formal robes, a shining coat of white armor under a flowing robe of swirling white and gold patterns. A heavy cloak is pinned over his shoulders and drapes behind him in a long train. The slant of morning light hits the balcony just right—a part of the palace's intentional design— and illuminates him in brightness.

Then I notice that he brought a prisoner with him. "Oh," I breathe, my heart seizing.

Two Inquisitors appear, dragging between them a boy with long dark hair, his slender frame weighed down with chains, his head tilted high as Teren now presses a sword against his throat. The boy's rich scarlet robes are torn and dirty. His face is solemn, but I recognize him immediately.

It's Raffaele.

It is my fault he's here.

Teren raises his free arm. "Citizens of Estenzia," he calls out. "It is with a heavy heart that I deliver this news." He pauses. "The king is dead. In his place, Her Majesty, Queen Giulietta, will rule. Tomorrow evening, the king's funeral will take place at the Estenzia arena. You are required to attend."

He pauses before continuing. "There will be changes to how we deal with traitors and abominations. Her Majesty does not tolerate crimes against the crown."

If Enzo had succeeded, he would have killed his sister, the queen, too. His nobles would have made their move, offering their support. He could be making his move *now*. But he won't. Not with Raffaele held hostage like this. And I realize, suddenly, that this is why Teren, not Giulietta, is addressing the crowd. She knows she has to protect herself.

The king's death begins to look more and more clear to me.

I look on as Teren tightens his grip on Raffaele. Raffaele winces as the sword digs into the flesh of his neck.

"Kneel," Teren commands him.

Raffaele does as he's told. His scarlet robes spill around him in a circle. The energy in my chest lurches painfully.

Teren nods at the crowd. "From this day forth," he says, "all *malfettos* are banned from the city. They will be moved to the city's outskirts and separated from society."

The crowd's silence breaks. Gasps. Mumbles. Then, shouts. Violetta and I just look on, our hands joined in fear. *What will the Inquisition do to them, once they're banished to the outskirts?*

Teren raises his voice over the chaos. "Anyone who turns in defiant *malfettos* to the Inquisition will be rewarded with gold. Anyone resisting this order, or found sheltering *malfettos*, will be executed."

Can I reach Raffaele? Can *any* of us? I study the square. It's impossible to get close enough without drawing attention, and with Teren holding Raffaele's life by the throat, we

can't afford to slip up. Too many Inquisitors surround the square for me to get anywhere close, especially in my weakened state. *We can't save him here.*

Violetta turns her head. A strange, thoughtful expression appears on her face. "There are other Elites out there," she whispers.

It takes me a moment to remember that her power means she can also do what Raffaele does—she can tell when another Elite is nearby. I glance abruptly at her. "Aside from Teren?"

She nods.

"How many?"

Violetta concentrates for a moment, counting. Finally, she replies, "Four."

Four. The others are here. Enzo is watching.

Teren scans the crowd as his voice continues to ring out across the square. "*Malfettos* are a scourge upon our population. They are lower than dogs. Unworthy." Teren bends down to grab Raffaele by his hair, yanks him back up on his feet, and presses his sword harder against Raffaele's throat. "People like this are a curse on our country. They are the reason why your lives are miserable. The more *malfettos* we get rid of, the better off our country will be. The better off *you'll* be." His voice rises. "Do you see this, Reaper?"

He's trying to lure us out. The crowd shifts, uneasy and on edge. People look up to the roofs and down the alleys. Just as they did at my burning.

Teren narrows his eyes. "I know you're watching. I've

heard that this worthless boy is precious to you. So I will make you a deal. Turn yourself in. If you don't, you will see me gut this boy right here on this balcony."

Enzo won't take the bait. We are completely trapped. I look desperately from Raffaele to the roofs where I think Enzo might be lying in wait, watching. There is no way to save him. None. We are going to watch him die.

Just as I think it is all over, a shout rises from someone in the crowd. Then, another. And up on the roofs, a shadowy figure stands up in front of the entire square.

It's Enzo.

His face is hidden behind his silver mask, but his words ring out clear and sharp. Cold with fury. I look on with my heart in my throat. "Let me make *you* a deal, Lead Inquisitor," he calls out. "And let us swear it here, on the gods. I challenge you to a duel. On the morning of the king's funeral, I shall meet you in open combat in the Estenzia arena. I shall fight you alone."

The crowd has gone completely still. They hang on his every word. Inquisitors on the roofs hurry toward Enzo, but I know he can disappear in the blink of an eye if any of them get too close. Teren must know it too, because he holds up one hand and signals for them to stop.

"If I win, Lead Inquisitor," Enzo continues, "then the Inquisition will release the boy you hold hostage. He will be pardoned of any accusations of wrongdoing and allowed to walk free, unharmed." There is a long pause. "If you win, then I will be dead."

It is going to be a fight to the death.

Teren and Enzo stay facing each other for a long time. Neither speaks. Finally, a slow smile spreads on Teren's face. He sends a single nod in Enzo's direction.

"Very well, Reaper. With the gods as our witness, let us duel."

Once upon a time, a prince fell madly in love with a demon from
the Underworld. When she disappeared back into the sea,
he ached so much for her that he walked into the ocean
and never returned.

—Kenettran Folk Tales, *various authors*

Adelina Amouteru

We head back to the safety of the catacombs. When evening starts to fall, stretching long shadows across the entire city, I finally dare to leave the tunnels again and lead Violetta farther into the city.

"Where are they headed?"

Violetta's voice is strained and breathless as she hurries along behind me, holding my hand. We make our way through the dark streets in a blind rush, relying only on what I remember of the city's layout. "They're growing fainter," she replies. "To the right. I think they might be going this way." She gestures toward where a series of buildings surrounded by archways begins. The university.

"That's one of their safe houses." I shouldn't be going back to the Daggers. But with Raffaele held hostage, and Enzo preparing to duel Teren tomorrow in the arena, I feel

the pull of the bonds I've formed over the past few weeks. My steps quicken. I cannot leave Raffaele to die like this. Perhaps Dante was the only one who wanted to get rid of me. Perhaps I can still be a Dagger, and they care about me, and I can still belong.

Lying to yourself again, my dear? My father's voice whispers in my head. I ignore him.

"This way," I say after a moment. We hurry on.

Finally, as we near the university, I pause to find the entrance to the catacombs again and lead us down. It will be too dangerous for us to get inside the university out in the open, while Inquisitors might be patrolling its halls. Through the catacombs, I find the worn stairs that lead up to the dark hall inside one corner of the university. I take the steps one at a time, careful not to trip. Behind me, Violetta is tiring fast. Her power must drain her much more quickly than mine does.

"They're here," she whispers.

I stop in front of the door at the top of the stairs, then place my hand on the gem embedded in the wood. It opens.

We emerge from the underground. The hall is so quiet that we can still hear the commotion outside the university's walls, the sounds of Inquisition patrols marching by, of raucous crowds. The next thing I hear are voices coming from within—voices that I know. I shrink into the shadows, and Violetta follows my lead.

The first voice I recognize is Lucent's. She sounds

frustrated. "He'll kill him before morning even comes—how can you believe a word he says?"

I pause for a second longer, collecting myself, and then I start hurrying toward the voices. Violetta follows behind me. They lead us into the university's main temple, where the doors are bolted shut. Light streams in from the stained glass high above us. And there, in the center of the looming space, stand several figures I know all too well.

They pause at the sight of us too.

I take a deep breath. Then I step out of the shadows.

※※※

"Where have you been?"

Lucent asks the question first. I have no idea how to answer. Where do I even start? Enzo requested a small room in the hall of the university temple's apartments for us, and now Violetta and I are holed up inside, resting on the tiny twin cots. Lucent stands at the doorway, questioning me with her arms crossed over her chest. Enzo sits in the lone chair in the corner of the room, while Gemma and Michel perch on the edge of one of the cots. Violetta stays close to me on the other cot, silent and still, trembling slightly. I'm glad she's too afraid to speak.

I glance at Enzo, who leans forward in the chair and rests his chin on top of his hands. He watches me in silence. "Teren threatened to kill my sister," I reply. "He was keeping her in the dungeons of the Inquisition Tower."

Enzo narrows his eyes. "When did your path first cross with Teren?"

Weeks ago. I can't bring myself to say it. "He threatened me during the Spring Moons, before he fought you."

Michel furrows his brows. "Why didn't you tell us?" he asks.

I hesitate. "I didn't think you would help me," I decide to say. And it's the truth. "It was too risky to involve everyone so close to the Tournament date."

Lucent sniffs and turns in the doorway so that I see her profile. She doesn't go so far as to accuse me of betrayal, but I can sense it in every line of her body. She doesn't trust me. Her respect for me has withered to make room for suspicion. I tell myself to stay calm. Even though Raffaele's capture is a large part of why I've come back to the Daggers at all, in this moment I'm relieved he's not here with the others.

He would probably sense the lies I'm weaving around myself.

My gaze wanders back to Enzo, who stays silent for a long time. He doesn't speak for me, but he doesn't speak against me either. Finally, he straightens in his chair and regards all of us.

"Teren is not going to keep his word," he says. "Make no mistake. When we duel tomorrow, he *will* use it as a chance to kill not only me, but the rest of us. He is not going to release Raffaele. He knows we will all be in the crowds at the arena, and he wants it to be the last standoff. He wants an all-out battle tomorrow."

Enzo is including me in the plans. I am still one of them.

"What exactly is the plan then, Reaper?" Lucent says. "The king is dead, and your sister has Teren under her thumb. The Inquisitors are rounding up every *malfetto* in sight. How do we take on Giulietta?"

"Giulietta will never show her face at the arena tomorrow," Enzo replies. "She'll be hiding somewhere, protected by her guards. Tomorrow morning, our remaining patrons will send their supporters to attack the arena. We'll rescue Raffaele, and I will kill Teren." His jaw tightens. "We are going to wage war." He glances at me. "I need your help."

When we kissed in the courtyard, I say to myself, *surrounded by rain and lanterns, did you mean it? What do you really want with me?*

Finally, I give him a small nod.

Beside me, Violetta stirs. Everyone's eyes shift to her. When she doesn't speak, I do it for her. "I brought my sister here not just to protect her," I say, "but because she can help us. She has something that can turn the tide."

Michel gives her a skeptical look. "Are you a *malfetto*?" He glances over her, searching in vain for a marking.

"She's an Elite," I answer. "I think she lacks markings because of what she can do." My gaze returns to Enzo. "She has the ability to take others' powers away."

Silence follows. And attention. Enzo leans forward in his chair, regards both of us thoughtfully, and then tightens his lips. I know that everyone is thinking the exact same thing.

Violetta can help us kill Teren.

"Well," he says. "Let's see what she can do."

Violetta's fever continues that night, a low burn that leaves her in a strange state of half consciousness. She murmurs for me now and then. I hold her hand until the whispers stop and her breathing evens out.

It's quiet in the university's temple hall. The others must have all retired to their chambers by now, although I doubt anyone is completely asleep. I want to venture outside, to get away from my sister for a moment and let the cool night air clear my senses. But the Daggers have locked us in our chamber. Lucent says it's for my safety, but I can sense the subtle hint of fear lingering behind her words. Walls are slowly rising between us.

The sound of steel ringing out in the hall catches my attention. I sit up, more alert now. For an instant, I think it might be Inquisitors. They've discovered our hideout here and are coming after us. But the more I listen, the more I realize that the sound is coming from one sword, its lonely sound echoing every few seconds from some distant chamber. I rise from the bed and press my ear to the door. It sounds like swordplay. I listen for a while, until it finally dies down.

Footsteps approach in the hall outside. I lean away from the door. Seconds later, a soft knock sounds out. It takes me a moment to answer. "Yes?"

"It's me."

Enzo's voice. I stay quiet, and a moment later I hear the lock click. The door opens a sliver to reveal part of Enzo's

298

face. He returns my stare for a moment before his gaze falls on Violetta's fragile form. "How is she?" he asks.

"She just needs rest," I reply. "I've seen her like this enough times. It seems to happen after she uses her powers."

"Come with me," he says after a moment. Then he leaves the door ajar and motions for me to follow him.

I hesitate, and for an instant I'm afraid that this will be the moment when Enzo finally gets rid of me once and for all. But he waits patiently, and after a while, I get up and follow him out of the chamber. One look at him sends a warm flush through me. He's clad in simple clothes tonight, his linen shirt hanging loose over his torso, its undone lacings revealing skin underneath. His hair is untamed and untied, a dark red mane falling slightly past his shoulders. One hand holds a sword. That's what the ringing sound had been in the hallway. Enzo must be practicing for the duel tomorrow.

I follow him down the hall with soft steps until we reach the door of his chamber.

We enter without a sound. In here, Enzo's figure is barely illuminated by soft candlelight. My heart hammers in my chest. I stand near the door while he wanders over to the tiny desk at his bedside and uses his energy to strengthen the candle's glow. His loose shirt reveals the skin of his lower neck. The silence sits heavily between us.

He gestures to the desk's chair. "Sit, please." Then he leans against the edge of his bed.

I sit. A long silence passes between us. Now that we're

alone, his eyes are gentle—not the hard, dark vision I'm so accustomed to—the same softness I'd seen when we kissed in the courtyard. He studies me. There's a cloud of fear hovering around him tonight, subtle but significant. Is he afraid of *me*? "Tell me. Why did you really run away?" he asks. "There was another reason, other than your sister. Wasn't there?"

He knows. A sudden fear floods through me. He doesn't know about Dante—how could he? He's digging for something else. Slowly, I let myself revisit the night when I covered the floor of my bedchamber with visions of blood, when I scrawled words of fury onto my wall. "Is it true?" I finally reply. "What Dante said to you in the hallway that night? About . . . getting rid of me?"

Enzo doesn't look surprised. He suspected my reason all along. "You were there in the hall," he says. I nod wordlessly. After a while, he clears his throat. "Dante's opinions were his own." Then, he adds in a softer tone, "I'm not going to hurt you."

Were. I shiver. Suddenly the room seems colder. "What happened to Dante?" I say.

Enzo pauses for a while, considering. Then he looks at me again. He tells me how they all scouted the city that night after seeing Inquisitors flooding the streets. How they split up. How all of them came back except one. How Lucent was the one to discover Dante's body in an alley.

The story stirs the whispers in my mind, calling them back to the surface so that for a moment I can barely hear Enzo through the hisses of my thoughts. *Dante deserved it*, the

whispers say. I murmur my condolences through a fog, and Enzo takes it all with a composed face.

How long can I keep up this lie?

We fall into a long silence. As the seconds drag by, I sense a new energy coming from Enzo, something all too familiar to me but foreign from him. I watch him for a while before I'm sure of what I'm feeling. *He's afraid.*

"Are you ready for tomorrow?" I whisper.

Enzo hesitates. It's so unlike him to have this aura of fear. It sends an ache through my chest, and I rise from the chair to move closer to him. Dante was wrong. I must mean something to him. He must care.

Enzo watches me drawing near. He doesn't move away. When I come to sit beside him, some of his tension seems to ease, and his expression softens, letting me in. "Teren's father taught me how to fight." He says it in a matter-of-fact way. "I am good. But Teren is better."

I think back to how the two confronted each other before— first at my burning, and then at the Spring Moons. Each time, their clashes lasted for mere seconds. What will happen tomorrow morning, when they face each other in a fight to the death?

"Has he always hated us so much?" I murmur.

Enzo gives me a wry smile. "No. Not always."

I wait for a moment, and soon Enzo begins talking again. He unveils the story of them as children, sparring together, and as I listen, the world around me fades until I feel as if I were standing in the palace courtyard from years ago, looking

on as a young prince and a Lead Inquisitor's son faced each other on a sunny afternoon. They were very young; Enzo was eight, Teren nine, both of them still unmarked. The blood fever had not yet hit Estenzia. Teren's eyes were a deeper blue back then, but lit with the same intensity. Beside them, the old Lead Inquisitor looked on and called out instructions as the boys dueled. He was careful not to criticize the crown prince, but his words landed harshly on his own son, hardening him. Enzo shouted at the man sometimes, defending Teren's skills. Teren would bow to Enzo after every match, complimenting him.

As I listen, I picture the difference between the two boys. Enzo himself must have still fought like a young boy, but Teren . . . his intensity sounded unlike a child's, even frightening.

"He struck as if to kill," Enzo says. "I liked training with him, because he was so much better than me. But he was not *cruel*. He was just a boy."

Enzo pauses, and the scene fades. "Years later, the fever swept through," he continues. "We both emerged marked. Teren's father died. After, I would wander into the courtyard and Teren would no longer be there, eager for afternoon sparring sessions. Instead, he spent his days muttering in the temples, mourning his father, building his self-loathing, taking in the Inquisition's doctrine that *malfettos* were cursed demons. I don't think he hated us, not yet, because neither of us knew yet about our powers. But I saw the shift in him, and so did my sister." His jaw tightens. "Ever since he became

Lead Inquisitor, he's hunted Elites, as well as those who help Elites."

Something in the way he says it sparks a memory. It takes all my strength to ask. "Daphne?" I say hesitantly.

Enzo looks up at me. A hint of something familiar dances in his eyes—and I wish I didn't know what it meant. The pain that comes from him, an emotion of darkness and anger and guilt and grief, glitters in the air as countless threads of energy.

"Her name was Daphne Chouryana," he says. "Tamouran girl, as you can tell. She was an apprentice at a local apothecary."

His words pick away at my heart, piece by piece, re-minding me that the things he loved about me might not have been me at all. He must have seen her in my face, in the olive of my skin. He must have seen her every time he looked at me.

"She would sneak illegal herbs and powders from the apothecary to help *malfettos* hide their markings," he goes on. "Dyes that temporarily changed hair color, creams that temporarily erased dark markings on skin. She was a friend to us. When we first discovered Dante, still wounded from battle, she nursed him back to health."

"You loved her," I say gently, sad for his loss and bitter for mine.

Enzo doesn't acknowledge this directly. He doesn't need to. "A *malfetto* prince is still a prince. I couldn't marry her. She wasn't from a noble family. It didn't matter, in the end."

I don't want to ask the details of what happened to her. Instead, I bow my head in respect. "I'm sorry."

Enzo nods back, accepting my condolence. "So it may go for all of us. We must move forward." He seems weary, and I wonder whether it has to do with thoughts of Daphne or grief over Teren. Perhaps both.

In the silence that follows, he leans toward me until we are separated only by inches. The glow in his eyes beckons me. There is a heaviness about them, a dark depth that I might never understand. He touches my chin. His heat flows through me again, and I realize how much I've missed it right as he bends toward me.

"I know who you are," Enzo whispers, as if he can sense the thought in my head. *Do you care for me only because of Daphne?*

No. He knows me. He cares for me because of who I am. The thought floods me with exhilarating speed, awakening all of my senses. His kisses are gentle this time, one after another, patient and exploring. His hands brush against mine, running up my arms, drawing me in. Nothing separates us except the thin fabric of my nightgown and his linen shirt, and when he pulls me into his embrace, his heat sparks against my skin. My alignment to passion roars, sending my energy hurtling through me, desperate to weave its dark threads into Enzo's own, ensnaring him. It makes me dizzy, the same way I felt the night in the alley, the night I am forcing myself not to remember. It is out of control. I can't stop it.

He pulls away. Then he leans his head against mine and

sighs. "Stay," he whispers. And I know that the aura of fear around him is fear of tomorrow, of what might happen to all of us, that perhaps he cannot save Raffaele's life, he cannot win against Teren, that in the morning he may step out of this place and never return. He is afraid, and it leaves him vulnerable tonight. I try to forget my own fears by putting my hands on his face, then running them down to clasp his neck.

After a moment, I nod without a word. He settles down beside me as I curl up on one side of the bed, and then he brushes my silver hair away from my forehead. Instinctively, I shrink away when his eyes settle on the broken side of my face, but he doesn't react. His fingers trail gently across my scars. They leave a path of warmth in their wake. It soothes me, leaving me drowsy. His eyes close eventually, and his breathing turns even. I find myself sinking into the comfort of early sleep too. I concentrate on the sensation until I feel nothing anymore, until I fall into a restless nightmare of demons, sisters, fathers, and words from a young Inquisitor with pale blue eyes.

I heard my sisters wailing through the night. They knew
what I had done, and they hated me for it.
                    —Dantelle, *by Boran Valhimere*

Adelina Amouteru

oday is supposed to be the first day of the Tournament
of Storms. Instead, it's an endgame with the Inquisition.

The main Estenzian square, usually left open and unclut-
tered, has been transformed into a sprawling marketplace of
makeshift wooden stalls and colorful flags, a sea of shops and
people that surrounds the main arena looming at the harbor.
But with today's Tournament now a funeral for the king and
a challenge to the Daggers, the atmosphere is ominous and
eerily quiet considering how many people are flooding in.
Here and there, lines of Inquisitors observe the masses. Teren
wants the public to see us dead, right before their eyes.

I walk with Violetta through the crowds. No invisibility
right now; it's too hard for me to hold such a shifting illusion
for as long as we'll need it—and with this many people, we'd
draw suspicion the instant others bump shoulders with us.

I have to save my energy for our attack. Instead, I've woven the illusion of different faces over each of ours. I changed my dark eye and the ruined side of my face into a flawless visage with bright green eyes, each of them framed with blond lashes instead of silver. I adjusted my skin color from dark olive to light cream, my lips to a pale pink blush. My hair looks red-gold, and my bone structure is different. Violetta, too, now has skin as fair as a Beldish girl's, and her dark hair is instead a coppery blond.

We are still not perfect images. I never had time to train myself in mastering the illusion of faces, and even though I'm improving rapidly, there are little things that seem off and unnatural. It should work, if no one stares too hard — but people who linger too long on our faces will frown, because they will know that something is off about us. So we move on.

By the time we've reached the general vicinity of the arena, sweat is running down my back.

The arena is enormous, perhaps the largest structure I've ever seen, rows and rows of archways stacked upon one another in a giant ring of stone. The number of Inquisitors grows as we near the arena. Teren has stationed an army of enforcers here. I try to keep my face down as much as I can, to imitate the rest of the crowd, and shuffle past the Inquisitors without looking at them. I half expect them to recognize me, to see through my shimmering illusion, but they seem to buy my appearance whenever they peer down at my face.

They are searching for the Daggers' allies. Threads of fear blanket the entire square, thickening right in the center of the arena.

"Stop," an Inquisitor says to me. I pause, remembering to look bewildered, and peer up at the Inquisitor. He stares down at my face. Beside me, Violetta stops moving. I suck in my breath and focus all my concentration on solidifying my illusion, emphasizing the subtle movements of my face, the pores of my skin and the details of my eyes.

The Inquisitor frowns. "Name?" he grunts.

I lift my chin and give him my most confident look. "Anne of House Tamerly," I answer. I nod at Violetta, who curtsies prettily. "My cousin."

"Where are you staying?"

I rattle off the name of a local inn I'd seen during the qualifying races. "My father is doing business in Estenzia for several months," I add. "We heard this morning that the king's funeral may also involve an excecution. Is it true?"

The Inquisitor casts me another dubious look, but people are crowding behind us and he has no time to waste. He finally grunts his approval at us and waves for us to continue. "Nothing you Beldish would appreciate," he answers. "Carry on."

I don't dare look back, but behind us, I hear him turn his attention to questioning the next person.

The arena had been built to hold tens of thousands of people. The archways stretch up toward the sky and down into

the ground, so that even though we entered the space from ground level, we now stand along a row of stone benches looking down at dozens of rows below us, benches that wrap around the arena in circles before ending at the bottom in a wide, central space. Hordes of people mill in the aisles. *Among them are our patrons' soldiers.* I can't tell which ones they are, but they are here, scattered and hidden among the masses. Waiting for Enzo's signal. I crane my neck, searching for him. Violetta shakes her head, letting me know she doesn't sense him nearby.

"Come on," I whisper, tugging her hand. "Let's get closer." We head down the rows until we are almost at the very bottom, then take our seats in the first row.

Before us stretches the arena's center. It is flooded with water, a deep lake with channels that filter out into the Sun Sea; the dark shapes of baliras swirl underneath the surface. Cutting above the lake is a wide strip of stone path stretching from where Violetta and I sit to the other side of the arena, with a larger round platform in the very center. During a typical celebration, balira riders will wait along the platform and call for their baliras, and when the enormous creatures burst from the water, the riders jump onto their backs and perform stunning acrobatics to a cheering audience. Masked revelers in elaborate costumes would parade along the path, magnificent in their glittering colors.

Not today. Today, white-cloaked Inquisitors line both sides of the stone path. In the water, baliras circle, their calls

muted, haunting and ghostly. I turn away, then scan the rest of the filling arena. There's a cloak of fear and anxiety that blankets the entire space. Some of the onlookers seem excited, restless for the promise of blood. Others stay seated, with their mouths pulled into grim lines, whispering among themselves. My restlessness rises with them. Threads glitter in the air, tempting me.

My breaths are starting to come in shallower gasps as I continue to hold our illusions steady across our faces. Violetta touches my shoulder. She nods toward the opposite end of the arena. "There," she whispers. I follow her gaze. *Enzo is somewhere in the crowd.*

The Daggers should all be in position by now, along with their supporters.

Finally, after what seems like hours, all the Inquisitors lining the arena draw their swords and hoist them into the air for a traditional salute. The crowds hush. I look toward the royal pavilion, where the king would have once appeared with his crown and golden cloak.

Instead, the pavilion stays empty. And at the far end of the arena, Teren strides in with Inquisitors flanking him. A helmet shields his eyes from view, transforming him into the fearful image of someone not quite human. Right in front of him, weighed down in chains and guarded by more soldiers, with a blindfold over his eyes and a gag in his mouth, is Raffaele. My heart begins to pound.

Teren stops in the middle of the arena, then holds up his hands to the crowd. "My fellow citizens!" His voice echoes

around the central structure. "It is with a heavy heart that we gather here today, not in celebration, but in mourning of our king's death." Not far from him, Inquisitors force Raffaele to his knees, draw their swords, and press the blades against his neck. "Your queen leads you now, Kenettrans. And with this new era, you will witness a historic moment, when our great and glorious nation is cleansed of the demons that have haunted us. That have tried to bring terror down on us."

Beside me, Violetta grips my hand tighter. I look down and see that her knuckles have turned white.

Teren turns in a grand circle, his white cloak trailing, and smiles at the quiet audience. "Reaper!" he shouts. "A deal is a deal. I have your little consort-friend here"—he pauses to bow tauntingly in Raffaele's direction—"and we are both waiting for you. Come out, demon." His smile fades, replaced with a chilling blankness. "Come out, so we can play."

I hold my breath. For a moment, nothing but silence blankets the crowd. The people shift uneasily, their eyes roaming for a sign of Enzo. My attention shifts to the long row of Inquisitors lining either side of the stone path over the water.

One of the Inquisitors near Teren breaks from the formation, then walks forward until the two stand barely ten feet apart. Some of the Inquisitors draw their swords—but most hesitate, thinking that the man is still one of them.

I grit my teeth and release the illusion of disguise on the newcomer. A sense of relief glides through me. Before everyone's eyes, the Inquisitor gradually transforms from

a white-cloaked figure to a tall boy in dark robes, his face hidden behind a silver mask and his hood pulled low over his face. Enzo.

Inquisitors lining the platform draw their swords, but Teren holds up a hand. He turns toward where Enzo now stands up. The crowd ripples with shouts, and I close my eye, savoring the wave of their fear. My strength builds.

The two face each other for a moment, neither speaking. Finally, Teren tilts his chin up. "How do I know this is your true self?" he shouts. "Is your little illusion worker hiding the other Elites here too?" Behind him, the Inquisitors press their swords tighter against Raffaele's throat.

"You know who I am," Enzo replies in a clear voice.

"Why should I believe you?"

"Why should *I*?" Enzo's tone turns mocking.

Then, Teren reaches up and removes his helmet, revealing his wheat-blond hair. He tosses the helmet away. "Show me who you really are, Reaper," he calls out, nodding at Enzo's silver mask. "Or your friend dies."

Enzo doesn't hesitate. He reaches up and pulls the dark hood of his cloak from his face, exposing his bloodred hair. Then he puts his hand on his mask, pulls it away, and unveils his identity to the crowd. He, too, tosses the mask aside.

"A deal is a deal," Enzo calls back.

Teren stares at him with a stony face. The crowd looks on. Everyone around us is stunned into silence. I sway, dizzy from the building tension. Our illusion of disguise shimmers at the edges of my vision.

"It's the prince!" someone shouts from the arena.

Others take up the cry, and the revelation rips through the audience. Even though I can feel the overwhelming fear darkening the people, I can also sense the crackle of excitement, the emotions from *malfetto* supporters in the crowd and our own patrons' fighters. Through the confusion, Teren nods at Enzo.

"No one will interfere," he shouts. "I will face you alone, as long as you are bold enough to do the same."

Enzo bows his head once in response.

Teren is lying. But so are we. This is a battle poised to erupt.

"It's been a long time, Your Highness," Teren says, pointing his sword at Enzo. I would have expected his tone to be mocking, but instead he's serious. Not a hint of amusement is in his voice. To my surprise, he bows his head at Enzo in genuine respect. "Let's see if you've gotten any better."

Enzo pulls long, gleaming daggers from the sheaths on his back. The metal of each weapon turns red, then white hot. Fire explodes from Enzo's hands and wraps both of them in a large ring, separating them from everyone else. The audience screams.

Teren lunges forward.

Enzo strikes out with his daggers, aiming for the eyes, but Teren puts up his shoulder and shields his face—the blow deflects harmlessly off his hard skin. Enzo rolls away, hops back to his feet, and whirls on his enemy again. They circle each other in a slow arc. Enzo twirls a dagger in one of his gloved hands.

"You seem hesitant this morning," Teren calls out. He strikes at Enzo with unnerving speed. Enzo dances out of the way, spins, and lashes out as hard as he can with both daggers. One of them manages to make impact, striking Teren somewhere on his side—but it looks as if someone were trying to stab through soft wood. Teren grunts, but the instant the blade leaves his side, he grins.

"Use your fire, Reaper," he taunts. "Give me a challenge."

Enzo attacks again. This time, his blades burst into flames, carving streaks of fire in the air as he lunges for Teren. He feints left, then twists in midair and slashes out at Teren's face. Sure enough, Teren jerks his head away from the blow—but Enzo moves along with him, twin blades burning, anticipating where he'll turn, and brings his second dagger viciously up toward Teren's eyes. The Inquisitor darts away barely in the nick of time. Enzo's blade scrapes against the side of Teren's cheek, leaving a gash that closes right up.

Teren smiles. "Better."

My turn. With a deep breath, I drop the disguises on Violetta and myself, then immediately cloak us in invisibility. Around us, people gasp in shock—but we are already on the move. I hurry to the small gate at the edge of the row, which leads into the lake's pathway. We cross over. Inquisitors line the pathway, poised to attack if given the command. I carefully make our way forward.

"Tell me," Enzo calls out over the roar of the flames. "Why do you turn your back on others like yourself?"

Teren doesn't reply right away. Instead, he draws his

sword and strikes out at Enzo. Enzo leaps to the side, but not before the sword's blade nicks a line in his arm. He conjures a burst of fire that swallows Teren whole—but Teren doesn't show any sign of pain. He steps out of the flames with a wicked smile, his skin crisping, darkening, and then returning to normal. The edges of his cloak fray and burn from the heat, but the clothes in contact with his skin stay untouched, as if behind some shield of protection.

"I never turned my back," Teren calls out. "I am the only one willing to help. Look at what we're doing right now, Reaper—our powers are curses from the Underworld, and we use them to destroy everything we touch."

"Destruction is a choice." Enzo raises one hand, calling the flames hotter, brighter, until the fire turns blinding white and engulfs Teren entirely. *If Teren can't see, he can't attack.* Enzo hefts a dagger. The fire suddenly vanishes—and in the abrupt absence, Enzo flings the dagger at Teren's eyes.

Teren deflects the dagger with his sword, then catches the dagger in midair and throws it back. Enzo ducks to the ground in a graceful sweep. "I am cursed, just as you are. Yet, while *you* continue to defend those born from the leftovers of the blood fever, *I'm* doing what the gods always intended." Teren's pale eyes seem to soak in the flames that surround them, shading them a terrifying color. His lips curl into a snarl.

Enzo pushes against Teren's blade. His muscles bulge under his sleeves. Teren is simply too strong—I can see Enzo's strength slowly ebbing away. Still, I can hear Enzo's voice

ringing out over the melee. "Perhaps you do it because you love your powers," he shouts, mocking, "and you want to be the only one with such a gift."

Teren's smile vanishes. "How little you know about me, Your Highness," he replies. "Even after all these years."

Enzo lunges forward and slashes at Teren's eyes. This time, his blade manages to cut the edge of Teren's eyelid before he darts away. When he looks at Enzo again, blood smears the film over his left eye, turning the pale iris bright red.

Teren launches himself at Enzo. He sidesteps with him, then plunges a dagger deep into Enzo's shoulder. I gasp. The flames around them falter. He shudders—but still manages to yank himself away. The blade tears out of his shoulder. Violetta and I are now so close that I can feel the heat from the fire. We are in position. *Is everyone else too?*

Teren's eyes burn. Enzo steps in front of Raffaele and turns to face Teren again, ready for another attack. Blood drips from his shoulder. Then—he raises a dagger high in the air and waves it once.

Our signal.

Several things happen at once. Arrows hit the two Inquisitors holding Raffaele down. A curtain of wind smashes into the other Inquisitors nearest Raffaele—it flings them all into the water in a chorus of shrieks. From deep within the lake, two baliras explode from the surface, translucent bodies arcing over the path where Violetta and I are crouching. I flatten against the stone. My sister follows. The baliras send

tides crashing against the platform, and rain down glittering water across the entire arena. Their eyes are black with fury, their calls thundering. One of them flips in midair, its enormous fleshy wings coming down on a line of Inquisitors at the end of the stone path. They are swept into the water. Another enormous wing sweeps right over our heads, flinging away the Inquisitors closest to us.

The other balira has a rider on board. Gemma. I look on as her creature turns, allowing her to reach down and clasp Raffaele's arm. She pulls him to safety on board the balira's back.

Our turn. Violetta reaches out with her energy at the same time I reach out with mine. She pulls Teren's powers away from him. Out on the platform, Teren's eyes bulge—he stumbles backward a step, then crouches down on one knee as if someone had struck a violent blow. Violetta sucks her breath in sharply. She won't be able to hold his powers back for long.

I drop our invisibility. For the first time, we are exposed in the arena. I focus all my concentration and reach out for Enzo's energy. In a flash, he transforms from himself into an exact copy of Teren.

The arena bursts into a scene of chaos. All across the stands, patrons and their fighters leap into combat, attacking Inquisitors wherever they stand, sending the people into a panic. Some of the Inquisitors still on the stone pathway in the arena's center look poised to join the duel between Teren

and Enzo—but with the two now identical, they can't seem to tell which one is which.

Enzo doesn't wait. He leaps forward, dagger raised. Teren manages to hold up his sword just in time to meet Enzo's blade, but in his sudden weakness, he can't deflect it. The two tumble backward onto the ground—Teren shrieks as Enzo's blade finally makes contact, white hot and sharp, slicing deep into Teren's shoulder and burning his flesh. Enzo's second blade seeks out his heart. In a rage, Teren slashes out at Enzo. Even now, he still manages to force the prince to dance away. He staggers to his feet. It takes me a moment to realize that he's laughing. He notices Violetta and me crouched at the edge of the platform. He scowls.

"About time you made your move," he shouts through the chaos.

The words have scarcely left his mouth when I notice that Inquisitors, hundreds—*thousands*—of them, are flooding into the arena. We were ready for him—but he was ready for us too. The people around us leap to their feet, screaming, and scramble for the nearest exit, but Inquisitors fence everyone in. It will be a bloodbath in here, whether or not we win.

I narrow my eye. The darkness building in me is overwhelming now, feeding on an entire arena's worth of terror and fury. I reach out, take hold of that energy, find Teren, and *pull.*

He freezes in mid-attack, then falls to his knees. He shrieks in pain as I conjure the most agonizing illusion I can muster.

Enzo engulfs him in flames, then lunges forward, aiming at his eyes.

This is it. My heart leaps in anticipation. *He's going to kill Teren.*

Something cold pushes violently back against my energy. I gasp. Teren's fighting me. My illusion on him wavers, then breaks. Violetta puts a hand on her forehead and stumbles backward. "I can't hold on," she says hoarsely to me, before collapsing to her knees. Out in the arena, Teren sucks in a deep breath of relief as his burned skin starts to heal over. He starts fighting back. The window to fatally injure him is closing. I look at my sister. Her eyes roll back, and, exhausted, she faints on the path. My concentration flickers.

"Violetta," I shout, grabbing her arm. Then I glance to where Enzo is fighting Teren. My illusion over Enzo has vanished too, and his dark-robed figure contrasts starkly against Teren's white uniform.

"Leave her!" When I look up, I see Michel standing over us, his eyes wild. He has joined us on the platform. He hoists Violetta up against him. "We've broken through one of the entrances—I'll get her out. Go!"

I hesitate for a split second before nodding. Then Michel spirits her away, and I turn back to the arena. Never in my life have I seen so many Inquisitors. Their figures swarm the stands, clashing with Enzo's fighters. In the chaos, I climb over the short wall separating the seats from the arena's center, land on the stone path dividing the water, veil myself

in invisibility, and rush toward where Enzo and Teren are fighting. My concentration snaps back into place, fueled by the panic, and Enzo again turns into a mirror image of Teren.

But I'm getting tired too. My powers are starting to slip out of my control.

I stop a short distance from them. Then I press my hands together, reach out, and weave a circle of energy threads around Teren. I conjure a dozen versions of himself, identical in every way, each of them lunging at the real Teren with daggers drawn. The illusion is brief, but it works. Teren hesitates for a moment, suddenly unsure of where to look. His enemy is everywhere all at once.

Enzo—the real Enzo—grabs Teren around his neck. He tries to stab at his eyes, but Teren manages to twist his face away at the last second. Enzo's blade slices across his neck, leaving a deep gash. Immediately, it starts to heal. Teren lets out a gurgling growl and slams his head backward, forcing Enzo off him, then staggers forward and spits blood from his mouth. I can't hold the dozen illusions anymore. The figures disappear, once again leaving Enzo alone with Teren.

Teren is breathing heavily. Even he has his limits. His eyes lock on to me again. I realize that I'm too tired to hold my own invisibility illusion.

"There you are," he says, his voice low and raspy, his chiseled face turned into a frightening snarl. His attention flickers away from Enzo as he dashes for me. "Little illusion worker."

Then it happens.

Teren lunges for me. His sword slashes me deep across my chest, slicing through my robes and into my skin. Pain hits me everywhere. I fall. My head hits the ground hard enough to send the world spinning. Suddenly, everything slows. I lift my hand and see it stained with my own blood. I try to reach for my energy, but everything moves too slowly, and my thoughts form in disjointed pieces. Broken illusions flash around me, my powers gone unsteady and uncontrolled. Through it, Enzo rushes forward to step between the two of us. *I have . . . hit my head . . .* Teren rushes at me with his sword. All I see are his pale, furious eyes. A nightmare.

I strike blindly out with my illusions. Teren's there, blurred before me. I try to scream at him—but I cannot form the thought. My powers spark wildly out of control. Teren's face changes into Dante's, then back again. A memory clicks into place. I suddenly see before me a million glittering threads. *I killed him in that dark alley, on the night the king died. I killed with an illusion of extreme pain.*

I reach down into my chest, find the last of my strength, and pull on Teren's energy. Let him feel agony like he's never known. Let him suffer. I put everything I have into this, letting my hatred of him go unchecked.

Teren lets out a wrenching cry of pain. He falls to his knees.

Wait. This isn't right.

I blink, confused, trying to clear my hazy thoughts. My

illusions continue to work on him, wild and uncontrolled and untethered, blind. *Blind.* Then I realize—why am I able to affect Teren? He cannot be injured. And Violetta isn't here. to stop him.

And that's when I realize, in horror, that I have attacked *Enzo* instead. Enzo was the one who had blurred toward me—he had moved toward me in an attempt to protect me. *Enzo* is the one that I sent staggering to his knees.

I yank my powers back instantly, but it is too late. Teren— the real Teren—seizes the moment. He takes his sword. He plunges it deep into Enzo's chest. It runs all the way through, the bloody point emerging from Enzo's back right between his shoulder blades.

No.

Enzo lets out a terrible gasp. Teren's mouth tightens in triumph. He clutches Enzo's robes in one fist, then yanks him closer, shoving the sword in deeper. I cannot move. I cannot think. I can't even scream. My shaking hand reaches out for him, but I am too weak to do anything else. All my powers—undone in the one moment when they would have mattered the most. I struggle to regain control, but it makes no difference now. Enzo trembles on the blade. Teren pulls him close and bends toward his ear. Somehow, in the midst of the arena's chaos, the Lead Inquisitor's words sound clear.

"I win," he says. For a moment, their eyes lock—Teren's, pale, pulsing, mad; Enzo's, dark, scarlet, dying. Then he pulls his blade out. Enzo collapses to the ground. I run to his

fallen figure, as if *this* might just be an illusion—but he stays still and unmoving. Somewhere, Teren's voice reaches me. "Thank you for your help," he says.

I put my hands on Enzo's face. His name falls from my lips, hoarse with pain. I had lashed out at him with all of my fury—but was it rage meant for Teren, or was it really my internalized anger at *Enzo,* for using me, for leading me on? *Maybe there's still a chance.* He fights, with the last of his strength, to return my gaze. What do I see there? Is it betrayal? I'm sobbing now—tears fill my vision and spill down my cheek. There is nothing to be done.

Enzo looks at me. He blinks rapidly as he tries to say something, but blood froths at the edges of his mouth. He coughs. Red speckles land on my arm. I look on in disbelief as his eyes meet mine one last time. Then his life fades away. Just like that.

My mind goes blank. The world turns silent.

The sky above us flickers, then turns a furious shade of scarlet, a vision of blood, deep and dark. I crouch, my hands ripping at the ground, my emotions unwinding, my energy surging to a level I've never felt before. My gaze fixes on Teren. I hurl myself helplessly against his invincible power, trying desperately to grasp on to him in some way, to *hurt him, hurt him, hurt him.* But I can't. I'm useless.

He could slay me right now, if he wanted to. But he no longer wears his eerie smile or his cold amusement. He looks serious, grave, and thoughtful.

"You don't belong with them, Adelina Amouteru," he says. "You belong with me."

Somehow, somewhere—a curtain of wind lifts me up into the air. I struggle against it, wanting to stay in the arena. I want to destroy Teren. But I feel Lucent's arms wrap around me, then her pulling me up onto the back of a balira. Below us lies the wreckage of the arena, the dead and dying, the smoke and carnage, the white cloaks littered in clusters, the bodies of the dead who had fought for Enzo.

None of that matters now. The prince is dead.

Teren Santoro

Teren looks up at the fleeing Elites as they spirit away the prince's body. Behind them are Inquisitors on the backs of baliras, chasing them down. Teren watches a moment longer, picturing Enzo's dead face as they go. The young prince's face was gray and lifeless, eyes shuttered, heart still. Blood stains the ground of the arena's platform.

Teren stays quiet. He does not smile. Enzo, whom he remembered from childhood, the boy who always defended him in front of his father. What a shame that he was the Reaper, all along. *It had to be done. Dirty* malfetto. *Now the world is a better place, and Giulietta can rule.* Teren's face remains a portrait carved from stone, but deep in his chest, he feels a twinge of loss.

What a shame.

Trust is when we plummet into the depths of an abyss and
reach out for each other's hands.

—Amaderan Poetry, *various authors*

Adelina Amouteru

I fade in and out of a strange, disturbed sleep filled with ghosts. Or illusions? I can't tell the difference anymore.

Maybe there is none.

Sometimes I see my father hovering over me, his face distorted and smiling. Other times, Violetta's tear-streaked face appears. And Enzo. *Enzo.* He hovers there, a little too far away, and I cry out for him, struggling against invisible bonds to reach him. *He's alive. He's right there.* Shouts come from somewhere in the distance. *Hold her down!* I'm in too much of a daze to dwell on anything other than the enormous creature carrying us across the sky and the silence and still-ness of those riding with me. I want to open my mouth and say something. Anything. But my state of half consciousness muzzles me. I run a hand along my chest and feel a thick bandage there, trying gamely to lessen my blood loss.

My vision blurs as I try to look around at the others, but I can't focus enough to see who they are. I look back up into the evening sky and close my eye. The world has faded to gray with Enzo's passing. The only feeling I'm aware of is Violetta's hand in mine, squeezing, and I squeeze back with what little strength I have. A few strands of my hair crisscross over my vision—they are dark gray, the darkest they've ever been.

I have a vague recollection of us leaving the balira's back, and of my changing surroundings. Evening light slants through tree canopies, and fireflies dance in the darkness. Occasionally, I glimpse a rolling hill, a gentle valley full of deepening green. The gates of an estate. The outskirts of Estenzia?

A wave of nausea hits me, and I close my eye again. Sleep threatens to pull me under.

The next time I come to, I'm lying in a twilit bedchamber, the air blue and waning, turning into night. For an instant, I think I've gone back in time—I've returned to the moment when the Daggers first saved me and took me to the Fortunata Court. It even looks like the same chamber. If I wait long enough, I'll see the maid come in and smile at me, and Enzo will follow in her wake, his dark eyes pensive and wary, lit with slashes of scarlet. He will lean forward and ask me if I want to hurt those who have wronged me.

Slowly, the chamber shifts until it looks like an unfamiliar room. My illusions are happening spontaneously again. It takes me a long moment to realize that this is not the

Fortunata Court, but some strange estate I've never been in, and that I'm not alone at all, but surrounded by the Daggers. I groan, then turn to look at the person sitting closest to me.

The instant I move, everyone backs cautiously away. Blades appear in their hands. I freeze. Their gesture sends a brief course of excitement through me, their fear stimulating my energy. Then the feeling vanishes, replaced with a sharp pain. My former friends. *They're afraid of me.*

The person sitting closest to me is Raffaele. He is the only one who doesn't jump away. His bruises and injuries are still prominent, his cheekbone blue and purple, his lip marred by a thin cut. Scars circle his neck. When Gemma approaches to pull him away from me, though, he holds up a hand and wordlessly stops her. She backs away. I look at them all silently.

"Where's my sister?" I finally whisper. My first words.

"Resting." Raffaele nods once at me when he sees my alarmed expression. "She's well."

The divide between me and the other Daggers is thick in the air. I realize through the fog in my head that they still aren't sure what role I played in Enzo's death. The words make me wince. My energy stirs, and Raffaele tightens his jaw.

"You killed Dante, didn't you?" Lucent says. Her voice holds none of the wry amusement that I remember, none of the reluctant friendship and trust that I'd started to earn from her. Now there's nothing but anger, held back only in deference to Raffaele. I've lost her completely. "How'd you do it?"

I open my mouth, but no sound comes out. I had indeed

killed Dante. I did it by twisting his pain illusions so severely that his heart bled. My silence is all that Lucent needs—her lips tighten, and a veil of fear and unease blankets the room.

"It was an accident," I choke out. The only thing I seem able to say, apparently.

"Were you working with Teren?" Lucent snaps. "Is that where you disappeared to when you ran away? Did you go off to see the Inquisition? Did you make some sort of pact with them?" Her voice rises. "He *thanked* you over Enzo's body. *You*—"

"No! I can explain." The thought makes the anger rise in me, and my illusions threaten to veer out of control again. I clamp down on them in time. But the gesture makes Raffaele turn concerned eyes on me. Gemma studies me while chewing her lip. Fear comes off her too. My heart twists. "I would never. It was an accident. I swear to the gods."

"Well, Raffaele?" Michel says, cutting through the silence that follows. "What do we do with her now?"

The way Michel addresses Raffaele and the way Gemma obeyed Raffaele's simple hand gesture tell me that the Daggers have anointed a new leader. Raffaele shakes his head at me once. His eyes are heavy with sadness. "You said you could explain," he says. "So tell us what happened."

I start to tell Raffaele about how I'd cloaked Enzo in invisibility, but he stops me with a subtle hand. "No," he says. His voice turns firm. "Tell us what happened, from the *beginning*."

My lips tremble. The truth. I hesitate, as always.

But then I crumble. In a stammering voice, I finally do.

I tell Raffaele about the evening at the Fortunata Court, when I first saw him perform. I tell him how Teren came to me in the audience and threatened me with my sister's life. I tell him how I took advantage of the qualifying races to go to Teren and tell him about the Tournament of Storms. I tell him how Teren found me again during the Spring Moons, and how I overheard Enzo and Dante's conversation about me. How I fled to the Inquisition Tower to free my sister. How I killed Dante in a dark alley. The release of all of my lies and secrets is a relief, exhausting me. I tell them how Teren lunged for me in the arena, how I threw up my hands in defense and conjured an illusion of indescribable pain on him. How I realized I was not attacking Teren at all, but Enzo.

My voice falters here. The retelling leaves my heart so pained that I can barely breathe, and in my sorrow I see a ghost of Enzo flickering in and out of the room, his dark eyes turned toward me, his expression haunting. I can feel the suspicion emanating from everyone, their unspoken thought that I am responsible for what had happened. That I am a monster.

I am so sorry. So very sorry.

Perhaps Teren had always known that I would do something like this.

When I finish, they are quiet. Lucent stares at me with an expression both disgusted and frightened. Gemma has retreated behind her, and Michel looks ready to stop me in case I try to hurt them here. I know what they're thinking,

even though they don't say it out loud. They want me dead. It would make them all feel much better. A thick, dark anger begins to build inside me. I claw for it. More fog lifts from my mind. I feel sparks of strength growing in me, pushing past the weakness of my blood loss and grief.

Finally, Raffaele speaks. There is a certain reverence the group gives him—with his words, the others quiet immediately, turning to him as if hoping he has the power to set everything right again. His voice is weak, but steady. "When I first tested you," he begins, taking one of my hands, "you aligned with fear and fury, passion and curiosity. Do you remember?"

He is using his energy on me. I can feel his soothing pull on my heartstrings, the gentle tug that warms me to him, calming me. I find myself leaning into his touch, squeezing his hand harder. That afternoon when we'd first met doesn't seem like so long ago. "I remember," I reply.

Raffaele goes on. A certain sadness enters his voice. "Your reaction to the nightstone and amber, to darkness, frightened me. It frightened me very much. Still, I wanted to believe that, somehow, you would be able to tame it to your will. Do you know how powerful you could be, if you mastered these two emotions and learned how to use them both in yourself and in others? I believed. I thought . . ." He hesitates for a moment. "I thought your alignment to passion would save you. Passion's energy is bright and warm, just like the color of its gemstone. It is a light in the darkness, a fire in the night. I thought at first it would make you *safer*, that if you were

around those whom you loved, you would be able to use your darkness to your advantage. I thought it would help tame you, and subsequently, that it would help you."

Tears prickle the corner of my eye. I know what path Raffaele's words are going down.

Raffaele lowers his jewel-toned eyes. "I was wrong. Passion is bright and warm . . . but passion has a dark side too. It links with fear. Our hearts fill with terror at the thought of harm coming to our loved ones, don't they? You cannot have love without fear. The two coexist. In you, your alignment with passion instead *fed* your fear and fury. It made you *darker*. The more you love someone, the more unsteady your powers become. Your growing passion for Enzo made you volatile. It led to you losing control over your powers, powers that had grown to dangerous strengths. That, coupled with your anger and bitterness, has made you incredibly unpredictable."

"What are you saying?" I whisper through my tears.

Raffaele continues to pull on my energy, and his gentle touch sends waves of sadness washing over me. He feels guilty, I realize. "Adelina," he murmurs. *Oh.* I gasp in sudden pain. I'm surprised that *this* is what finally breaks my heart. He has never, ever called me just *Adelina* before, not even when we first met. He is breaking his affectionate ties with me. "I advised Enzo from the very beginning to kill you. He refused."

I begin to cry. A memory comes to me of my afternoon with Raffaele, when we sat together along the golden waters

of Estenzia's canals and watched the gondolas go by, when he sang me my mother's lullaby. *Dante was right*. Raffaele, kind, beautiful, sensual Raffaele, whom I cared about with all my heart, the only person in the world I thought I could trust entirely, the person I returned to the Daggers to help save, had never trusted me in return. *Kindness with strings attached*. He was the last thread suspending me in the light. Without him, I can feel myself spiraling downward, falling to a place where I can no longer pull myself back up.

"Even you," I whisper through my tears. "How could you?" I don't need to ask to know that Raffaele must have also suggested that Enzo kill the boy who couldn't control the rains. In some ways, Raffaele had always been the Daggers' leader. "Were we ever friends?" I say in a small voice. "Did you ever care about me?"

Raffaele winces. I can tell it pains him to tell me this truth, that even as he yearns to give me some comfort, he holds back and hardens his heart. "I stand by my advice to him. I trained you slowly because I didn't want you to embrace your full powers. I knew, early on, that it could bring all of us suffering—including you."

Who will ever want you, Adelina? Did you honestly think you could escape who you are? You will never fit in anywhere. My father's ghost materializes beside me, his breath heavy and cold against my skin, his familiar voice hissing in my ear. No one else reacts to his presence, though. He is an illusion that tortures only me.

"We can fix it," I say. My hand clenches harder around

Raffaele's. One last, frantic attempt. "You told me once that there were rumors of an Elite who could bring the dead back to life. Right?"

Raffaele shakes his head. "You're deluding yourself, Adelina," he says gently, and I know that he isn't talking about the impossibility of bringing Enzo back. He's talking about Enzo's love for me.

He cared. He risked his life for me. In desperation, I reach out with my energy and conjure an illusion of emotions around Raffaele, trying to convince him that Enzo loved me, if even briefly, if even in a moment of weakness—trying to convince him that *he* cares for me. My words come faster. "I'll learn how to rein in my powers—I promise, I can do it next time. Just give me one more chance."

Raffaele closes his eyes. I feel him resisting the illusion being woven around him. "Don't," he whispers.

"Please," I whisper back in a breaking voice. "You've always been kind to me. Don't leave me behind, I beg you. I will be lost without you. What will I do? How will I learn?"

When Raffaele opens his eyes again, they look glossy with unshed tears. He reaches out to smooth hair away from the ruined side of my face. "You have goodness in your heart," he says. "But your darkness overwhelms it all; your desire to hurt, destroy, and avenge is more powerful than your desire to love, help, and light the way. I have reached the limits of my knowledge. I don't know how to train you."

Beauty and pain go hand in hand, my father always said. For an instant, I fantasize about making Raffaele feel the pain

that he's giving to me, forcing him to cower before me in agony. How satisfying that would be. My energy swells in anticipation. Then I recoil in horror at the spark of joy I felt at such a depraved act. He's right about me. He's always been right.

Raffaele tightens his lips. Tears no longer shine in his eyes. Maybe I imagined them all along. "You can stay the night here," he says. "But in the morning, you and your sister need to leave. It is my job to protect the Daggers, and I no longer feel that we can be safe with you among us. I'm sorry."

He's casting me out. I'm no longer one of them.

Darkness swirls within me, washing at the shores of my consciousness. I see all the times I trained with Enzo, how he saved my life and took me in, how we kissed, the glow of his silhouette in the darkness, the way his hair would fall, loose and unruly, over his shoulders, his gentle expression. Then I see the stormy night when my father made a deal to sell me, the first time I called on my illusions in the middle of pouring rain, the real reason why Enzo chose to save me on my execution day, all the times I was hurt and abused, left behind and abandoned, the iron stake and the fire and the people chanting below, wishing me dead and gone, Teren's pale eyes staring back at me, the Daggers, my training, Dante's sneering face, Raffaele's betrayal. The ambition churning in me reaches its peak, displacing my sorrow, fusing with my anger and hate and fear, my passion and curiosity. The whispers that lurk in the back of my mind now claw their way out into the open, their fingers long and bony, gleeful

for the freedom I'm giving them. *Are the Daggers any different from your father, who wanted to sell you to settle his debts?* they hiss at me. *From Teren, who wanted to use you to get to the Daggers?* Even the training cavern, hidden underground, was not a far stretch from the Inquisition's dungeons.

Perhaps I'd simply switched one dark prison cell for another. No one ever gives me their kindness without hoping for something in exchange.

Are they any different?

Are they all the same?

They all want to use you, use you, use you until they get what they want, and then they will toss you aside.

Everything Raffaele saw in me on my testing day is true. Together, my alignments with energy swirl inside me, shifting and powerful. I am shaking.

Raffaele feels the rising power in me, because a note of fear hovers over him. Still, he doesn't move. He faces me with grim determination, refusing to back down. *Don't. Concentrate. Control it.* The only way to clamp down on my energy is to erase my emotions, and so I fold them each away, one by one. My sorrow turns to anger, then to ice-cold fury. My soul curls in on itself in defense. I am gone. I am truly gone.

I am not sorry.

"You have no right to judge me," I whisper, looking around at the others. "You belong to a society that thrives on murder. You're no better."

Raffaele only returns my look with his level gaze. He nods at the others to leave. Lucent starts to protest, then sighs and

casts me one last glare before following Gemma and Michel out the door. Raffaele and I are the only ones left in the room. For a moment, however brief, the gentleness on his face fades away to reveal something hard and dark.

"Murder is a means to an end," he finally says, tilting his head slightly at me. This time, the gesture looks more cunning than flirtatious. "Not an activity of pleasure."

If you cast me out of the Dagger Society, then I will form my own. I am tired of losing. I am tired of being used, hurt, and tossed aside.

It is *my turn* to use. *My turn* to hurt.

My turn.

"You're making a mistake," I say. My voice emerges flat and cold. The voice of someone *new*. "By not killing me now."

"No," Raffaele replies. "I'm not."

He finally stands. His hand separates from mine. He walks toward the door with his signature grace, then stops right before it.

"Adelina," he says, turning. The look in his eyes threatens to break me. "I loved him too."

Then he leaves me, and I am truly alone.

I pledge myself to the Rose Society until the end of my days,
to use my eyes to see all that happens, my tongue to woo others to
our side, my ears to hear every secret, my hands to crush my enemies.
I will do everything in my power to destroy all who stand in my way.
    –The Rose Society Official Initiation Pledge, *by Adelina Amouteru*

Adelina Amouteru

Night has fallen, and it is quiet again. Out in the estate gardens, a few candles flicker in mourning for Enzo. I don't know where the other Daggers are; perhaps they've long ago left this place. Perhaps they've fled to the Skylands, where Beldain might give them shelter. Tomorrow morning, things will be different—the uprising has been crushed, Giulietta will rule as the queen of Kenettra, and Teren will bring his wrath down on all *malfettos*. Enzo's supporters have gone into hiding to lick their wounds. Violetta and I will flee Estenzia. Where we'll go, I'm not sure. I'll settle in another port capital, perhaps, one far from here. Maybe I'll start my own society to strike back against Teren. Maybe we'll run across other Young Elites. The Daggers can't be the only ones.

I sit before the mirror of my vanity in my chamber, leaning weakly against my chair. My chest wound hurts every time I breathe. The knife tucked into my boot is my only remaining weapon, and now I take it out and set it on the vanity's surface, its point facing me. Through the window, I can see the dark blue silhouettes of the estate gardens. Enzo walks down there, gliding through the grass surrounding the main fountains. His sapphire robes trail behind him. I know he's not real, that it's only another vision that I cannot control.

Everyone will talk about me. Word of the prince's death is going to spread through the country like wildfire—Lucent has already sent doves to deliver the news to other Dagger patrons. People will say that the prince had fallen for me, and that I killed him in order to help Teren gain the throne. They will accuse me of tricking Enzo into loving me, and then trying to seize his position of power. I will be whispered about. I will have enemies lurking in every shadow.

Let them talk. Let their fear of me grow. I welcome it.

I stare silently at my reflection in the mirror, studying my long silver locks, the broken side of my face, all of it illuminated by the blue-white hue of moonlight. I think back to the night when I screamed at my reflection and shattered my mirror with my brush. Has anything changed since then? My father's ghost blurs in and out of the mirror's reflection, gliding behind me, his face a dark, menacing portrait. I try in vain to make him go away, but I can't. My powers overwhelm me, creating visions of things I don't want to see.

I suddenly seize the knife on my table. Then I grab a lock of my hair and frantically begin to cut it off. Strands glitter across my vision—for a moment, I can't tell if they are strands of energy or strands of my hair—and then fall, shining, to the floor. A strange fever seizes me; my wound twists in protest under my bandages, tearing open again, but I don't care. I hate everything about my markings, I want them gone, they have brought upon me all of the pain and suffering in my life, they have taken from me everything that matters. In this instant, none of my powers give me joy. I am still alone, broken and small, the butterfly fighting for life in the grass. Maybe it will be for the best if Teren wins. Let him destroy us all. Let our markings die out from this world and end our fight.

I have to get rid of this marking. Again and again I slice away, chopping off locks of my hair and spilling the broken strands all around me. In my frenzy, the blade nips at my fingers and my scalp, leaving cuts as it goes. I sway in my chair, then fall to the floor. Red blurs across my vision, mixing with the gray.

"Adelina!"

Somewhere in the midst of my frenzy is a small, clear voice. Then Violetta is here in my room, her smooth hands reaching for mine, her pleas falling on deaf ears. I jerk away from her grasp, jump to my feet, and continue to slash away at my hair. "Let go of me," I hiss, tasting salt and water on my lips.

Someone seizes the blade from my hands, leaving me helpless. In blind fury, I lash out at my sister with my illusions, trying to force her to return the knife to me—but Violetta wrenches my power away. The sudden rush of energy leaving my body robs me of my breath. I gasp, then brace myself against my table as my knees crumple. Violetta's arms are around me; she's lowering me carefully to the floor. All around us are locks of my hair, painted silver and gray by the moons. Violetta pulls me into a tight embrace. I cling desperately to her, terrified.

"I can feel myself losing," I whisper, my voice cut by broken sobs. "The darkness seeps in a little more every day. What have I done? How can I be like this?"

"I can make it stop. I can eventually learn to take it away from you forever." Her soft words cut through the angry voices poisoning my mind. She hesitates. "I can save you."

Teren's exact words come out of my sister's mouth. I flinch away. "*No,*" I snap. "Give it back."

Violetta's eyes glow with tears. "It will destroy you."

Let it. I don't care. "Give my power back, I beg you. I can't live without it."

Violetta studies my face. It is not often that I see our resemblance . . . but here, in this pale moonlight, her eyes become mine, my hair becomes hers, and the sadness on her face breaks my heart as surely as mine must break hers.

Finally, Violetta lets go; my energy comes rushing back to me, giving me life and freedom. I seize the threads and

hold them close. This is all I have that is mine. "Just leave me alone," I mutter over and over again. "Just leave me alone—"

My words cut off when Violetta wraps her arms around me again.

"Mi Adelinetta," she whispers in my ear. "Do you remember how we used to lie in the long grass, counting the stars as they emerged in the evening sky?" I nod against her shoulder. "Do you remember how we used to dance in Mother's old bedchamber? Do you remember how we used to hide in the closet and pretend we lived far, far away?" Her voice starts to tremble. "Do you remember how I sat up with you late into the night, binding your broken finger as best as I could? Do you remember?"

I nod, biting back my tears. *Yes.*

"You are not alone." She tightens her embrace. "All my life, I have tried to protect you."

And then I realize that all I ever wanted, kindness with no strings attached, had only ever come from Violetta. I do not know why I never saw it. In all this world, only she has done things for me, bad or good, with no thought of her own gain. We are sisters. Despite all we've been through, all that we have held against each other, we are sisters until death comes for us.

Something breaks inside me, dissipating the ugly whispers that plagued me moments earlier, and the gates holding back my tears break down. I hug Violetta fiercely, as if I might die were I to let go. Grief envelops me. I begin to

weave. I form an illusion all around us, a vision of things that I dream of and things that don't exist. The room shimmers and then disappears, replaced instead with the sun-drenched gardens of our old family home. My hair and lashes are no longer silver, but dark like my sister's and mother's, and my face is unbroken and perfect. Violetta giggles at me and tucks a flower behind my ear. Our father comes to greet us from inside the house—he is a whole and healthy vision, a fantasy of someone I never knew, with laughter in his voice, the scent of wind and wood on his coat instead of the familiar perfume of wine. Beside him is our mother, an amused smile on her lips, a vision of the women we will grow into. I run into their arms. My mother puts her hands on my cheeks and kisses me. My father hugs me and lifts me high in the air. He spins me around in a wide circle. I throw my head back and laugh with him, because I am his daughter and he is my father, and he is not ashamed of me. He loves me wholly, the way it should have been.

I hold the vision for as long as I can. I would have held it forever, happy to lose myself in it for the rest of my life.

Finally, I release the illusion. It slowly fades away around us, the sun and grass replaced with moonlight and wooden floors, my mother and father replaced with Violetta, her arms still wrapped tightly around me, her skin warm. I lean against her, weak and exhausted, bleeding, my energy spent. Neither of us speaks.

Tomorrow morning, I will lead us out of Estenzia. I will

find others like ourselves. I will turn us against Teren with such fury that he will beg for forgiveness. Tomorrow, I will take on all of these things. I will be unstoppable.

But tonight, we stay where we are, holding on, lost in the dark.

EPILOGUE

City of Hadenbury
Northern Beldain
The Skylands

Maeve Jacqueline Kelly Corrigan

Far north of the island nation of Kenettra, on the high Skyland plains of the nation of Beldain, Crown Princess Maeve dips her hands in holy water in preparation for a prisoner's execution. She squints up at the clouds covering the sky, then out at the long length of bridge that leads from her and the Hadenbury Palace gates out into the city. The winds are strong, for a summer day. They whistle against the gates behind her, singing some haunted tune, and the smattering of people who have gathered for the executions huddle closer together on either side of the gates, braving the cold and peering curiously over the heads of soldiers.

Maeve gathers her furs higher around her neck, bracing herself against the winds in front of the gates, and then turns her attention to the chained man groveling at her feet. Tiny ornaments dangling in her hair clink together in the wind. Third prisoner today. She sighs. *If I'm going to spend a*

day killing people, I should at least be on the battlefield. Shooting arrows into weak, staggering prisoners is no fun at all.

Behind her, in a perfect line, stand her six older brothers. At her side, her white Beldish tiger sits languidly, staring at the prisoner with lazy golden eyes, her fur long and thick and slashed with gold stripes. They match the fierce lines of gold painted across Maeve's own face. Amazing, really, how much a skinny adolescent tiger taken from the forests of the northern Skylands can grow in a year.

She leans a hand against the hilt of her sword. "Do you have a confession?" she says to the prisoner. Her voice rings out low, harsh, and grating, just like her mother's, loud enough for the audience to hear. "Speak, so that I may decide whether you are deserving of a swift death."

Maeve can barely understand the prisoner's reply through his sobs. He crawls as close to her as he can, until the guards flanking him shove him back. He manages to brush dirty fingers against the edges of her boots. "Your Highness," he manages to say through his shaking voice. He turns his head up to her, eyes wet and pleading, and wipes at the lines of dirt and blood painting his face. Maeve wrinkles her nose in disgust. Hard to believe this man was once nobility. "I have my confession. I—I have shamed this land which Holy Fortuna has blessed. I do not deserve to live. I—Your Royal Highness, I am your humble—"

"Your confession, Sir Briadhe," she interrupts, her tone bored. She wears her braids high in warrior fashion today,

fierce ropes of entwined locks that run along either side of her head, pushing her hair up like the hackles on a wolf's back. Half of her hair is dark blond; the other half is midnight black. The great goddess Fortuna, keeper of Beldain, had blessed her with this marking, among other things.

The prisoner's sobbing continues. He confesses through trembling lips, something about adultery and affairs, rage and murder, how he had killed his fleeing wife with a dagger in her back. How he kept stabbing her even after she was dead.

The audience murmurs in low voices as he speaks. When he finishes, Maeve's eyes sweep the scene, pondering the appropriate punishment. After a moment, she looks back down at the prisoner. "Sir Briadhe," she says. She pulls the heavy crossbow from her back. "I will make you a deal."

The man glances up at her, a sudden rush of hope lighting his eyes. "A deal?"

"Yes. Look behind you. Do you see this long bridge that we stand on? How it leads beyond the palace grounds and into the city?" Maeve nods off into the distance as she starts to notch an arrow to her crossbow. "Make it to the end of the bridge before I count to ten, and I will strip you of your title and let you live in exile."

The prisoner gasps. Then he crawls to Maeve again and starts to kiss her boots. "I will," he says in a rush. "I will, thank you, Princess, thank you, Your Highness."

"Well?" Maeve says as the man's guards haul him up onto

his feet. She tightens her grip on the crossbow. The guards step aside, leaving the man to sway on his own. "You had better get going."

She hefts the crossbow to her shoulder and begins to count. "One. Two."

The prisoner panics. He whirls around, picks up his chains, and starts to run as quickly as he can. He stumbles over his chains in his haste, but manages to catch himself in time. The crowd starts to chant, then shout. Maeve squints down the line of her crossbow. She continues to count.

"Seven. Eight. Nine."

The prisoner is too slow. Maeve lets her arrow fly. *Equal crime*, her mother always said, *equal punishment*.

It hits him squarely in his calf. He screams, then collapses in a heap. Frantically he pushes himself back onto his feet, then staggers onward. Maeve calmly notches another arrow, then lifts it and shoots again. This time, she aims for his other leg. It strikes true. The man falls hard. His sobbing pierces the air. The crowds cheer. The prisoner is a few yards from the last post—he starts to drag himself on his elbows.

Prisoners are always so damn desperate when they stare death in the face.

Maeve watches him crawl for a moment. Then she kneels down to her tiger. "Go," she commands.

The tiger pounces from her side. Moments later, the prisoner's wails change into high-pitched screams. Maeve looks on as the audience cheers. The sight brings her no joy. She holds up her hands for silence, and the shouts cut off sharply.

"This is no occasion for applause," she calls out in disapproval. "The queen does not tolerate cold-blooded murder in the great nation of Beldain. Let this be a lesson to you all."

One of her brothers straightens from his casual stance and taps her on her shoulder. Augustine. He hands her a parchment. "News from Estenzia, Little Jac," he says over the noise. "The dove arrived this morning." The nickname lifts Maeve's heart for an instant. It always reminded her of her childhood with her band of brothers, trailing after them in her furs and dresses, mimicking their swagger and hunting stances. Then her heart tenses. Lately, Augustine has only called her Little Jac when troubling news arrived, like when their mother first fell ill.

Maeve reads the letter in silence. It's from Lucent, and addressed not to the palace but directly to Maeve herself. She stays quiet for a long moment. Then she sighs in frustration. "Kenettra has a new ruler, it seems," she finally replies. She clicks her tongue in disapproval, then whistles for her tiger to return.

Her brother leans closer. "What happened?"

"The king was assassinated," Maeve replies. "Not by the crown prince, but by Kenettra's Lead Inquisitor. And the prince is dead."

Augustine leans back and rests his hand on his sword's hilt. "That changes our plans, doesn't it?"

Maeve nods without answering, her lips tight. She had hoped that being one of the Daggers' biggest patrons would mean that after Enzo took the throne, he would carry out his

promise of reigniting trade between Kenettra and Beldain. *If I'm to gradually win control of Kenettra, I'd rather do it without sacrificing thousands of soldiers.* Besides, she preferred to see someone who supported *malfettos* on the island nation's throne. But now the crown prince is dead. "It's a complication," she finally says. "Still, perhaps it will be easier this way."

"And what's this mention of a White Wolf?"

"Some new Elite," Maeve mutters, distracted, as she re-reads the letter. *Killing off Fortuna's chosen ones? Those Kenettrans get more barbaric every year.* She turns around and hands the parchment back to her brother. "Give this to the queen."

"Of course."

"And gather the others," she adds. *Time to call her Elites into action.* "If we still want to make a move, we'll need to do it soon."

Augustine folds his arms across his chest and smiles. "With pleasure, Your Highness."

Maeve watches him go. *Lucent.* She misses Lucent desperately, their intimate conversations and their friendly duels and their wild forest adventures. Lucent would track the deer; Maeve would deliver the killing shots. Lucent would scowl; Maeve would tease. Lucent would kneel to pledge her loyalty to the crown; Maeve would help her to her feet. Lucent would shy away from her kisses; Maeve would pull her back.

Lucent fled to Kenettra after the queen banished her; Maeve grew quiet and cold in her absence.

As the guards clean up after the execution, Maeve heads back into the Hadenbury Palace. Her brothers continue on to their mother's bedchamber, their voices excited as they talk about the news, but Maeve takes a different route that steers her away from the palace's apartments, out across the courtyards, and toward a small, separate manor. Her mother married two husbands and birthed seven sons before finally getting a daughter. Maeve has waited her whole life to step into her birthright . . . but becoming the queen of Beldain means that her mother will first have to pass away. She winces at the thought.

Still, she chooses to avoid visiting the dying queen with her brothers. Maeve was not in the mood for another lecture on choosing a husband so she could start birthing an heir.

Two soldiers standing guard at the manor house bow low to her. They escort her up the familiar halls until they finally reach a quiet floor. Here, Maeve takes the lead while the nervous guards stay several feet behind her. She approaches a narrow door with iron bars stretching across its wood, then pulls out a key strung around her neck. On the other side of the door, she hears someone stir. The keepers back away. Even her pet tiger refuses to get closer.

The lock clicks open. Maeve pushes aside the iron gratings and swings the door open with a faint screech. She enters alone, closing the door securely behind her.

The room is dark; shafts of blue light beam in from be-tween the windows' iron gratings. In the chamber's bed, a figure stirs at her entrance and sits upright. He looks tall and thin, his hair rumpled. Her youngest brother.

"It's me," Maeve calls out gently. The young man in bed squints sleepily at her. In the light, his eyes shine like two glowing disks, the color not quite of this world. He doesn't reply.

Maeve stops a few feet before the end of the bed. They stare at each other. She knows that if she opened his chamber door and gave a command, his eyes would turn black and he could very well kill everyone in the palace yard. But she doesn't, and so he remains quiet.

"Sleep well, Tristan?" she says.

"Well enough," the young man finally replies.

"Do you know what I heard today? Kenettra has a new ruler, and the country's Young Elites are at war."

"Tragic," Tristan replies. Somehow, over the last few months, his conversations had finally faded away into brief sentences. Every day, the light in his eyes grew more distant.

She swallows, trying to ignore the way his silence twists her heart. They were only a year apart, she and Tristan, and he used to be so talkative, to the point where she'd shout at him to leave her alone. They spent such long days in the forest with Lucent. She closes her eyes and thinks back five years. The accident. Tristan's death. Lucent's banishment. Maeve's discovery.

She still remembers how she visited the Underworld in

her nightmares, shortly after Tristan was killed. She'd had dreams of the realm of the dead before, but that night's was different. She was there, *physically* there, swimming through the dark waters in an attempt to find her brother. She'd found him. And she pulled him back to the surface. A miracle, a power from the gods. *Magic,* people would call it now, the gift of the Young Elites. But she never told anyone what she did—everyone simply assumed that Tristan had never truly died in the first place. She kept her power a secret, even to her mother, even in her rare letters to Lucent. Only her society of Elites knew. If word got out, the palace gates would swarm with people from all over the world, begging her to revive their loved ones. Better to keep a low profile.

For the first few years after he returned, Tristan was himself again. Alive. Normal.

Then, slowly, he began to change.

Maeve smiles sadly at her brother's silence, then touches his cheek. She can feel his strength even now, a strange, unnatural power coursing through his body that she alone, who chose to bring him back, has the power to unleash on the enemy of her choice.

"Come," she says. "I need to pay Kenettra a visit."

Acknowledgments

The *Young Elites* began as a hero's journey—a boy takes on the task of mastering his powers and vanquishing the villain. The story didn't work, though, and I was left struggling in the middle of nowhere, trying to figure out why. One day, as I mulled this over with my agent, Kristin Nelson, she said, "Hey, what about this Adelina girl? She's an interesting side character."

"Oh, yeah," I replied, distracted. "She's a fun bad girl to write. I hope I can keep her around if I redo this."

Kristin said, "Maybe she should be the star."

Sometimes, all it takes to see the right path is a flash of brilliant insight from someone else. I realized the problem was that I didn't want to tell a hero's journey; I wanted to tell a villain's.

So thank you, Kristin, for your wit, wisdom, and wonderful friendship. The book would not exist without you.

Subsequently, I never would have been able to turn that lopsided first draft into a proper story without the steady guiding hand of my editor and friend, Jen Besser. You are awesome in every possible way.

For your razor-sharp feedback—thank you JJ, Amie, and Jess Spotswood, for pushing me to become a better storyteller. I love your brains, and I love your books.

I never would have saved myself from many, many embarrassing copyediting mishaps without the incredibly smart Anne Heausler at my side. If I don't know something, I know that you will.

Thank you to the lovely folks of Team Putnam and Team Penguin, for tirelessly championing the book and getting it into the right hands. Shenanigans with you guys are better than a thousand Lil Jon concerts.

Writing can be a lonely, underestimated, and often haphazard profession. I'm lucky to be surrounded by friends who not only empathize but comfort and cheer. Beth, Jess, and Andrea, you are my forever sisters/elementals. Margie, Mel, Kami, Tahereh, Ransom, Leigh, and Josie—that is a lot of awesome in one sentence. Jess Brody, Morgan, Jess Khoury, Brodi, Jen Bosworth, Jenn Johansen, and Emmy, long live the mighty Steamboat 8. Amie, I crave your awesomeness like I crave cake. Which is all the time.

Finally, I cannot be a happy person without my daily support system. Thank you, friends, fam, Mom and Andre. And thanks, Primo. I still feel weird calling you my husband. Good-weird. Really good-weird. Love you.